Reconstructing the American Welfare State

David Stoesz
and
Howard Jacob Karger

with a Foreword by
James O. Midgley

Rowman & Littlefield Publishers, Inc.

ROWMAN & LITTLEFIELD PUBLISHERS, INC.

Published in the United States of America
by Rowman & Littlefield Publishers, Inc.
4720 Boston Way, Lanham, MD 20706

British Cataloging in Publication Information Available

Library of Congress Cataloging-in-Publication Data

Stoesz, David.
Reconstructing the American welfare state /
David Stoesz, Howard Jacob Karger ; with an introduction by James Midgley.
p.   cm.
Includes bibliographical references.
1. Public welfare—United States.
2. United States—Social policy.   3. Welfare state.
I. Karger, Howard Jacob, 1948- .   II. Title.
HV95.S826   1991
361.6' 0973—dc20   91-32471 CIP

ISBN 0-8476-7679-X (cloth, alk. paper)
ISBN 0-8476-7727-3 (pbk., alk. paper)

Printed in the United States of America

∞ ™ The paper used in this publication meets the minimum requirements of
American National Standard for Information Sciences—Permanence of
Paper for Printed Library Materials, ANSI Z39.48–1984.

Reconstructing the American Welfare State

For Dotty and Paul for their love and support over the years.

DS

For my father, Samuel Karger, who taught me how to ask the important questions.

HJK

Contents

Part One
The Evolution and Crisis in American
Social Welfare Policy

Part Two
Conservative and Liberal Prescriptions for Welfare

Figures and Tables

FIGURES

TABLES

Foreword

James O. Midgley

The idea that the state should be involved in the promotion of human welfare is not a new one. Examples of rulers enacting legislation to protect citizens or to promote their well-being have been found in the artifacts of many ancient civilizations. These provisions were usually contained in prescriptive (or proscriptive) legislation and, while they presumably had the force of law, they were not implemented by a specialist cadre of officials assigned to manage some prototypical welfare bureaucracy. Such programmatic responsibilities were, in any case, believed to lie within the proper province of religious authority. By religious injunction, the temples, churches, monasteries, and mosques provided for the destitute, succored the orphans, and housed the discarded. It was only during the Renaissance that the role of the state as a provider of welfare expanded. Throughout Europe, at this time, the emerging city-states introduced measures to deal with the growing problem of mendicancy within their boundaries; and in 1601 in England, the enactment of the forty-third statute of the reign of Elizabeth signaled the introduction of the first comprehensive, national public program for the suppression and remediation of destitution. The enactment of the Elizabethan statute is often recognized as a landmark in the history of social welfare not only because it was the first major attempt to apply the considerable resources of the state to deal with a pressing social problem, but because it legitimized state intervention in social welfare.

Although state intervention in human welfare is not, therefore, a recent innovation, it was only during the twentieth century that the principle of state-sponsored welfare was widely institutionalized. Emulating formative Elizabethan innovations, legislative measures touching on other human problems were enacted with increasing frequency during the late nineteenth and early twentieth centuries. These dealt with education, public health, employment, housing, income maintenance, and other social concerns, and gradually resulted in the creation of new governmental agencies responsible for their implementation. The first official bodies designed to foster public health were established in many cities during the early decades of the nineteenth century, while public authorities charged with the education of children proliferated during the century's middle and latter decades. Governmental agencies responsible for managing the asylums and other institutions also evolved at this time. At the federal level in the United States, the first major social agency was the Children's Bureau created by President Taft in 1912, following an initiative by the redoubtable Hull House women and their collaborators. There were similar developments in the other industrial countries and also, to some extent, in the colonial territories of the European powers. Here, welfare legislation formulated in the metropolitan countries were frequently copied verbatim; and thus, in spite of seeking to address local problems, social programs were often unsuited to domestic cultural and economic realities. In Latin America, governments began to establish human service agencies on a limited scale after they secured independence from Iberian rule at the beginning of the nineteenth century. In Peru, for example, the independence government first appointed a director of public charity in 1826 to implement the provisions of the Constitution of 1822, which charged the state with the responsibility of providing for the poor.

The gradual and apparently inevitable extension of state involvement in social welfare was not universally applauded. Many expressed direct opposition to the intrusion of the state in human affairs, regarding welfare as the proper domain of the charities and churches. In an age of utilitarianism and laissez-faire, the implications of state interventionism were recognized, and statist intrusion was soundly rejected on the ground that it would damage the productive process, foster dependency, and weaken the nation's moral fiber. On the other hand, there were those who believed that the engagement of the state in social welfare was an appropriate expression of the collective conscience, and that the state offered the most effective vehicle for the implementation of rising collectivist impulses. While wary of interventionism, others took a more instrumental (and cynical) view, believing that the involvement of the state would dampen popular discontent and ameliorate the worst excesses of capitalist economic growth. All three perspectives found expression in the implementation of social policy in the industrial countries at the turn of the century. Bismarckian innovations in social security are widely regarded by social historians as an expression of the *instrumental* view, while the introduction of various social programs by European liberal and social democratic governments exemplify the *collectivist* perspective. The anti-welfare *individualist* attitude was probably strongest in the United States; but here too, the expansion of governmental welfare provision continued apace.

World War I and the global economic depression that succeeded it gave further impetus to the proliferation of the state welfare endeavor. World War I demonstrated that assumptions about the health and welfare of the populace could not be taken for granted. The British had made this discovery somewhat earlier when the low nutritional standards, poor education, and ill health of military recruits for the Boer War were recognized to be inconsistent with the status of a superpower, and an impediment to its imperial designs. After the world war, the problem of unemployment—previously regarded as a function of individual preference—was shown to be determined by wider economic and social forces over which individuals had no control. The failure of the returning heroes to find jobs could hardly be attributed to simplistic notions of indolence or moral deficiency. These and other contradictions were amplified during the Great Depression when millions of respectable citizens lost their jobs, homes, and savings. It is difficult for today's generation, which has blithely assumed prosperity to be a normal condition of life, to appreciate the impact of these events on popular attitudes at the time. Although prevailing individualist beliefs were hardly abandoned, Americans in the cities and in the countryside recognized that hard work, sobriety, and perseverance could not guarantee security and well-being. Little wonder that those who advocated welfarism either through crude populist appeals or the advocacy of more sophisticated socialist doctrines gained rapid electoral support. It was, however, the political centrists who carried the day. Both in Europe and the United States, liberals and social democrats were able to use their political machines effectively to mobilize electorates in support of the welfarist agenda.

The New Deal exemplifies the institutionalization of welfarism in American society. Contrary to deeply rooted traditional American anti-welfarist attitudes, Roosevelt's legislative and administrative programs were widely endorsed. Measures designed to create employment, manage the economy, provide a variety of human services, and foster income security were introduced in rapid succession despite opposition from various quarters. Judicial and party political objections were overcome, the disapprobation of fashionable elites and the business community was ignored, bureaucratic and managerial obstacles were surmounted, and budgetary resources were mobilized. Within a relatively short period of time, the American welfare state had been shaped; and in spite of the vagaries of war, recession, prosperity, changing political realities and new cultural beliefs, it has retained its essential characteristics up to the present time. The nascent European welfare states that emerged at about the same time also evolved rapidly and have also retained their essential original features, although in most cases they differ significantly from the American model.

THE NOTION OF A WELFARE STATE

Although the term "welfare state" has gained popular currency in the English language, its provenance is uncertain. British scholars claim it as their own, contending that the term first came into general use after the implementation of the recommendations of the Beveridge Report in 1942. In the United States the term has a somewhat unfavorable connotation but is equally familiar. This is true also in other English-speaking countries as well as in Europe, where the notion of the welfare state is now widely accepted.

Definitions of the term abound, but there is little agreement either in popular usage or in scholarly circles as to its correct meaning. The lack of a standardized definition is partly a function of the general inability of social scientists to agree on basic terminologies, but also of the real difficulties inherent in encapsulating the term's various meanings, connotations, and nuances within a simple categorical statement. A major obstacle to defining the term is its incurably normative character. In spite of their efforts to maintain a dispassionate analytical perspective, scholars concerned with the study of social policy have a proclivity for evaluative judgments. This is equally true of their efforts to define the welfare state. For some commentators, the welfare state is an article of faith. For others, the concept misrepresents the "true" goals of social policy. For some, it is a term of derision either because it exemplifies the undesirable institutionalization of welfarism in modern society or because it represents the unfortunate successes of welfare capitalism.

There are, however, certain commonalities in the various definitions of the welfare state that have been formulated over the past 50 years. At a fairly elementary level of analysis, most explicate the statist, welfarist, and organizational components of the concept, paying particular attention to its various social-sector components and to its policy objectives. Most also relate the term to its historical context and most allude to its wider economic and political implications, although few have yet accentuated the concept's cultural dimensions. Most also recognize the pluralistic character of the welfare state, and it is here that normative considerations tend to complicate matters. For some, the normative dimension finds expression through a minimalist *residual* conception while, for others, an all-embracing *institutional* conception is articulated.

The minimalist or residual view conceives of the welfare state as a society in which governments intervene in human welfare by providing a variety of social services that ensure the needs of citizens will be met. Many definitions of this kind emphasize the notion of minimum standards, limiting state interventionism to guaranteeing a basic level of welfare for all. The market economy, the family, and other institutions are regarded as the primary and appropriate mechanisms for the promotion of welfare, and state involvement is focused on those who are unable to utilize these institutions effectively. Also, the residualist conception does not advocate other forms of intervention intended to affect productive processes, the distribution of incomes and wealth, or the fostering of collectivist attitudes. Firmly rooted in individualist values, it favors an accentuated form of welfare pluralism in which commercial, voluntary, and nonformal welfare provisions are encouraged and ordered to form a coherent welfare safety net. Government involvement is articulated with these forms of provision; and although the state assumes ultimate responsibility for welfare, other modes of service provision are actively promoted.

The institutional view, on the other hand, conceives of the welfare state as a society in which state intervention is encompassing and proactive; instead of focusing primarily on those in need, state programs are comprehensive and designed directly to affect the welfare of all. Definitions of this kind emphasize the overarching role of the state in providing universalist human services of a great variety, regulating and managing the economy, redistributing resource flows, and subsidizing both social and economic goods. Expressing collectivist ideologies, the institutional conception regards the welfare state as an integral element of a larger strategic design in which nationalization, economic planning, redistribution through fiscal and other measures, and the participation of the unions and other popular organizations in economic and social management are essential components. Although the institutional model accommodates welfare pluralism, it relegates commercial, voluntary, and nonformal provisions, and subsumes them to state initiative.

Both conceptions of the welfare state are ideal-typical and—like the socialist and capitalist archetypes—seldom find pure expression in the real world. Nevertheless, real-world approximations can be found in, for example, the Scandinavian model on the one hand, and that of the United States on the other. In spite of their differences, both conceptions are also based on a mixed-political-economy paradigm of society. Although the individualist and collectivist elements in both approaches are evident, neither gives pure expression to these two ideological traditions. While the residual conception accommodates welfarism within the structures of capitalist society, the institutional approach seeks to modify these structures

by (as some have derisively observed) "reforming" capitalism. By insti-
tutionalizing welfarism and implementing other large scale interventionist
strategies, the proponents of the institutional model seek to create a new
societal formation that, despite its tendency toward managerial centraliza-
tion, enshrines liberal democracy and retains the market as a primary productive mechanism. And it is largely because both models are essentially
revisionist versions of the Western capitalist archetype that both have been
heavily criticized. The right argues that the welfare state has weakened
capitalism and caused widespread economic and social stagnation. The
left, on the other hand, believes that the welfare state has failed to reform
capitalism and that poverty, inequality, and deprivation continue to characterize the Western experience. The present welfare crisis reflects the
failure of proponents of the welfare state to secure legitimacy for their
views among those on either the political right or left and effectively to
translate their ideas into practice.

THE CRISIS OF THE WELFARE STATE

Although the rhetoric of crisis has been overworked in contemporary
social science, few would claim that the welfare state is in sound condition
today. Indeed, during recent years, the literature of social policy has made
frequent reference to the apparently intractable problems facing the welfare state, and the challenge these pose to its proponents.

As several social historians have demonstrated, the years immediately
following World War II were characterized by widespread popular opti-
mism. Having lived through a time of devastating conflict, Americans
celebrated the peace and believed that the nation's military and global
superiority would prevent future conflagrations. The memory of the Great
Depression was still fresh, but was tempered by pervasive prosperity and
the existence of the welfare state. The mushrooming suburbs, political
stability, the availability of new consumer goods, high levels of employment, rising life expectancy, gains in health care, and the existence of a
comprehensive state-managed welfare safety net, all worked to engender
a positive outlook among many.

By the 1960s, the mood had changed. The assassination of a popular
president, civil disobedience and brutal opposition to a cause that much
of middle America did not understand, and new international conflicts in
Southeast Asia, Africa, and Latin America were troubling portends of changing
times. By the end of decade, as urban violence became widespread, as the
media sensationalized the student movement and the counterculture's excesses,
as trade union activity appeared to be more militant, and—above all—as

the Vietnam conflict reached unprecedented proportions, popular disquiet became endemic.

Disquiet was most evident in conservative political circles, where contemporary uncertainties were readily blamed on the demise of traditional values and the rejection of the social and moral order by the young. Although conservatives had previously participated in creating what has been described as the postwar "liberal" consensus, many now questioned the ingredients of this consensus. Tolerance, they believed, had led to permissiveness; the acceptance of change had weakened cherished traditional values; state welfarism had diminished self-reliance; and economic interventionism had damaged the natural working of the productive process. Although Barry Goldwater became a symbol of conservative resolve to return the nation to its traditional halcyon ways, his poor performance in the 1964 election suggested that the conservative counterattack was premature. But Goldwater laid the groundwork for the emergence of a conservative movement that would later secure political power and shake the very foundations of liberal consensus politics and its statist and welfarist premises.

The political left was not entirely happy with the centrist consensus either. While many on the left recognized that the liberal consensus had brought stability and prosperity, they were impatient with the pace of change, contending that injustice, deprivation, and inequality remained endemic in American society. The unsettled conditions of the 1960s were, they believed, symptomatic of deeper ills that could only be remedied through significant changes in popular attitudes, social institutions, and political processes. They too were critical of the welfare state, claiming that it had singularly failed to solve the social problems of the time. Others of a more militant persuasion argued that, because the welfare state had been conspiratorially manipulated by elites in order to exercise social control, it had no useful social welfare functions and should be abolished. Its replacement by a just and equal society through revolutionary means if necessary was the only viable means of attaining the ideals of a true welfare society. More serious was the Marxian left's conclusion that the welfare state could not continue to serve as an agent of capitalism because the rising demand for services would create a "fiscal crisis of the state" which would ultimately sap capitalism of its vitality.

Initially, debates about the problems of the welfare state were largely confined to intellectual circles; but in time they began, through the popular media and the efforts of political campaigners, to permeate public consciousness. While the left had little direct impact on popular attitudes, its view that the welfare state had failed miserably to meet human needs was used by anti-welfarists in their campaigns. Conservatives could claim with justification that, with the exception of a few faithful centrist New Deal liberals, there was little support for the welfare state from either the left or the right. Equally significant was the argument that rising demands for state services would eventually outstrip the capacity of the state to respond. Agreeing with the Marxian analysis, conservative intellectuals argued that the increasing burden of taxation required to fund ever more expansive social programs would eventually overload and cripple even the best intentioned government. If a major crisis was to be avoided, the widespread belief that the state could provide for all had to be negated. To avert a fiscal crisis of the state, a crisis of the welfare state had to be induced.

The great oil shocks of the 1970s further damaged centrist consensus politics and further debilitated the welfare state ideal. With rampant stagflation, rising unemployment, increased trade union militancy, deindustrialization, and other changes related to new global economic realities, welfare budgets became increasingly strained. In addition, public confidence and the sense of security that characterized the 1950s dissipated rapidly. The Watergate scandal demonstrated that even the nation's most pivotal institutions were affected. As in the 1930s, political leaders who offered dramatic solutions to the crisis of confidence sweeping the land secured significant popular support.

The ideology of the New Right provided solutions of this kind. By advocating commonsensical economic recipes based on familiar individualist doctrines, Ronald Reagan appealed to the instincts of many voters. His emphasis on traditional American values, patriotism, the centrality of the family, and the importance of community offered the prospect of a return to security and stability. His personal style was engaging and reassuring, and his ability to exploit populist sentiment through the promise of strong leadership attracted widespread support. When the president claimed that the welfare state was responsible for many contemporary ills, many Americans believed him.

The Reagan administration imposed severe budget cuts on the welfare state and damaged many of its constituent programs. For the first time since its inception, the welfare state experienced a serious fiscal crisis. Although previous conservative presidents such as Richard Nixon had introduced changes to the welfare state, these had not significantly altered its character. Despite budgetary deficiencies, the fiscal and economic woes of the 1970s had not seriously disabled the welfare state. On the other hand, the Reagan administration inflicted severe damage. While the president did not—as some of his advisors had hoped—succeed in abolishing the welfare state, the Reagan years culminated in a major crisis of confidence in its elemental principles. In addition to the incapacitating effects of the budget cuts, the agenda of weaning the public from its faith in the state as a final guarantor of welfare had been implemented. As a result of the cuts, even the notion of the welfare state as a residual safety net was effectively challenged. Although the constituent programs of the welfare state survived (albeit in a weakened condition), its legitimacy had dissipated.

The crisis of legitimacy of the welfare state affected various constituencies. As a result of the permeation of New Right ideas throughout the conservative movement, the welfare state retained few adherents on the center right. In addition, public perceptions of the welfare state became increasingly negative. Those who derived benefit from the welfare state were also affected, becoming increasingly critical of its meager provisions, punitive ramifications, inefficient management, and stigmatizing consequences. Left-liberal intellectuals who had previously championed the welfare state were put on the defensive; and while they criticized the Reagan administration for its shameless lack of compassion, many privately doubted whether their defense of a crumbling, inefficient, and unsatisfactory system was justifiable. Those on the radical left seldom contemplated these issues, and instead used the attack on the welfare state as a campaign slogan with which to berate the Reaganites. Most devastating, however, was the defection of many liberals from the welfare state ideal. When those who have been most closely associated with the advocacy of state responsibility for welfare come to question these premises, the welfare state is indeed in crisis.

RESOLVING THE CRISIS

While proponents of the welfare state ideal have frequently invoked the notion of crisis when discussing the problems facing the welfare state, radical New Right advocates do not share their concerns, except, of course, to bemoan the fact that in spite of their efforts the apparatus of the welfare state remains intact. For the New Right, the abolition of state welfarism remains a cherished goal. Theirs is not—as has sometimes been claimed—a residualist conception, but rather an abolitionist one in which the very notion of state responsibility for welfare is abrogated. Unlike established liberal, conservative, and socialist approaches, which differ primarily in the degree to which they institutionalize state welfare responsibility, the New Right transcends the idea of the welfare state, arguing instead that governments have no right or obligation to be involved in the business of welfare. While some New Right adherents reluctantly accept that the state must subsidize voluntary and commercial welfare activities, others are willing to retain only the harshest poor-law provisions. Generally, however, the New Right favors a charity model of welfare in which those in need are catered for through philanthropic, commercial, or nonformal effort.

During the Reagan years, successive attempts to abolish the welfare state through indirect measures failed to reach their desired goals. Budgetary cuts, administrative delays and obstacles, new procedural definitions, and other tactics undoubtedly damaged the system; but as suggested earlier, they did not terminate state welfare responsibilities. There were numerous policy proposals for the replacement of state welfare with alternative methods of provision; although some offered viable policy options, they were politically untenable. The large conservative think tanks were particularly inventive in formulating policy proposals of this kind; but with the Democratic opposition in control of the Congress, and the risk of massive public opposition to the abolition of favored social programs such as Medicare and Social Security, the New Right's abolitionist agenda could not be implemented.

Ironically, the New Right's failure to abolish the welfare state has exacerbated the welfare crisis. Devastating cuts, ever more restrictive and complex managerial procedures, the decline in morale among welfare administrators, the disaffection of clients, and the dissipation of popular confidence and legitimacy have crippled state welfare programs. There are, of course, conservatives who continue to believe in the welfare state and who oppose the radical abolitionist impulse of the New Right. While retaining a residualist conception of the welfare state, they continue to advocate the involvement of government in social welfare. But they too have become disillusioned, and convinced that a major overhaul is needed. However, apart from proposing minor modifications to specific programs, traditional conservatives have failed to formulate coherent proposals for responding to the welfare crisis.

This is true also of traditional liberal New Dealers. Many were thrown on the defensive by the New Right onslaught, and could do little except decry the attack on the welfare state and continue defiantly to proclaim its virtues. After again securing a majority in Congress, they were able to maintain a reasonably effective rear-guard position and to protect core welfare provisions from further fiscal damage. As has been suggested already, those on the radical left adopted a similar stance but achieved little more than to hurl their choicest expletives at the Reaganites. On the other hand, some Democrats—the revisionist neoliberals—began to extricate themselves from their party's long-standing commitment to the welfare state. Riding the conservative tide, they sought credibility with their electorates by criticizing the welfare bureaucracy, deprecating the apparent pervasiveness of welfare dependency, and advocating a greater measure of commercial, voluntary, family, and personal involvement in welfare. Many publicly proclaimed the death of the New Deal, arguing that policies and programs introduced 50 years earlier in response to the crisis of the Great Depression were outmoded and unsuited to the nation's needs as the century drew to a close. But in spite of their pronouncements, few had credible or workable alternatives that would form the basis for a truly current and humane welfare agenda. Their uncritical support for the so-called welfare reform initiative of the late 1980s belied their declarations of commitment to formulating new policy approaches that would deal effectively with the crisis of the welfare state.

RECONSTRUCTING THE WELFARE STATE

Apart from advocating the abolition of the welfare state, there is a dearth of radical proposals for responding to the welfare crisis. Although the guerrillas of the New Right continue to cling dogmatically to their faith, the prospect of abolition has receded further as George Bush popularizes new notions of a "kinder, gentler America." Traditional conservative supporters of the minimalist welfare state have had few ideas for improving the situation, and the traditional liberal center and the radical left are apparently devoid of innovative solutions. While neoliberals claim to have identified new and exciting policy proposals, these amount to minor adjustments and are designed more to appease popular opinion than to address basic problems. The failure to find solutions to the welfare crisis has engendered an attitude of despair among many proponents of the welfare state, who wonder whether the idea of the welfare state is workable in American society after all.

In the absence of bold, imaginative, and coherent solutions, the welfare crisis will perpetuate itself, and policy proposals are likely to result in little more than an occasional tinkering with a problem that requires major solutions. It is obvious that imaginative and comprehensive solutions are required. At the risk of being presumptuous, this book offers solutions of this kind. Instead of seeking to treat the symptoms of the crisis, it proposes a major overhaul. Instead of patching, it seeks to reconstruct the American welfare state.

David Stoesz and Howard Karger are two highly innovative thinkers in the field of social policy who have devoted years of careful study to the American welfare state and its problems. Authors of a highly successful textbook on the subject, they have published on issues of welfare reform, the effects of international economic developments on the welfare state, the problems of income maintenance, the social policy agendas of the leading conservative think tanks, and the commercialization of welfare through the involvement of large for-profit corporations. They are uniquely qualified to analyze the current welfare crisis, and to offer bold and imaginative solutions.

There are three major premises on which their argument rests. First, they note that the modern welfare state is based on programs that are outmoded and no longer suited to the realities of the time. In this regard they agree with the neoliberal critique, and seek both in their analysis and policy prescriptions to take account of contemporary needs, problems, and conditions. Second, they argue that the welfare state is the incremental accretion of a historical evolution of various policies and programs that consequently do not fit together in a coherent and workable way. Viewing the structured neatness of many European welfare states with some envy, they nevertheless recognize that the political, social, and cultural conditions that facilitated the emergence of comprehensive welfare states in Europe simply do not pertain in the United States. In a lively preface, replete with powerful imagery, they argue that the cultural uniqueness of the American experience requires indigenous responses that specifically address domestic needs and realities. Third and finally, they believe that core principles appropriate to the requirements of American society must shape any attempt to reconstruct the welfare state. These principles are expounded in the concluding part of the book, and are applied to formulate a variety of new and highly innovative programmatic proposals for a reconstructed welfare state. While some scholars and practitioners of social policy may disagree with Stoesz and Karger's conclusions, theirs is a vision for a new, appropriate, and humane welfare state that deserves serious consideration and extensive debate.

Preface

In 1966 Robert Venturi's *Complexity and Contradiction in Architecture*
appeared—a slender volume advocating an essentially American vernacular in building design.[1] For Venturi, structural design in the United States
had suffered from the influence of European stylists. In the shadow of
World War II, refugees of the German Bauhaus had come to the United
States, bringing with them new possibilities for construction and design—
huge geometric buildings that were elegantly parsimonious. In the great
industrial cities, working Americans soon found themselves gawking upward at "modern architecture." The feeling was unsettling; the buildings
dwarfed the observer and seemed intimidating at the same time, indiffer-
ently throwing back the mirrored image of the onlooker. Yet, "forward-
thinking" corporate executives, and later governmental officials, found
themselves somehow wanting until their headquarters could be lodged in
these magnificent monuments to simplicity. An "edifice complex" ran
rampant. Soon, modern architecture was everywhere. Massive, vertical
blocks sheathed in reflective glass overwhelmed the more modest and familiar
buildings of native design. No American city seemed complete until its
skyline was mastered by these monoliths.

In contrast to the austere sterility of European design, Venturi advocated a "messy vitality" of more ordinary style. Countering Mies van der
Rohe's functionalist aphorism "Less is more," Venturi parodied, "Less is
a bore." Then, to make the point, Venturi chose the typical American
"main street" for inspiration, including garish neon signs and roadside produce
stands—even a handicraft shop built as a yellow duck.[2] By juxtaposing the
steel, glass, and granite high rises of America's power elite with the country's
own indigenous constructions, Venturi reminded us that these latter forms

have important virtues that are absent in modern design: they are democratic and human in scale. Ultimately, Venturi's cause was to invent a postmodern, populist architecture consonant with the American experience—an accomplishment for which he was awarded the Pritzker prize in 1991.

As spatial engineering is a cultural construct, so is social engineering. For the better part of a century, American social philosophers have looked to the state to assure that their compatriots were protected against the caprices of capitalism, mishap, and just plain bad luck. The articulation of this philosophical stance has consumed the entire careers of many committed people, sheaves of public legislation, and billions of dollars in appropriations. Most Americans understand this philosophical inclination by way of the major social programs—Social Security, Medicare, Aid to Families with Dependent Children—and the agencies that administer them: the Departments of Health and Human Services, Labor, and Housing and Urban Development. They comprise what we know as the American welfare state.

Yet, reliance on the state—the federal government, in this instance—for social provision has not been uniformly well received in the United States. In Europe, the national government has proven an effective and durable source of social welfare. In fact, the track record that European social advocates had already established before the world depression of the 1930s was such that American intellectuals sought to replicate it in the United States through the New Deal. But the European conception of the welfare state grafted poorly onto American culture. Policy analyst Marc Bendick concluded this when he observed that contrary to Europe, in the United States, the emphasis consistently has been on the local, the pluralistic, the voluntary, and the business-like over the national, the universal, the legally-entitled, and the governmental. Given such a consistent pattern of anti-governmental bias in the American response style, it is unfortunate that much of American social policy has looked to Europe for models of both specific programs and general approaches. Reflecting political, social, economic, and intellectual circumstances very different from those in the United States, most European nations have evolved an approach to social welfare services that is strongly state centered. . . . When presented explicitly to the American public, the European welfare state approach has won few adherents outside of academic circles.[3]

Such antipathy toward government has presented enormous problems for American social activists who propose solutions to social problems through *public* policy. Immediately, they find themselves ensnared by a host of thorny issues: the public is skeptical, if not a little paranoid, about the intrusion of government in social affairs; citizens tend to become frustrated at the bureaucracies that proliferate with social legislation, especially when *they* have to negotiate the red tape; and taxpayers revolt when they perceive that the drain of social programs on their income shows no indication of abating. These complaints compose a large part of the indictment that conservatives have prepared against the American welfare state. Less well known are the reservations of those having direct experience with its programs. With the exception of correctional facilities, probably no institution is held in more contempt by those dependent on it than the welfare department. Tragically, social programs are viewed as obstacles by the very people who need them so badly. For their part, professional social workers often view the public social services as an occupational stopover between graduate school and the more lucrative (and pleasant) jobs in the private sector. More often, social workers avoid the public welfare sector altogether. A letter written by a group of Missouri public welfare workers in response to a proposed statewide licensure amendment for social workers illustrates the aversion of trained social workers to the public sector.

> In regard to the . . . licensing of social workers bill: We would be agreeable to the bill ONLY if current DoSS [Department of Social Service] social workers were exempt. As of April, 1985, we had only 9 out of 70 workers and supervisors with a degree in social work. . . . The rest of us would likely be forced to resign should this bill pass without this amendment.[4]

The turnover of social workers in the public social services is so high that clients often do not know who their social workers are, and social workers often do not know the rudiments of the programs they operate. For example, the Department of Family Services in Missouri, a typical midwestern state, had the following turnover rate in 1984: in St. Louis City, the turnover rate was 10.7 percent; in St. Louis County, 15.5 percent; and in Greene County (Springfield), 19.2 percent. The overall turnover rate for Missouri's Department of Family Services in 1985 was 13.9 percent[5]—a figure that compared unfavorably with the private sector, where the separation rates ranged from 0.8 percent in the smaller firms to 1.6 percent among financial institutions.[6] Among the casualties of the ensuing confusion are accuracy in the payment of benefits and the safety of abused children. From the perspective of most parties who have examined the matter closely, the American welfare state begs for an overhaul.

Reconstruction of the American welfare state has been on the conservative policy agenda since the Reagan administration assumed office in 1980, leaving liberals on the defensive with regard to social programs. For more than a decade now, conservatives have found it high sport to dismantle, defund, or simply rout programs for the poor. The hallmark of this strategy was Charles Murray's *Losing Ground,* which proposed scrapping most of the social welfare programs.[7] Still, despite a decade of legislative and budgetary "deconstruction," conservatives have yet to propose a viable alternative to the American welfare state.[8] At best—and this is an accomplishment, considering the conservative demagoguery of the past— the *neo*conservatives have demonstrated considerably more sophistication in the social welfare debate. In this respect, the hoary rhetoric of an anti-welfare paleoconservatism has given way to a neoconservatism that is every bit as adept in debating social welfare as is the practiced oratory of the liberal welfare statists. Much to the chagrin of those liberal philosophers who held a monopoly in organized compassion, a ragtag band of religious fundamentalists has proved an effective phalanx in the endeavor of the old right to retard the growth of the state in relation to the business sector.

As the poverty programs withered, liberals fared worse. Writing on the eve of the 1980 presidential election, Irving Howe dismissed the Reagan candidacy as the last gasp of American paleoconservatism.[9] What liberals lacked in foresight, they made up for in tenacity: defending social programs preoccupied them throughout the 1980s.[10] Still, it seemed beyond the capability of the liberals to present a structural critique of the American welfare state.[11] Besieged by a hostile Reagan administration and a compliant Democratic Congress, liberals simply had their hands full trying to protect increasingly meager benefits from further savaging. Now as we approach the end of the century, conventional conservative and liberal prescriptions for welfare seem to have been exhausted. The welfare debate has reached an impasse.

This ideological inertia is reflected in the social legislation of the era. With the Bush administration well under way in completing a third term of the Reagan presidency, the American welfare state has stagnated: 1988 brought the Family Support Act, substantial welfare reform in rhetoric only; 1989 saw the repeal of Catastrophic Health Insurance, the first recall of a major social program in the history of the American welfare state. Aside from nostalgic appeals for more altruistic participation in nonprofit agencies—"a thousand points of light"—the Bush administration has done virtually nothing substantive to enhance the welfare capacity of the nation, whether by public *or* private initiative. Fiscal constraints imposed by the budget deficit, the savings and loan bailout, and the Gulf War have almost certainly precluded the deployment of new social programs. Predictably, the social debris attributed to an unattended welfare state continues to foul America's cultural ecology.

Our modest attempt to offer proposals for the reconstruction of the American welfare state follows in a pragmatic tradition. Respecting the structures inherent in a democratic-capitalist political economy, we have sought to maximize their welfare potential. Thus, this strategy might be described as an exercise in "radical pragmatism." For those accustomed to more orthodox prescriptions, what we propose will be unacceptable—or worse, incorrect. Yet, conventional ideology has made glaring errors in social philosophy. Liberals have become overreliant on the state as a source of social provision, treating the private sector with suspicion, if not disdain. Conservatives denigrate governmental programs en masse—proclaiming the supremacy of free enterprise—and give scant consideration to the voluntary sector. Given what is called "welfare pluralism" or "the mixed economy of welfare," any attempt to reconstruct the American welfare state must address contributions of the voluntary, governmental, and corporate sectors.

Moreover, prescriptions must clearly define rewards and penalties apportioned through social policy. Intentions are not enough. President Bush's appeal for "a thousand points of light" is just so much lip service without a substantive proposal—such as a Volunteer Tax Credit or a National Service Corps—to bolster nonprofit social agencies. Much of the stalemate in the welfare debate can be overcome, we argue, by more creative thinking *about* and clear articulation *of* institutions that already exist. The inability of policymakers to do this is reflected in the public's dissatisfaction with much of public policy—particularly *welfare* policy. In a democratic polity, it is desirable for social policy to reflect the preferences of the public. The alienation of the public from government in general suggests that philosophy is "behind the curve" in social affairs, and nowhere more so than in questions of social welfare. There is no reason why welfare philosophy should be poor philosophy.

Americans need to think seriously about social welfare. Since the last major era of welfare reform—the War on Poverty—social, economic, and political factors have conspired to justify a reinvention of how Americans respond to a variety of needs. If domestic factors alone are insufficient to compel such a reexamination, international events demand it. The United States can no longer conduct domestic policy in a vacuum, independent of international economic considerations. Accordingly, our purpose is to examine critically the liberal version of the American welfare state, assess the merits of the conservative critique, and then propose a conceptualization apropos of the postindustrial era.

By integrating and reinforcing the social capacity of the voluntary, governmental, and corporate sectors we endeavor to construct a coherent version of welfare that is as post-New Deal as it is post-Reagan. Moreover, we seek to build a social institution that is democratic, productive, accessible, and relevant to the real circumstances of Americans. In the manner that Robert Venturi has proposed a relevant spatial architecture, we argue for a contemporary social architecture anchored in the American experience.

Reconstructing the American Welfare State is divided into three parts. Part One addresses the evolution and crisis of American social policy. Chapter 1 examines the philosophical basis of welfare, including the evolution of the welfare state and the structure of social welfare. Chapter 2 examines the twin crises of the American welfare state: the fiscal crisis and the legitimation crisis. As such, this chapter examines the effects of Reaganism on the welfare state, the fiscal crisis of the state, the impact of the global economy on American welfare, and the public's loss of confidence in the ability of welfare state programs to solve social problems. In Part Two the conservative and liberal responses to the welfare state crisis are evaluated. Chapter 3 examines conservative efforts to reshape American social welfare, including the failure of conservatives to fashion a viable alternative to the governmental welfare state. In particular, the chapter looks at the role of conservative think tanks in structuring the welfare debates of the 1980s and evaluates the political success of the New Right and their major welfare proposals. Chapter 4 assesses the liberal and left responses to the crisis in welfare. As such, the chapter evaluates the historic role played by liberals in the formation of the American welfare state, and analyzes the inability of liberals and the left to formulate viable welfare proposals to meet the welfare crisis of the 1980s. In Part Three we propose social programs that are more consonant with the American experience. Chapter 5 includes the rationale for reconstructing the American welfare state, as well as the primary principles around which welfare programs should be organized. In Chapter 6 we configure a set of social welfare initiatives to illustrate the reconstruction theses. In Chapter 7 these initiatives are then reinterpreted as a social welfare model that can serve as a guide for future welfare legislation.

ACKNOWLEDGMENTS

DS: Many people have made this book possible. Our students and colleagues who sat through various lectures on these topics in the classroom and at conferences provided us with both a sounding board and a critique for our ideas. As a way to address their contributions as well as the adverse circumstances in which many human service workers toil, we will contribute 10 percent of royalties from this book to policyAmerica, a nonprofit group endeavoring to formulate social policies that are optimal for all Americans. Our editor, Jonathan Sisk, deserves credit for having believed in this book since the beginning, and a humble thanks to Pat Merrill who reacquainted us with punctuation, syntax, and so forth. James Midgley, a first-rate scholar and dear friend, made the book possible. In addition, thanks to Larry Litterst and Michael Sherraden for their insightful critiques. Melissa Martin helped even when her required hours were exhausted.

HJK: An apology to Connie Karger for having to eat cold suppers while waiting for me to finish "just one more sentence." A special thanks to Saul Karger for having the patience to put up with a distracted father and for playing patiently in the living room while I wrote. He taught me much about love and patience.

NOTES

1. Robert Venturi, *Complexity and Contradiction in Architecture* (New York: Museum of Modern Art, 1966).
2. Robert Venturi, Denise Scott Brown, and Steven Izenour, *Learning from Las Vegas* (Cambridge, Mass.: MIT Press, 1972).
3. Marc Bendick, *Privatizing the Delivery of Social Welfare Service* (Washington, D.C.: National Conference on Social Welfare, 1985), pp. 1, 6.
4. Letter from Missouri Division of Family Services employees to senator and state representatives, Communication Workers of America, District 6, St. Louis, Mo., March 25, 1985. Quoted in Howard Jacob Karger, *Social Workers and Labor Unions* (New York: Greenwood Press, 1988), p. 151.
5. Missouri Division of Family Services, "Social Service Worker Turnover, Calendar Year--1984," Jefferson City, 1984, n.p.
6. Bureau of National Affairs, "Report 4th Quarter, 1985," Washington, D.C., March 6, 1986, n.p.
7. Charles Murray, *Losing Ground* (New York: Basic Books, 1984)
8. Stuart Butler, "A Conservative Vision of Welfare," *Policy Review* (Spring 1987).
9. Irving Howe, *Beyond the Welfare State* (New York: Schocken Books, 1982).
10. Among the liberal standard-bearers worth noting are Marian Wright Edelman of the Children's Defense Fund and Robert Greenstein of the Center on Budget and Policy Priorities.
11. This point was made most effectively by Lawrence Mead, "The New Welfare Debate," *Commentary* (March 1988), pp. 44-52.

Part One

The Evolution and Crisis in American Social Welfare Policy

1

The Idea of the Welfare State

David Stoesz

If H. L. Mencken were reporting on welfare politics today, he would liken the contemporary welfare state to a corporation—one that was going broke. Indeed, during the past decade the welfare state has been more criticized than at any time in modern history. Much to the alarm of those who have championed state intervention to assuage the dislocating tendencies of capitalism, even the cornerstones of welfarism—Social Security and Medicare—have come under assault. And no industrial nation has been exempt; even Northern European welfare states have been pared. "The welfare state everywhere is in a period of retrenchment," concluded Robert Kuttner.[1] Ironically, those programs intended to expand individual opportunity, strengthen the family, and support community institutions have been accused of corroding individual initiative, eroding the family, and subverting the community. Spearheading the attack on social programs are conservatives who have appealed to economic individualism, cultural traditionalism, and populism to halt the expansion of the American welfare state.[2]

At this point there is little dispute that, while the conservatism of the 1980s has not rolled back the welfare state, it *has* contained the program expansion that had characterized the institution for more than half a century. This is no small matter. A long-held precept of liberalism—as well as its rebuttal to radical populism—has been that, through incremental additions, economically marginal and politically disenfranchised populations could be folded into the protections assured by the governmental welfare state. It was this idea that led the English social philosopher Richard Titmuss to hope that the welfare state, as an instrument of government, would eventually lead to a "welfare world."[3] Ultimately, governmental programs, which were the basis of the welfare state, were treated by most

3

welfare philosophers as synonymous with social welfare. This convention was followed in the United States, as well. For American social philosophers, government programs designed to ameliorate the caprices of capitalism were both desirable and inevitable. In their classic *Industrial Society and Social Welfare*, Harold Wilensky and Charles Lebeaux suggested that "under continuing industrialization all institutions will be oriented toward and evaluated in terms of social welfare aims. The 'welfare state' will become the 'welfare society,' and both will be more reality than epithet."[4] Accordingly, from the New Deal through the War on Poverty, the notion that government should be the primary institution for promoting social welfare was to become a persistent theme among American welfare philosophers.

The American welfare state was defensible to the extent that it offered social and economic security to an ever larger number of vulnerable citizens; its validity was contingent on its expansion. Yet, five decades into the legislative experiment, reports seemed to question what Americans had gotten for their investment in the welfare state. Initially, these focused on one of the few indicators that had extensive validity: infant mortality. In the spring of 1983, the *New York Times* editorialized that unacceptably high rates of infant deaths were found in the nation's poorest communities: "in parts of Detroit, 33 out of 100 children don't live until their first birthday; in the Avalon Park section of Chicago, the rate is 55 out of 100."[5] The Worldwatch Institute found that the infant mortality for African Americans in Washington, D.C., was higher than that of Trinidad and Tobago, Jamaica, Cuba, and Costa Rica.[6] The infant mortality rate in parts of Detroit was the same as Honduras, one of the poorest nations in Central America.[7] The highly regarded Children's Defense Fund examined the infant mortality rate of nations for the period 1980-85 and ranked the United States seventeenth.[8] Confidence began to fade in the nation's social programs.

Yet, as important as infant mortality is, there is more to social welfare than the health and nutrition afforded to expectant mothers and infants. In what is probably the most ambitious attempt to fashion a comprehensive picture of national development, the University of Pennsylvania's Richard Estes charted the social progress of nations of the world. Following a classically liberal understanding of social development, Estes incorporated multiple indicators of social development in addition to support for welfare programs—among them, access and adequacy of education, health care, economic development, political participation, and opportunities for women. By the time the statistics had settled, the most comprehensive understanding of the social development of the world's nations had been constructed. Of particular interest, however, was Estes's ranking of na-

tions for 1979-80, *before* the anti-welfare biases of the Reagan administration affected social legislation in the United States. After a half-century of investment in the American welfare state, the United States ranked
twenty-third. Predictably, the more integrated welfare states of Northern
Europe dominated the top ten. In the second ten were Canada, France, and
the turbo-economies of Japan and West Germany. Associated with the
United States in the third tier were nations such as Costa Rica, Portugal,
and Cuba.[9] Compared to many nations of the world, the actual performance of the United States failed to correspond with the image it preferred to present to its citizens. On closer inspection, the reality of the
American welfare state was that its inadequacy was so extensive that many
economically retarded areas of the United States resembled the developing nations of the Third World.[10]

During the 1980s, the welfare state came under increasing scrutiny not
ony in the United States, but also in the nations most committed to the
concept.[11] "At its present levels, the welfare apparatus has simply become
too expensive for most governments—and their taxpayers," reported *Time*.

> Across the Continent, social security systems are grappling with fiscal crisis, in
> part because ponderous, costly bureaucracies have mushroomed to administer a
> vast array of programs that sometimes neglect the essential to serve up what is
> merely desirable. . . . Bloated beyond its architects' intent, welfarism is threaten-
> ing bankruptcy in some countries.[12]

More scholarly assessments reinforced the impression that the welfare
state, as ideological currency, had run its course. In an analysis of the
welfare states of nine nations, Robert Morris concluded that since the 1970s
government commitments to universal programs—particularly pensions
and health care—had been maintained, but that the welfare state's redistributional function had been significantly limited.[13]

The prospect that the welfare state was running aground seemed incomprehensible to many American liberals. Accustomed to increasing benefits and expanding eligibility to governmental social programs, welfare
state advocates were effectively disarmed when the institutional base of
their ideology—the state—was discredited. This occurred, paradoxically,
shortly after theoreticians such as James O'Connor[14] and Ian Gough[15] had
predicted a restructuring of welfare since the state was finding itself unable
to socialize the increasing costs of monopoly capitalism. Of no small note
was a similar conclusion—albeit attributed to different causes—reached
by conservative public-choice theoreticians, who posited that the welfare
state was inevitably overdrawn by the increasing demands of beneficiary/
constituent groups.[16] Thus, the New Right of the 1980s seems to have

exploited a degree of consensus reached by left and right economic theorists a decade earlier. Overspent and outdated, the welfare state was due for an overhaul.

THE EVOLUTION OF THE WELFARE STATE

Much of the turbulence characterizing the debate over the welfare state can be attributed to its internal complexity, perhaps best reflected in the term "welfare pluralism."[17] Following the pluralist tradition, the welfare state is an institutional accommodation to industrial capitalism, and it is inevitable that the private sector would figure prominently in its evolution. Titmuss recognized this a generation ago when he identified three categories of welfare: (1) social welfare (personal social services and grants to the impoverished); (2) fiscal welfare (e.g., tax exemptions for dependents); and (3) occupational welfare (fringe benefits connected to the labor market, such as pensions and health insurance).[18] For Titmuss these categories operated as distinct systems that tended to "divide loyalties, to nourish privilege, and to narrow the social conscience."[19] Despite the institutional diversity in social policy suggested by welfare philosophers during the first half of the century, welfare pluralism was eclipsed by a "welfare statist" consensus that emerged following World War II. Liberal adherents of the American welfare state were gratified as government social programs expanded, fueled by economic prosperity. Little noticed by welfare statists, private-sector welfare activity also increased.

By the 1980s, conceptualizations of welfare were including the private sector as a valid category. According to Sheila Kamerman, the "mixed welfare economy" included not-for-profit agencies, governmental social programs, and the market.[20] Michael Walzer—in his "theory of social assignments"—proposed four entities that are central to understanding welfare: the family, the market, the state, and the social sector.[21] Walzer's classification is virtually identical to that employed by Norman Johnson in his book on welfare pluralism.[22] David Stoesz presented a "structural interest" approach, identifying four sectors: the voluntary sector, the governmental sector, the corporate sector, and private practice.[23] In each of these formulations, the state is but one component; much of welfare activity can be attributed to nongovernmental institutions.

Welfare pluralism has significant implications for the welfare state. Assuming the validity of private actors within social welfare, it can be argued that there is no a priori reason why services must be reserved for the state. In effect, welfare pluralism converts social welfare to an institutional crap game: it becomes anyone's bet as to the optimal assignment of social responsibility. As might be imagined, welfare pluralism wreaks havoc with the liberal preference for a welfare state dominated by government. As welfare statists have seen, welfare pluralism has proven a powerful lever that conservatives can use to pry welfare programs away from government. Historically, the old right preferred to assign social responsibility to the private nonprofit sector, and more recently to the private for-profit sector. The New Right prefers sectarian agencies, the business sector, and, of course, the family as a basis of welfare provision. The very existence of private entities, in other words, provides the right with a variety of alternatives whenever it wishes to critique its nemesis, the liberally inspired governmental welfare state. In fact, a strong case can be made that conservatives who seek alternatives to government have more "institutional candidates" for the provision of welfare than do pro-welfare state liberals.

Hypothetically, a society can mobilize a variety of sources for welfare provision: theocracies have focused on religious organizations; capitalist economies rely on business; for communist nations, social welfare is properly a governmental responsibility. The need for social welfare—a primary function for all societies—can be addressed through a range of organized activities. A central question for democratic societies is precisely which organized activities are selected to provide specific welfare services. To the extent that such decisions involve governmental institutions, a legislative mandate is required; hence, the issue becomes a focus of public policy. To the extent that the public is affected by nongovernmental entities such as private nonprofit organizations and commercial firms, the society's welfare—as broadly defined—is also concerned. Thus, it becomes a central question for welfare theoreticians to decide which institutional candidates should be assigned responsibility for social welfare, and how much. Obviously, in a pluralistic democratic-capitalist nation such as the United States, the answer to this question presents a myriad of possible answers.

The rationale for social welfare in the United States has evolved according to the emphasis placed on those institutional candidates available to meet social needs. During particular periods a consensus evolves about the primary method for addressing need; in effect, these serve as a basis for articulating a solution to social problems. Harold Wilensky and Charles Lebeaux structured their work around a "residual conception" of welfare in which the family and market were prominent, and an "institutional conception" in which the state protected citizens against social and economic insecurity.[24] Recently, David Stoesz added a "functional conception" in which welfare is defined more closely in line with requirements of economic productivity.[25] These conceptions reflect a "consensus" around which welfare has been organized. While a consensus represents a general agreement about how to address need, it also allows a measure of diversity in doing so. This is to be expected in democratic societies. Significantly, the institutional articulation of each welfare consensus tends to be additive: older solutions to need remain as newer solutions evolve.

At the same time, each consensus is apropos of a given historical period. Since much of welfare has been predicated on social and economic circumstance, we would expect the welfare consensus to change with dislocations in these spheres. Accordingly, the *residual* consensus of welfare was discredited by the collapse of industrial capitalism during the world depression of the 1930s; the *institutional* consensus of welfare is in the process of being discredited by the flourishing of global capitalism during the 1980s. This is illustrated in Figure 1.1, a chart that identifies the primary eras of welfare and their institutional and ideological manifestations. Note that the institutional manifestations of each conception of welfare reflect the ideological cleavages typical of the American polity: liberalism and conservatism.

The Residual Consensus

Drawing on progressivism, the residual consensus of welfare called upon the altruism of private citizens and the self-interest of the business community.[26] Private citizens were asked to give time and money toward social betterment as a demonstration of civic virtue. The wealthy established philanthropies, contributing substantial sums for social welfare.[27] Settlements, such as London's Toynbee Hall and Chicago's Hull House, and the Charity Organization Societies—not to mention the numerous religiously based aid associations, such as the Salvation Army—proliferated. Such voluntary agencies routinized philanthropy, effectively socializing charity. Beginning with Denver's Associated Charities in 1887, the concept of a community appeal spread until more than 200 cities had community chests by the 1920s.[28] The culmination of the "federation movement" saw community chests standardized in the form of the United Way organizations that are evident in every American city.

During the same period, business recognized that investments in employee welfare were not only morally defensible but, in a competitive labor market, economically essential. The provision of health insurance, pensions, vacation leave, and other benefits soon became an important fixture of the modern corporation.[29] Speaking before the U.S. Chamber of Commerce in 1918, John D. Rockefeller suggested that industry be regarded as a form of social welfare. "The soundest industrial policy," he proposed, "is that which has constantly in mind the welfare of employees as well as the making of profits, and which, when human considerations

Figure 1.1

The Evolution of Welfare

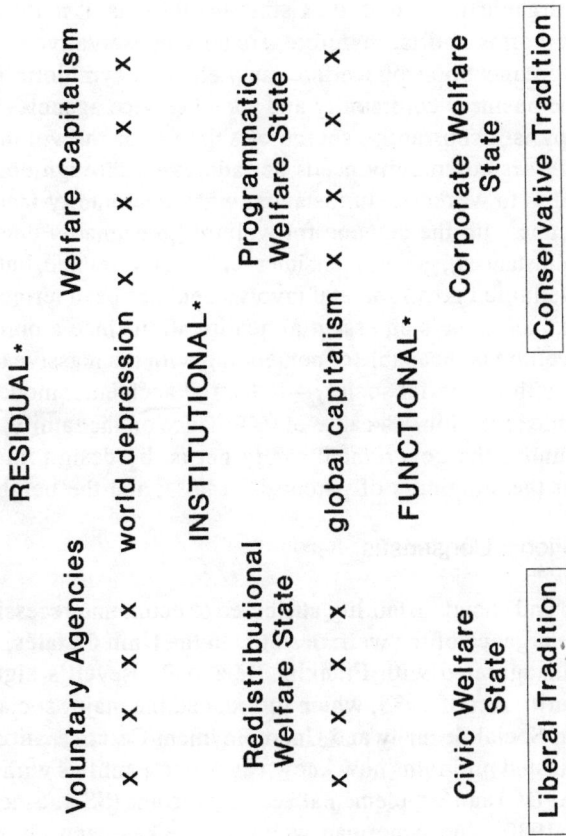

RESIDUAL*   Welfare Capitalism

Voluntary Agencies   world depression   x   x   x
x   x   x

INSTITUTIONAL*

Redistributional   global capitalism   x   x   x
Welfare State
x   x   x

Programmatic
Welfare State

FUNCTIONAL*

Civic Welfare   Corporate Welfare
State   State

| Liberal Tradition | | Conservative Tradition |

* Designates conceptions of social welfare

demand it, *subordinates profits to welfare.*"[30] The importance of welfare capitalism is recognized by the state, as evident in tax benefits—called "tax expenditures"—offered to the business community for providing benefits to workers, the provision of which would otherwise fall on government.

Social welfare, from a residual perspective, is a particularly local phenomenon. Provision to the needy is assigned to existing institutions—the family and employers—that have firsthand knowledge about the nature of an individual's distress and the merit of his or her claim. Because residual welfare is organically bound to existing institutions, it tends to reinforce community norms and is, therefore, socially conservative.[31] Evident in the residual conception of welfare, as well, is a symbiotic relationship between the business community and social service agencies. Corporate philanthropy is a substantial source of support for the voluntary sector, which addresses community needs not addressed through employer-provided benefits to workers. In instances when community institutions are unable to cope with the demand for welfare (presumably due to extraordinary circumstances), government intervention is warranted, but in a limited manner. Delimited governmental involvement has been termed the social "safety net," and this is an essential qualification since a purely residual notion of welfare is incapable of contending with the massive dislocations associated with industrial society—industrial accidents, modern warfare, and economic recession. Because of its reliance on the family, employers, and community, the government safety net is, by design, marginal—an apology for the stinginess of parents, the boss, and the neighbors.

The Institutional Consensus

Political and social instability attributed to economic recession precipitated the emergence of the welfare state. In the United States, the welfare state was inaugurated with Franklin Delano Roosevelt's signing of the Social Security Act of 1935, which introduced the major social insurance programs of Social Security and Unemployment Compensation as well as the means-tested programs now known as Aid to Families with Dependent Children (AFDC) and Supplemental Security Income (SSI). Since its origins in the mid-1930s, the American welfare state has been an amalgam of ideologically disparate programs. Unlike European welfare states such as Britain, the American welfare state did not emerge from a coherent social vision. Instead, Franklin D. Roosevelt created a patchwork welfare state in response to the social volatility of the Depression and the need to salvage what remained of capitalism. The early work programs such as the Civilian Conservation Corps and the Works Progress Administration were interim measures designed to occupy workers until a viable labor market was restored. Grant programs for the poor—what is now Aid to Families with Dependent Children and Supplemental Security Income—were peripheral to the primary focus of the New Deal: the social insurance programs. Yet, even then securities provided through the fledgling American welfare state were uneven. Unemployment insurance was not generous in its provisions, and Social Security actually excluded certain groups of workers (domestics and agricultural workers) for a time—a testament to institutional sexism and racism. Excluded altogether from the New Deal was a national health program. Thus, Roosevelt crafted what (except for Social Security) he envisioned as a temporary welfare state, whose major programs would be dismantled after the Depression.[32] Despite the ambivalence of its founders, however, the welfare state remained intact because it addressed important social needs. Perhaps as significantly, this pastiche of public policy—as incoherent as it was—proved a relief to progressive activists who had been struggling for decades to leverage child-labor, maternal-health, sanitation, and factory-safety legislation through balky *state* legislatures only to find these already field-tested programs often ruled unconstitutional by a regressive Supreme Court when they were enacted by the *federal* legislature.[33]

By the 1950s the welfare state had become an important edifice in the American social landscape; liberals then labored to expand its protections to additional groups of citizens, and to integrate its administrative features. Expectations that the welfare state would lead to greater equality, social justice and the redistribution of income and resources, seemed to occur naturally after Roosevelt's presidency. In its most focused form, these aspirations were articulated during the Great Society and War on Poverty programs of the 1960s—a period that came to represent the halcyon days of liberal influence in social welfare policy. Enduring welfare policies of the mid-1960s include the Food Stamp Act and the amendments to the Social Security Act that introduced Medicare and Medicaid. At the same time, aggressive social plans designed by some of the best minds of the period departed from traditional welfare policy, promising a poverty-free America and a nonstigmatized, community-based, and easily accessible system of social welfare. To realize these objectives, the Johnson administration developed various programs, including Volunteers in Service to America (VISTA), a domestic peace corps; Upward Bound, a program that encouraged poor and ghetto children to attend college; the Neighborhood Youth Corps for unemployed teenagers; Operation Head Start, a program that provided preschool training for low-income children; special grants and loans to rural families and migrant workers; a comprehensive Community Action Program (CAP) designed to mobilize community resources; the Legal Services Corporation; the Model Cities

Program; Job Corps, a manpower program that provided job training for disadvantaged youths from age 16 through 21; and the Economic Development Act of 1965, which provided states with grants and loans for public works and technical assistance. A key phrase in Johnson's Great Society program was "the maximum feasible participation of the poor"—a concept that informed poor communities they should invoke self-determination in their attempt to empower themselves politically and economically. Ingrained within these programs was a belief that the welfare state could ensure equality of opportunity and a redistribution of social, economic, and political resources. In one of a few rare instances in recent American history, rhetoric was backed up by fiscal resources. From the early 1960s to 1975, the number of federal domestic aid programs rose from 200 to 1,100. In their first year of operation, only 15 of the 65 local agencies in the Model Cities Program were able to spend more than 50 percent of their funds.[34]

America's brief flirtation with bold social welfare initiatives ended by the early 1970s, and with that change the euphoria of social welfare planners turned to anguish. Pressed to justify the massive expenditures of the 1960s, liberal welfare advocates had few successes to point out. While AFDC rolls doubled, social problems such as drug addiction, crime, teenage pregnancy, child abuse, and mental illness continued to soar. By 1968 the Great Society programs had become unpopular with the American public, and stinging critiques of its losses began to appear regularly in newspapers and magazines.

With Richard Nixon's election as president in 1968, the American welfare state took a contradictory turn. The bold yet brief social experiments of the War on Poverty ended as programs were terminated, reduced, or reassigned to mainstream federal bureaucracies. At the same time, the more established social programs—Social Security, Medicare, Medicaid, AFDC, and Food Stamps—expanded dramatically.[35] In addition, the Nixon administration brought forth several new social programs: Supplemental Security Income, the Comprehensive Employment and Training Act, the Community Development Block Grant Program, and the Rehabilitation Act.[36] Few supporters rose in defense as Nixon systematically crushed the Great Society initiatives of the Johnson administration. Planners formerly associated with the Great Society were mute by the early 1970s; like war criminals, they became reticent about their supposed fiscal "crimes." Some poverty warriors adhered to principle and sought to fine-tune the social programs that remained intact. Even here, disturbing cracks were appearing in the foundation of the American welfare state. When four field experiments were launched to determine the effect of implementing a guaranteed annual income program, the most ambitious of these found "significant reductions in average hours worked" by beneficiaries[37]—a conclusion that squared nicely with critics of welfare programs who claimed that benefits subverted the work ethic. Disillusioned by the much touted failure of the Great Society, many liberals abandoned ship or retreated into obscurity. In retrospect, social activists discovered that the institutional view of social welfare—essentially, the liberal version of the welfare state—had foundered on a philosophical point. The bifurcation of welfare state benefits—social insurance versus means-tested grants—introduced a dualism that would continually bedevil welfare advocates. When confronted with the problem of allocating benefits, welfare state architects had a difficult choice: benefits could be allocated according to the principles of either equity (benefits being related to contribution) or equality (benefits being not predicated on contribution). The former was frequently invoked in the form of social insurance through which the state mimicked the way in which business provided for the pension and health care needs of workers. But in the state's doing so, the problem of benefits for those not participating fully in the labor market remained. In order to solve this problem, the welfare state had to redistribute resources.

Charles Atherton makes a useful distinction by differentiating the "programmatic" welfare state, which apportions resources to specific needy populations without explicitly addressing the skewed distribution of wealth, from the "redistributive" welfare state, which seeks equality through transferring assets from the wealthy to the poor. It is the redistributive notion of the welfare state to which leftists subscribe, because it emphasizes social justice.[38] Yet, using welfare state programs to promote egalitarianism has not been easy, leaving frustrated welfare statists to portray the American experience as the "semi-welfare state"[39] or the "reluctant welfare state."[40] Ultimately, the redistributive welfare state seems to be more dependent on economic growth than welfare statists might have hoped. The reason for this is that in democratic-capitalist nations the public objects to redistributive welfare programs that are funded from taxes during periods of economic insecurity. Although the national economy expanded during the 1980s, the American middle class saw its economic fortune fall as tax cuts failed to keep pace with increases in Social Security taxes and as incomes, at best, held steady.[41] To be blunt: equality demands prosperity.

By the early 1980s, the redistributive welfare state was in trouble. Citing conservative political victories in Scandinavia, Britain, and the United States, Gosta Esping-Anderson concluded that "the voters have not only rejected flawed and expensive programs, they have renounced the very idea of the welfare state. It seems an out-dated and naive vision whose time has come and gone."[42] Significantly, there seems to be agreement even among pro-welfare theorists on both sides of the Atlantic that the welfare state is in a period of stagnation, if not contraction.[43] In the United States this is particularly so; the Reagan presidency recognized a convergence of social, political, and economic circumstances that could be traced as far back as the Carter administration, and it exploited this national frustration to halt further expansion of the welfare state.[44]

The Functional Consensus

The grand vision of a welfare state guaranteeing "a general equality of living conditions"[45] faded with the rise of global capitalism and its institutional manifestation, the "stateless corporation." The institutional consensus that protected the welfare state was predicated on an industrial capitalism in which there was congruence between the political and economic sectors. Government had confidence that social policy could be framed in reference to economic considerations about which it had some measure of influence because the economy existed within the nation-state. The essential question was the extent to which the state elected to intervene in the market. With the globalization of capital, however, national government lost this influence and with it the capacity to control welfare. If business determined that welfare costs were prohibitive, capital and labor could be transferred to more favorable sites, usually in another country.[46]

For Robert Reich, the international market is represented by "global webs" of management, production, and finance that disregard traditional political boundaries. "National governments seeking to levy income taxes on parts of global webs are often baffled," Reich observed. "As more and more enterprises become parts of global webs whose internal accounting systems record the transfers of intermediate goods and related services, earnings and revenues can appear in all sorts of places (often, not coincidentally, *where taxes are lowest*)."[47]

The second economic convulsion of the century—the globalization of capitalism—fundamentally changed social welfare. But since it did not take the form of a recession, many welfare advocates failed to recognize its significance. Global capitalism has ushered in an era of functional welfare, essentially bringing social welfare more in line with requirements of economic productivity. As the U.S. market share of basic industries was lost to foreign competitors, it became increasingly difficult for government to socialize the resultant costs. Not only did the state have less revenue as a result of a decreasing tax base, but government also had to contend with the accumulation of social debris left behind. This situation put an enormous fiscal strain on the welfare state. Means-tested programs for the poor were hardest hit because they were funded by general revenues. Since taxpayers are more politically influential than the poor, poverty programs are usually the first victims of a fiscal reprisal. But social insurance programs were also vulnerable. If the involuntary contributions (payroll taxes) that subsidize programs such as Social Security and Medicare have been hiked to the point that contributors are gagging, workers will be receptive to containment of the welfare state. Usually considered safe from the budget knife, even social insurance programs have been trimmed when select subgroups of beneficiaries have been targeted. As the economic base of the United States eroded, the nature of social welfare changed as well. It was no longer politic to propose open-ended commitments of universal entitlements to welfare; only carefully targeted investments in human capital were plausible.

With the economy falling away from the polity, political leaders were seen in a Darwinian scramble to fashion protective economic pacts— "corporatism" in Britain, "industrial policy" in the United States. The negotiation of social and economic policy by the state, business, and labor was proposed as a "social contract" that stabilized the tendency of democratic-capitalist economies to fragment.[48] The implications of this for the welfare state were elaborated by O'Connor, who predicted the emergence of a "social-industrial complex" through which welfare policy would be formulated.[49] During the 1980s, analysts from every point on the ideological continuum endorsed an industrial policy. Some called for an industrial policy heavily influenced by the federal government.[50] Others, showing allegiance toward labor and community, advanced more populist initiatives.[51] To the right, Kevin Phillips proposed a variant in which the corporate sector was dominant.[52] Playing a middle ground, Robert Reich opted for greater coordination among principles—a de facto industrial policy, without calling it as much.[53] Yet, for all the intellect aimed at developing a national economic recovery policy, a decade of deliberation failed to deliver such a policy. At the national level, the Reagan and Bush administrations pursued a laissez-faire tack, seeking further integration of the U.S. economy in international capitalism. At the state level, the sole effort to develop industrial policy was rejected by Rhode Island voters in the mid-1980s. The nation's economic priorities remained firmly under the control of corporate institutions. Proponents of an American industrial policy watched in disbelief as the U.S. economy went rudderless for a decade and the more organized economies of Japan and Germany steamed past.

While multinational corporations explored new markets overseas, human service corporations exploited the rapidly expanding service sector at home. Largely unnoticed, the business sector began exploiting health care with the passage of Medicare and Medicaid in 1965. Through the 1970s, for-profit firms made substantial inroads in several areas: nursing homes, hospital management, health maintenance organizations, child daycare, and home care. During the 1980s, continuing care communities and corrections became human service markets.[54] Human service corporations grew as a result of the increasing demand for care by consumers and the willingness of the state to contract out service provision. The proliferation of proprietary human services posed specific problems for the welfare state, however. First, through "preferential selection," for-profit firms skimmed from the client pool candidates for care who represented less serious impairments and who promised payment for care through fee-for-service or insurance. To the extent that commercial firms selected to care for those who were more profitable, uninsured clients with more complex disorders were referred to public institutions. Second, human service corporations avidly bought out other firms in order to expand service territory, diminish competition, and acquire capital. To the extent that the state contracted out care to the commercial sector, it had little choice but to meet the fee schedule of a small number of providers. The only alternative was for the state to deploy its own system of providers—a decidedly more expensive option in the short run. Third and finally, for-profit firms enjoyed advantages in administration as a result of computer technology and management information systems that allowed them greater efficiencies. Eventually, private nonprofit providers had to adopt competitive practices in order to survive.[55]

By the 1990s, the corporate sector was well positioned to challenge the governmental welfare state. The expansion of the global economy made it increasingly difficult for the federal government to control production and tax capital for purposes of advancing the general welfare. Without necessary revenues, the American welfare state withered. Regarding domestic policy, the corporate sector demonstrated a seemingly endless appetite for exploiting human service markets. To the extent that human services fell under the auspice of the corporate sector, the influence of the state in social affairs ebbed. Thus, as the governmental welfare state showed a decreasing capacity to provide for the needs of many Americans, the corporate sector filled the void. For progressives, suddenly the unthinkable was possible: the sequel to the New Deal and the War on Poverty was not another generation of liberally inspired government social programs. It was a *corporate* welfare state.

RECONSTRUCTING SOCIAL WELFARE

By the 1990s, welfare advocates found themselves on new conceptual ground. The redistributional aspects of the American welfare state had been dealt punishing blows by the Reagan administration through budget cuts in poverty programs during the 1980s. With the repeal of Catastrophic Health Insurance in 1989, the promise of new social insurance programs—the backbone of the programmatic welfare state—seemed doubtful. While governmental welfare initiatives were held up by hostile politicians and a skeptical public, corporate welfare prospered as evident in the proliferation of for-profit human service corporations. At the same time, the fiscal capacity of government was subverted as what had once been "American" corporations shed their tax obligations to the U.S. government by shifting operations overseas.

In their efforts to understand dramatic reversals in domestic policy, social observers began to associate excessive individualism and bureaucratization with the nation's ills. The growth of "megastructures"—notably the state, corporations, big labor, and professional associations—contributed to social insecurity by trivializing individuals, who increasingly looked to religious organizations, the family, civic associations, the neighborhood for support.[56] Meanwhile, the consumption binge of the 1980s fueled a "culture of narcissism" through which Wall Street parvenus became models of American success.[57] In the attempt to locate a common ground for social policy, the necessity of a "new civic consciousness" became more apparent.[58] In casting about for a new orientation for social policy, progressives acknowledged that an American welfare state modeled after its European counterparts was insufficient for the task at hand. Senator Daniel Patrick Moynihan, himself a warrior on poverty, stated as much when he called for the creation of a postindustrial orientation for social policy. *"The issues of social policy the United States faces today have no European counterpart nor any European model of a viable solution. They are American problems, and we Americans are going to have to think them through by ourselves."*[59] An indigenous solution to the nation's social problems was needed; solutions fashioned a half-century ago from an imported institutional model were no longer a valid guide for social welfare policy.

In this respect, forward-thinking social activists realized that they must seek to restore public confidence in social welfare by following a dual track. Welfare policy must be reconstructed so that social programs would be consistent with the requirements of international competitiveness. In addition to reinforcing national productivity, social programs must be designed to support work, family, and community. The case for reconstructing social welfare was compelling enough. Progressive critics of traditional welfare programs pointed out that the nation had little choice in the matter; economic and political factors compelled the restructuring of social welfare. The United States could no longer afford to make universal grants to populations without considering how these effect productivity, since the nation's competitive standing in the global economy would not allow it. Architects of social programs could no longer afford to disregard the importance of work, family, and community in designing welfare programs, because the public would not support such programs. As social activists had done before, it was once again time to reinvent the nation's approach to social welfare.

After a decade of ebbing political support and fiscal reprisals exacted against the American welfare state, the need for reassessment should be abundantly clear. Our solution to this set of circumstances—termed "the civic welfare state"—is described in the last section of this book. Lest Santayana's warning—"those who cannot remember the past are condemned to repeat it"—go unheeded, the reconstruction of social welfare must begin with an assessment of the crisis of the American welfare state and the ideological forces that are pulling it apart, the subjects to which we now turn.

NOTES

1. Robert Kuttner, *The Economic Illusion* (Boston: Houghton Mifflin, 1984), p. 263.

2. Midgley, "The New Christian Right, Social Policy, and the Welfare State," *Journal of Sociology and Social Welfare* 17 (Winter 1990).

3. Richard Titmuss, *Commitment to Welfare* (New York: Pantheon, 1968), p. 127.

4. Harold Wilensky and Charles Lebeaux, *Industrial Society and Social Welfare* (New York: Free Press, 1965), p. 147.

5. "Poorer, Hungrier," *New York Times* (April 10, 1983), p. 20E.

6. Kathleen Newland, *Infant Mortality and the Health of Societies* (Washington, D.C.: Worldwatch Institute, 1981).

7. Kathleen Noble, "Are Program Cuts Linked to Increased Infant Death?" *New York Times* (February 13, 1983).

8. Dana Hughes, et al., *The Health of America's Children* (Washington, D.C.: Children's Defense Fund, 1987), p. viii.

9. Richard Estes, *The Social Progress of Nations* (New York: Praeger, 1984), pp. 106–9.

10. Ira Sharkansky, *The United States: A Study of a Developing Country* (New York: Longman, 1975).

11. Gosta Esping-Andersen, "After the Welfare State," *Public Welfare* 44 (Winter 1983).

12. Frank Painton, "Reassessing the Welfare State," *Time* (April 15, 1981), p. 32.

13. Robert Morris, *Testing the Limits of Social Welfare* (Hanover, N.H.: University of New England Press, 1988).

14. James O'Connor, *The Fiscal Crisis of the State* (New York: St. Martin's Press

15. Ian Gough, *The Political Economy of the Welfare State* (London: Macmillan, 1979).

16. Buchanan and R. Tollison (eds.), *Theory of Public Choice* (Ann Arbor: University of Michigan Press, 1972); James Buchanan and R. Wagner (eds.), *Democracy in Deficit* (New York: Academic Press, 1977); President's Commission on Privatization, *Privatization: Toward More Effective Government* (Washington, D.C.: U.S. Government Printing Office, 1988).

17. Norman Johnson, *The Welfare State in Transition* (Amherst: University of Massachusetts Press, 1987).

18. Richard M. Titmuss, *Essays on the Welfare State* (Boston: Beacon Press, 1969).

19. Richard M. Titmuss, *Commitment to Welfare* (New York: Pantheon, 1968), pp. 42, 52.

20. Sheila Kamerman, "The New Mixed Economy of Welfare," *Social Work* (January/February 1983).

21. Michael Walzer, "Toward a Theory of Social Assignments," in W. Knowlton and R. Zeckhauser (eds.), *American Society: Public and Private Responses* (Cambridge, Mass.: Ballinger, 1986).

22. Johnson, *Welfare State in Transition*.

23. David Stoesz, "A Theory of Social Welfare," *Social Work* 34 (January/February 1989), pp. 101–7.

24. Wilensky and Lebeaux, *Industrial Society and Social Welfare*.

25. David Stoesz, "The Functional Conception of Social Welfare," *Social Work* 33 (March 1988), pp. 58–59.

26. Roy Lubove, *The Professional Altruist* (New York: Atheneum, 1969).

27. Brian O'Connell, *Philanthropy in Action* (Washington, D.C.: Foundation Center, 1987); Theresa Odendahl, *Charity Begins at Home* (New York: Basic Books, 1990).

28. William Trattner, *From Poor Law to Welfare State* (New York: Macmillan, 1974).

29. Neil Gilbert, *Capitalism and the Welfare State* (New Haven, Conn.: Yale University Press, 1983), p. 3.

30. Norman Furniss and Timothy Tilton, *The Case for the Welfare State* (Bloomington: Indiana University Press, 1977), p. 156; original emphasis.

31. Stoesz, "Theory of Social Welfare."

32. Jacob Fisher, *The Response of Social Work to the Depression* (New York: Schenkman Books, 1980).

33. Kenneth Davis, *FDR: The New Deal Years 1933–1937* (New York: Random House, 1986).

34. Neil Gilbert, "The Welfare State Adrift," *Social Work* 31 (July/August 1986), p. 252.

35. Although Nixon ended many of the experimental programs of the Great Society, he did not curb welfare expenditures, which grew at a healthy rate during his administration. See Diane DiNitto and Thomas R. Dye, *Social Welfare: Politics and Public Policy* (Englewood Cliffs, N.J.: Prentice-Hall, 1987).

36. Bruce Jansson, *The Reluctant Welfare State: A History of American Social Welfare Policies* (Belmont, Calif.: Wadsworth, 1988).

37. James Seaberg, "Family Policy Revisited," *Social Work* 35 (November 1990), p. 552.

38. Charles Atherton, "The Welfare State: Still on Solid Ground," *Social Service Review* 63 (Fall 1989), pp. 167–79.

39. Michael Katz, *In the Shadow of the Poorhouse: A Social History of Welfare in America* (New York: Basic Books, 1986).

40. Jansson, *Reluctant Welfare State.*

41. Kevin Phillips, *The Politics of Rich and Poor* (New York: Random House, 1990).

42. Esping-Andersen, "After the Welfare State," p. 28.

43. Ramesh Mishra, *The Welfare State in Crisis* (New York: St. Martin's Press and Sussex, England: Wheatsheaf, 1984); Julian LeGrand and Ray Robinson, *Privatization and the Welfare State* (London: George Allen and Unwin, 1984); Herbert Gans, *Middle American Individualism* (New York: Free Press, 1988); Michael Sandel, "Democrats and Community," *New Republic* (February 22, 1988).

44. Sidney Blumenthal and Thomas Edsall (eds.), *The Reagan Legacy* (New York: Pantheon, 1988); Phillips, *Politics of Rich and Poor*; James Midgley (ed.), "The Reagan Legacy and the Welfare State," special issue of the *Journal of Sociology and Social Welfare* (forthcoming 1992).

45. Furniss and Tilton, *Case for the Welfare State*, p. 20.

46. W. Holstein, "The Stateless Corporation," *Business Week* 3159 (1989).

47. Robert Reich, *The Work of Nations* (New York: Knopf, 1991), pp. 114–15; emphasis added.

48. Gough, *Political Economy of the Welfare State*, p. 149.

49. O'Connor, *Fiscal Crisis of the State*, p. 54.

50. Lester Thurow, *The Zero-sum Society* (New York: Basic Books, 1980); Robert Kuttner, *The Economic Illusion* (Boston: Houghton Mifflin, 1984); Robert Kuttner, *The Life of the Party* (New York: Viking, 1987).

51. Samuel Bowles, David Gordon, and Thomas Weisskopf, *Beyond the Wasteland* (Garden City, N.Y.: Anchor, 1983); Gar Alperovitz and Jeff Faux, *Rebuilding America* (New York: Pantheon, 1984); Bennett Harrison and Barry Bluestone, *The Great U-Turn* (New York: Basic Books, 1988).

52. Kevin Phillips, *Staying on Top* (New York: Random House, 1984).

53. Robert Reich, *The Next American Frontier* (New York: Times Books, 1983); Robert Reich, *Tales of a New America* (New York: Times Books, 1987).

54. David Stoesz, "Corporate Welfare," *Social Work* 31 (July/August 1986), pp. 245–49.

55. David Stoesz, "Human Service Corporations," *Administration in Social Work* 13, 3/4 (1989), pp. 190–92.

56. Peter Berger and Richard Neuhaus, *To Empower People* (Washington, D.C.: American Enterprise Institute, 1977).

57. Christopher Lasch, *The Culture of Narcissism* (New York: W. W. Norton, 1979).

58. William Sullivan, *Reconstructing Public Philosophy* (Berkeley: University of California Press, 1986), p. 156.

59. Daniel Patrick Moynihan, *Came the Revolution* (San Diego: Harcourt Brace Jovanovich, 1988), p. 291; original emphasis.

2

The Crisis of the Welfare State

Harold Jacob Karger

By the end of the 1980s, American welfare advocates had become all too familiar with the social, economic, and political manifestations of institutional failure. Social advocates found themselves on the defensive during the Reagan era, salvaging welfare programs that been under assault throughout the decade. Some remembered the stirring years of the War on Poverty and looked forward to an eventual return to liberal social policy initiatives. Welfare advocates held faith in the cyclical nature of social legislation, reassured by liberals such as Arthur Schlesinger, Jr., that the pendulum of public sentiment would swing in a more beneficent arc, restoring the liberal momentum that had spawned social programs during the New Deal and the War on Poverty. Unfortunately, few looked beyond the United States, where theorists had not only identified the internal contradictions of the welfare state, but also predicted its demise. For theorists educated in the tradition of the European left,[1] it came as no surprise that the American welfare state had reached an impasse: escalating demands for benefits and services outstripped revenues, which were increasingly scarce as the economic base declined. This economic conundrum contributed to a political convulsion as elected officials struggled to pare benefits to which the public had become accustomed. Public disaffection from social programs increased as benefits declined, while taxes appeared to remain high. It became more plausible to believe that nongovernmental sources of assistance (or that individuals using their taxed income more prudently themselves) were better vehicles to advance the common good.

Eventually, the very legitimacy of the welfare state came into question. Economic, social, and political forces contributing to the disassemblage of the welfare state were reinforced as the institutional foundation and the carefully crafted matrix of social provisions began to unravel. After such a discouraging decade, it is not surprising that welfare advocates would seek solace in a long-awaited swing of the ideological pendulum—a swing that would return compassion, integrity, and beneficence to social policy. Had they been more introspective in analyzing their predicament, however, an altogether different analogy would have come to mind: a double helix with the connecting elements falling out of the middle.

THE LOSS OF LEGITIMACY

No analysis of the welfare state was more prescient than that of Ramesh Mishra, a policy professor at Canada's McMaster University. Mishra identified three conditions that signaled a crisis in the welfare state: (1) a government fiscal crisis that was increasingly difficult to moderate, leading to cutbacks in welfare benefits; (2) the emergence of a political philosophy that viewed welfare expenditures as a barrier to economic growth; and (3) a crisis of legitimation in which the capacity of the welfare state to solve social problems rapidly deteriorated, resulting in a loss of public confidence.[2] Unfortunately, the American welfare crisis fits squarely within Mishra's framework. For one, the American welfare state has been in the throes of severe budgetary cutbacks since the late 1970s, with particularly sharp reductions inflicted during the 1980s. Mishra's second criterion was met by the growth of neoconservatism within the Republican party and its corollary—neoliberalism—within the Democratic party. Finally, both the American public and client groups showed less faith in the capacity of the American welfare state to function as a sound and dependable social institution.

Indeed, the stability of the American welfare state rested with its capacity to maintain a tenuous balancing act. The German theorist Claus Offe recognized as much when he examined the welfare state in relation to competing visions of social welfare. Offe argues that the social welfare state is "a constantly moving compromise between the values of security and humanitarianism . . . on the one hand, and individual initiative and self-reliance in the competitive order on the other."[3] The fuzzy goals of the American welfare state become only more muddled by a lack of clarity in the objectives of social programs. Moreover, instead of explicitly stating the goals of the welfare state, proponents have preferred to use vague language. For example, one welfare advocate defined social welfare as "those organized activities that are primarily and directly concerned with the conservation, the protection, and the improvement of human resources."[4] The purposeful obfuscation of social welfare goals has been important for several reasons. For one, vague goals allowed welfare state administrators to shape the social welfare state to fit the mercurial moods of American political opinion. In periods of political liberalism, such as the New Deal and the War on Poverty, the welfare state moved to the forefront of progressive social and political reform. In conservative periods, such as the 1980s, the welfare state was portrayed as a benign form of state charity. Instead of being proactive in these latter times, the welfare state was defined as the rescuer of last resort and a glimmer of compassion in an otherwise callous free market. Regardless of the political milieu, however, the fit between American values and the welfare state has always been uneasy. Yet, several themes have persisted: an emphasis on the "worthy poor," low benefit levels, and the chronic underfunding of social programs.

It comes as no surprise, then, that the American welfare state is constantly challenged from without and within—by those seeking to contain its scope versus those demanding increased protections. Conservatives are the most outspoken external critics of the welfare state, viewing social welfare as a tax burden and a drain on the nation's economy. Hence, the emphasis on privatizing social services, cutting entitlement programs, and redefining the welfare state as a safety net rather than a series of universal programs designed to enhance the quality of life for all citizens.[5] The notion of universal entitlement programs is particularly repugnant to conservatives, who prefer welfare receipt to be contingent on dire need. For most anti-welfare conservatives, the relationship between the welfare state and capitalism is untenable—a particular irony since much of the stability enjoyed by democratic capitalism can be directly attributed to the social stability encouraged by welfare state programs.

While representing a different orientation, client groups have also emerged as critics of welfare state programs. Dissatisfied with arcane bureaucratic procedures and scanty benefits, client groups have registered well-grounded grievances against the welfare state. For clients receiving benefits from social programs, the coverage of the welfare state is less adequate than the public often appreciates. Social Security fails to pull many pensioners out of poverty; Medicare's health-care provisions are nowhere near comprehensive, and still a premium is exacted from beneficiaries. The provisions of programs targeted for the poor are notoriously inadequate. Concerning groups left to fend for themselves in a competitive environment for which they are poorly prepared—minority youth, undocumented workers, dependent children, the illiterate—the welfare state provides essential benefits for which they are often ineligible. In those instances where they may be entitled to benefits, eligibility requirements are so irrelevant to client circumstance that the result is less often desperately needed assistance and more often publicly voiced frustration. While the grievances of welfare clients have a ring of truth, the seemingly insatiable public appetite for services increases the burden for a welfare state that is already laboring under insufficient resources. Despite these attacks on the legitimacy of the welfare state, many clients view social programs as a source of essential benefits to which they have a rightful claim.

Accelerating demands for benefits contribute to a negative image of the welfare state as an unlimited insurance company that is expected to underwrite all needs, risks, and failures. From this perspective—one advanced by public-choice theorists—the welfare state is seen as having an addictive effect on subgroups who need and use welfare services. Gays lobby for more money for AIDS research, advocates for the homeless demand more shelters and low-cost housing, and defenders of public assistance recipients argue for increased income-maintenance benefits. Each group sees the welfare state as having the capacity to solve its problems, *if* only more money were allocated.

And it is true that, as the scope of the welfare state is diffused by encompassing more entitled groups, its impact on any given social problem or client group is lessened. The resource limitations of the welfare state, coupled with the diversity of its constituency and the range of problems it must handle, ensures that it will fail to meet the expectations of many if not most of the groups who depend on it. Sadly, the disillusionment, frustration, and anger of clients deepen with each new policy failure.

Little of this has been lost on a less than bemused public that is expected to understand somehow all the manifestations of these competing forces. The dilemma is only exacerbated by the news accounts televising the vociferous demands of pensioners and the poor contrasted with seemingly endless trips to and from committee rooms as elected officials try to reconcile an increasingly precarious budget situation. In short, the failure of the welfare state to tackle the hard social problems facing American society has contributed to a crisis of legitimation.

Riven by disagreement about its purpose and its performance, the American welfare state was more vulnerable to conservative criticism in the 1980s than at any point in its 50-year history. Conservatives, for their part, repackaged their critique of the welfare state. In place of the anti-welfare diatribes of the 1950s, neoconservatives fashioned an argument that was not only consistent with American values but that also included plausible alternatives to liberally inspired programs. Most significantly, liberals— once the progenitors of America's most noble experiment in promoting the common good—were soon on the defensive, besieged by conservative politicians, religious fundamentalists, and irate taxpayers. To their dismay, welfare advocates found little support for social programs. Under assault, few rallied to defend the welfare state—an irony that liberals would sooner forget. The American public, the very constituency for which a half-century of social legislation had been constructed, was abandoning it.

REAGAN AND THE FISCAL DILEMMA
OF THE WELFARE STATE

The American welfare state experienced dramatic growth in the 1960s as a result of a basically sound and growing economy. However, the liberal consensus that had guided the U.S. welfare state since the New Deal began to disintegrate in the wake of the economic slowdown of the 1970s.[6] The recession of the 1970s seemed to confirm what conservatives had been saying all along: the size, scope, and comprehensiveness of the welfare state was a major burden that drained society of vital investment capital through high levels of taxation. Moreover, conservatives maintained that the welfare state ruptured social cohesiveness by encouraging a strong dependence on welfare state programs. Stuart Butler of the Heritage Foundation summed up the critique when he faulted government programs for a breakdown in the mutual obligations between groups, a lack of attention to efficiencies and incentives in the way programs were being operated and benefits awarded, an induced dependency of beneficiaries on programs, and a growth of the welfare industry and its special interest groups—particularly professional associations.[7]

In building their case against social programs, conservatives benefited from a convergence of social, political, and economic circumstances. As early as the Carter presidency, opinion polls foreshadowed the credibility crisis of the American welfare state. In 1976, for example, most Americans opposed spending for social welfare, regardless of age, education, gender, and political affiliation. Significantly, *even those earning less than $10,000 a year opposed funding welfare programs*. Only nonwhites approved welfare expenditures.[8] By the end of the Reagan presidency, the public was more favorable toward welfare, but fiscal concerns remained paramount. In a 1988 study, researchers from the Public Agenda Foundation solicited responses from 545 adults about specific solutions (with hypothetical costs included) to particular social problems: welfare reform, early childhood intervention, the working poor, and long-term care. The report concluded that, "while a majority wants the government's role to be expanded in certain ways, there are definite limits to what people are willing to pay for expanding government's role in social welfare. . . . Significantly, only a minority indicated a willingness to pay more than $25 per year for any of the proposals. This was true even for the most popular of them, the proposal to provide government assistance for long-term care."[9]

Public antipathy toward welfare helped fuel the "traditionalist movement" and the political agenda of the New Right.[10] A loose amalgam of secular conservatives, religious fundamentalists, and traditionalists began in the late 1970s to build a broad populist base to promote family, flag, and faith at the same time railing against liberal positions favoring abortion, the separation of church and state, and children's rights. Substituting protest and telemarketing for fire and brimstone, evangelicals were instrumental in the early victories of the Reagan revolution.[11] While traditionalist influences at the national level ebbed during the late 1980s, there was little indication that "movement conservatives" had run out of steam. They simply refocused their objectives at state and local levels around specific issues, such as abortion.

The traditionalist thrust in politics received a boost with the 1988 presidential candidacy of televangelist Pat Robertson. Although he lost in the primaries, Robertson's interest in politics persevered. In 1990, Robertson founded the Christian Coalition to "train conservative Christians to shape government policy." Drawing recruits from his 1.8 million-member presidential campaign mailing list, Robertson was expecting to have 150,000 members in 500 chapters by 1991.[12] As a sequel to the now defunct Moral Majority, the Christian Coalition represents a major effort to routinize traditionalist aspirations in politics. As such, it will function to continue to pull Republican party politics in the direction of the social agenda of the New Right.

Much to the dismay of welfare state advocates, public antipathy and traditionalist hostility led to the erosion of political support for social programs. After four decades of cultivation, Democrats who had once exploited Harry Hopkin's dictum—"tax, tax, spend, spend, elect, elect"—suddenly found the welfare state a liability. Many Democrats reneged on their carte blanche support of entitlement programs, having discovered that "liberalism" was associated with publicly funded programs for the poor. Democrats, the traditional defenders of New Deal-type social programs, followed public sentiment as it swung to the right—a shift in ideology that continued throughout the 1980s. By the end of the decade, only 29 percent of the electorate identified themselves as liberal, while 40 percent identified themselves as conservative.[13] The political consequences of this shift in public opinion were enormous. "The power of the national consensus that underpinned the Democratic Party's liberal, post-New Deal coalition has been weakened, if not, to some degree, dissolved," observed *Washington Post* editor Thomas Edsall.[14] Sensing public disaffection from the traditional liberal inclination in social affairs, Democratic operatives had second thoughts about their party's public policy legacy. "The values and ideas associated with the New Deal and the Great Society still float about in public discourse," reflected Democratic pollster Stanley Greenberg, "but they are no longer embedded in a common historic experience or a convincing story."[15] A conspiracy of events, then, preceded the conservative tide that was to prevail in social policy during the 1980s.

The conservative argument played to a receptive audience, and in 1979 Ronald Reagan was elected to the presidency of the United States. Running on an anti-welfare plank, Reagan appealed for a return to the halcyon days of yesteryear—a largely imaginary period when hard work ensured success, self-reliance was the cornerstone of society, neighbor helped neighbor, government was unobtrusive, and social and personal values were clear and mutually agreed upon. Reagan's approach to the welfare state was rooted in the same simplistic rhetoric: get rid of welfare chiselers, trim bloated welfare budgets, end unnecessary and redundant programs, stimulate self-reliance in welfare recipients, and force the slothful to work.

Flushed by electoral victory and a Republican Senate, Reagan began to fulfill his campaign promises by slashing welfare expenditures, developing stringent regulations to limit coverage, and making proposals to cut entitlement and social insurance programs. In Reagan's bold and punishing budget cuts of 1981, AFDC funding was reduced by 11.7 percent and stiffer eligibility requirements were enacted. The Food Stamp Program was reduced by 18.8 percent (other food programs were reduced by 13.3 percent), and strikers and students became ineligible for benefits. The duration of unemployment insurance was reduced by 13 weeks.[16] As a result of Reagan's budget cuts and other fiscal policies, the poverty rate climbed to 15.3 percent in 1984—higher than any year since before the War on Poverty programs in the middle 1960s.[17]

Support for Reagan's initiatives came not only from traditional conservatives, but also from a large and disenfranchised group of blue- and white-collar workers, many of whom were registered Democrats. Even before Reagan's presidency, a conservative political and social agenda had enjoyed wide support by the late 1970s. This phenomenon occurred for several reasons. First, many traditional middle-class workers were sliding into a lower standard of living as a result of decreased or stagnant real incomes, high levels of under- and unemployment, and an increase in single-parent families.[18] Many of these workers grasped at the issue of lower taxes in a desperate attempt to shore up their eroded standard of living.[19] Second, stereotypes of "welfare cheats" and "well-off" AFDC recipients flourished because of the physical and social isolation of the poor. Third, liberal affirmative action programs—associated with the social welfare state—became a dreaded symbol for many middle-class white males struggling to hold onto their increasingly precarious economic standing. Fourth and lastly, many of Reagan's younger supporters had always lived in a welfare state and thus took its privileges for granted. These people had little idea of the dangers of life outside of the protective umbrella of the American welfare state.

Several major changes occurred as a result of the budget cuts of the early 1980s and the general fiscal policies of the Reagan administration. For one, despite the economic recovery of the middle and late 1980s, a poverty rate of more than 13 percent (32 million people) existed for most of the decade—a number higher than in the recession years of 1974 and 1975. In 1978 the poverty rate was 11.4 percent, with an unemployment rate of more than 6 percent. By 1988 (at the height of the economic recovery) the poverty rate was 13.1 percent, but the unemployment rate had dropped to around 5 percent.[20] Thus, poverty rates no longer directly responded to labor market conditions, which suggested that many of the poor were impervious to the ebb and flow of economic life. In other words, there seemed to be a growing lumpenproletariat that remained poor despite the prevailing economic conditions in the United States. With increasing frequency, social commentators spoke of an American "underclass."

During the eight years of Reagan's presidency there was a clear retrenchment in the welfare state. With the exception of the Family Support Act, a marginal enhancement of the Aid to Families with Dependent Children Program (AFDC),[21] and a flirtation with Catastrophic Health Insurance, no major social welfare programs were initiated and the existing ones operated on inadequate budgets. Despite Reagan's claims not to have reduced benefits for the needy, total appropriations for low-income entitlement programs fell by 57 percent from fiscal year 1981 to 1989, after adjusting for inflation.[22] As a result, even though poverty rates increased from 1978 to 1984, AFDC rolls dropped—from 11.4 million recipients in 1975 to 10.6 million in 1984. This situation was worsened by the failure of AFDC benefits to keep pace with inflation, having fallen more than 31 percent in the typical state from 1970 to 1987. At present, two-thirds of the eligible poor receive no AFDC benefits, and more than half the eligible poor get neither Food Stamps nor Medicaid coverage.[23]

Despite Reagan's public posturing, he was not able to dismantle the major components of the welfare state. Means-tested programs took direct hits, but remained intact; social insurance programs were basically spared. Apart from some erosion, the fundamental programs and services of the American welfare state—although battered—remained intact. While conservatives accomplished only limited objectives through budget cuts, their real success lay with undermining the ideological and the fiscal bases of the welfare state. Specifically, Reagan was able to sabotage the welfare state not by direct budget cuts, but by creating the largest federal debt in American history.

The scope of the federal debt often seems difficult to comprehend. While the 1989 gross national product (GNP) of the United States was slightly over $5 trillion, the federal debt was rapidly approaching $3 trillion. In other words, the federal debt equaled three-fifths of the entire GNP in 1989. In 1988 the world traded a total of $2.7 trillion worth of goods— less than the $2.83-trillion U.S. federal debt in the third quarter of 1989. Broken down, the federal debt totaled over $13,000 for every man, woman, and child in the United States. By creating enormous deficits (from about $50 billion a year in the Carter term to $145-200 billion a year in the 1980s), the Reagan economic legacy paralyzed the growth of public services well into the next century. Perhaps more to the point, this federal debt made the creation of new fiscal-based social welfare programs almost inconceivable regardless of any emerging social problems. Indeed, the enormity of the problem failed to register with politicians until the 1990 budget debacle when a stalemate between Congress and the White House actually shut down the federal government for a brief period.

THE GLOBAL ECONOMY AND THE AMERICAN WELFARE STATE

The domestic events that crippled the American welfare state during the 1980s had their roots in international economics. Once the world's undisputed economic leader, the United States is now struggling to maintain an economic presence in a highly competitive world economy.[24] In 1980 the United States had a $2-billion trade surplus; by 1984 other countries were gradually catching up with its productivity, and that surplus turned into a deficit of $102 billion.[25] To maintain prosperity and finance an increasingly (if relatively) unproductive economy, the United States turned to massive foreign borrowing. In 1982 America had net foreign assets of $152 billion; by 1986 it surpassed Brazil to become the world's largest debtor nation.

The economic problems of the United States were complicated by several factors. From 1960 to 1980, America's share of the world's manufactured exports fell from 25 to 17 percent. By 1988 the United States had dropped to the third largest exporter ($320 billion), behind West Germany ($323 billion) and ahead of Japan ($256 billion). Even with a 27-percent increase in exports in 1988 (due mainly to a drop in the dollar), America imported $460 billion worth of goods, making it the world's largest importer.[26] (In comparison, Germany imported $251 billion in 1988 and Britain $189 billion.) By the early 1980s the United States imported 50 percent of its consumer electronics, 30 percent of its automobiles, and a large proportion of cameras, shoes, tools, tires, machinery, and clothes.[27] Apart from the trade deficit, another striking imbalance appeared. In terms of dollar value, Japan's number-one export to the United States was motor vehicles, followed by heavy equipment, iron and steel plates, and consumer electronics. In contrast, the leading exports of the United States to Japan were soybeans, corn, fir and hemlock logs, coal, wheat, and cotton.[28] In essence, the United States was becoming an agricultural exporter struggling to compete in an industrialized global economy.

Despite these economic problems, free-trade exponents continued to tout the advantages of unfettered corporate activity in the international arena. Conservative economists Alvin Rabushka of the Hoover Institution and Steve Hanke of Johns Hopkins University outlined the requirements for success in the new economic community: (1) a laissez-faire economic approach emphasizing free trade and markets, no tariffs, and a commitment to the free movement of capital; (2) an emphasis on research and development; (3) dramatic reductions in corporate and progressive income taxes; (4) a decrease in governmental regulations and in the power of regulatory agencies; (5) a privatization of the economy by selling off publicly owned industries, utilities, and transportation systems; (6) a reduction in the role of government in the marketplace, including slashing or eliminating public employment programs; and (7) a decrease in welfare activities, including major cuts in entitlement programs.[29] Clearly, the internationalization of capital had significant, if downplayed, implications for domestic policy.

The consequences of the global market for American domestic policy became clearer during the 1980s. For example, although 20 million new jobs were created in the 1980s, they were not with the Fortune 500 companies, which cut their workforces by 3.5 million. Many of the new jobs created in the past decade were low-paying service positions in the secondary labor market.[30] Thus, despite a 6-percent unemployment rate, more than 44 percent of the jobs created in the United States between 1979 and 1985 paid less than $7,400 per year.[31] Instead of achieving economic self-sufficiency, many workers in these low-paying jobs remained eligible for basic welfare benefits. Thus, because of its mandate to provide services for economically dislocated workers, government implicitly assumes the social costs of corporate competition in the new global economy. For Robert Kuttner, the gradual erosion of the American economy as U.S. corporations forsake their domestic obligations in favor of a furtive chase for ever cheaper production locations abroad poses a specter as traumatic as the Great Depression. Kuttner aptly names this protracted retreat from prosperity "the slow bleed."[32]

At the same time, the capacity of government to shoulder more of the burden associated with corporate competition in the global market declines as the state pares its expenditures. As the federal government backs away from its welfare commitment, costs are "devolved" to states and localities. In 1989, for example, only 31 percent of the short-term unemployed in the United States received benefits—a figure that compared unfavorably to the 75 percent who received benefits in the 1970s.[33] Moreover, laying off or terminating workers affects merchants, banks, landlords, and the tax base of state and local governments. As might be expected, this scenario contributes to a deterioration in psychological health and social relations. Previous studies had already linked economy-related changes to an increase in mental illness and suicide rates and a rise in the crime rate.[34]

As troubling as the global market was for communities that had lost jobs and tax revenues as corporations moved manufacturing abroad, pervasive changes within the national labor market also became apparent. Thomas Donahue of the AFL-CIO observed

> a trend toward replacing long-term employees with part-time and temporary ones who have no personal stake in the company's success, no permanent home workplace, only the most transitory and superficial relationships with their fellow workers, and—of course—no regular benefits, vacations, holidays, or company life and health insurance plans, and no retirement benefits at the end of a working lifetime. If that trend prevails, there's a serious danger that a large piece of our society will be split three ways: At the top, a highly paid professional, managerial and technical group, made smaller and more tightly knit by computer networks. Next, a layer of outside contractors providing materials and services that the corporate elites would rather buy than provide in-house. And at the bottom, doing the work, a permanent floating population of rootless functionaries, moving from job to job or to the unemployment line, who would be closer to the Marxist idea of a dispossessed proletariat than anything that America has seen so far.[35]

The creation of an American lumpenproletariat presaged greater dilemmas for an already overextended welfare state. Because low-paid and marginal workers have few of the traditional employment protections accorded a stable workforce, they require more social welfare benefits, including various forms of income support. Moreover, with scant retirement benefits and insufficient incomes to create their own retirement plan, this group would likely consume high levels of welfare benefits when they retire. By allowing corporations to create a floating labor force, government appeared to enter into a new social contract with business, effectively mortgaging the nation's future.

By the early 1990s, the consequences of the global economy for domestic social policy were increasingly clear. The expansion of the international economy influenced domestic policy in two primary ways. Bennett Harrison and Barry Bluestone have written extensively about the effect of international capital on the manufacturing sector. In the face of international competition, American industry responded by abandoning core businesses, investing offshore, shifting capital into highly speculative ventures, subcontracting with low-wage contractors both domestically and abroad, and substituting part-time workers for full-time employees.[36] This economic crisis was manifested by "deindustrialization," a widespread and systematic disinvestment in the nation's productive capacity. Harrison and Bluestone argued that "the essential problem with the U.S. economy can be traced to the way capital—in the forms of financial resources and of real plant and equipment—has been diverted from productive investment . . . into unproductive speculation, mergers and acquisitions, and foreign investment."[37] Indeed, high-income production jobs declined by 1.4 million between 1970 and 1982.[38] Permanent job losses in Ohio included a 20-percent loss in primary metals manufacturing, a 10-percent loss in electronic equipment manufacturing, and a 19-percent loss in transportation equipment manufacturing. The loss of high-paying manufacturing jobs corresponded to increased poverty levels in the traditional industrial states. In Pennsylvania, New Jersey, and New York the poverty rates climbed from 10.4 percent in 1978 to 13.4 percent in 1985; in Michigan, Ohio and Illinois they went up from 10 percent to 14 percent.[39] In the wake of deindustrialization lay empty factories, displaced workers, bankrupt communities, and widespread social dislocation.

Accompanying deindustrialization is the emergence of what Robert Reich calls a "global web" of production, marketing, and financial institutions. As blue-collar jobs are shifted abroad, they are replaced by service-sector jobs at home. Reich estimates that "routine production services" (similar to manufacturing jobs in the industrial sector) account for 25 percent of employment; "in-person services" (routine people-processing activities) account for 30 percent; and "symbolic-analytic services" (traders in financial and intellectual capital on which international capital depends) account for 20 percent. For the United States the global market has meant decreases in better-paying, routine production jobs and increases in low-wage, in-person service positions.[40] Because this job substitution is gradual and its effects on specific communities is differential, the impact of these economic events for the nation is not always visible. During recessions, however, the globalization of capital presents serious problems for social welfare. Specifically, less economically secure workers are more likely to be casualties of a contracting economy. The compounding factor, however, is that because of the globalization of capital a significant portion of corporate wealth is no longer located within the nation's authority for purposes of taxation. Moreover, because of their mobility, corporations can blackmail government into tax concessions by threatening plant closures, relocating operations offshore, or laying off large numbers of workers. According to Unisys Corporation Chairman W. Michael Blumenthal, the "stateless" corporation is more facile than the multinationals of a generation ago, moving production and research units "around the world without particular reference to national borders."[41] As a result, government is denied the essential tax revenues necessary to ameliorate the distress felt by workers, their families and communities.

IMPLICATIONS FOR THE WELFARE STATE

The interaction of a conservative political climate at home and global markets abroad effectively straightjacketed the American welfare state throughout the 1980s. Policies that favored consumption over investment, the private over the public, and laissez-faire over regulated markets not only reversed a liberal orientation to social policy but, when translated into welfare legislation, also diminished the comparatively weak protections that the American welfare state afforded its citizens. Despite evidence that the global economy was posing difficulties for domestic policy, the Reagan, then Bush, administrations chose to rely on the private sector to chart a course through what was becoming increasingly rough waters. This course complemented the goals of free-marketeers who expected localities themselves to dispose of the detritus that had washed to their shores as a result of the disruptive effects of international capitalism.

Data generated during the 1980s showed that the American welfare state as a social institution had lost ground. While a few individuals and corporations increased their fortunes (the incomes of the top 1 percent having risen from $174,500 in 1977 to $304,000 in 1987, a huge 74-percent rise),[42] the middle class and public institutions grew relatively poorer. Moreover, laissez-faire labor policies encouraged greater income inequality. For example, in 1960 the average CEO was paid 41 times more than a shop floor worker; by 1988 that CEO earned 91 times more than the factory worker.[43] Between 1973 and 1984, families with incomes over $50,000 per year increased from 14.9 to 15.6 percent. During that same period, the proportion of families with incomes below $20,000 increased from 32.1 to 36.4 percent. These changes occurred while the traditional middle class—families with incomes of between $20,000 and $50,000 per year—fell from 53 to 47.9 percent.[44]

While the rich were getting richer, real earnings for most Americans either stagnated or fell. For example, while the yearly earnings of the top 20 percent of American families rose from 1978 to 1987 (after adjusting for inflation) more than $9,000 (to almost $85,000), the income of the bottom 20 percent dropped by $576 (to $8,800).[45] The examination of family income over an 11-year period provides even bleaker figures. From 1973 to 1984 the incomes of the poorest fifth of families with children fell 34 percent. It is estimated that from 1980 to 1984 there was a net transfer of $25 billion in income from poor and middle-income families to the richest fifth of the population.[46] While this widening disparity is alarming to liberals, many monetarists and supply-side economists argue that income inequality is socially desirable. For these economists, social policies that promote income equality encourage coercion, limit individual freedom, and damage the economy. Furthermore, income inequality is seen as the desirable outcome of the marketplace: it reflects differences in rewards based on individual talent and initiative. According to free-market economists, income differentials provide an otherwise unmotivated labor force with an incentive to work hard.[47] This growing income disparity has enormous impact for the welfare state because not only is the number of people eligible for entitlement programs growing, but much of the clientele of these programs were once middle class.[48]

Instead of ensuring a healthy public and private sector, major U.S. tax cuts and procorporate fiscal policies in the 1980s led to uneven economic growth. In effect, the private sector grew wealthier at the expense of the public sector. One of the outcomes of this neglect was a decaying physical infrastructure. Another was a less competitive workforce. Given a $3-trillion federal debt, it was unlikely that the federal government could undertake a substantial renovation of the American infrastructure, at least not without a significant restructuring of military, social, and economic priorities. In the end, the American public sector was more impoverished than before the economic upswing of the 1980s.

Apart from the economic data, perhaps the most striking feature of the welfare state crisis is impressionistic. For despite the continued erosion of the standard of living of the middle class, Americans failed to perceive government social programs as a vehicle for redress. During the very period of vulnerability, when welfare state philosophers would have expected the public to demand vociferously the basic protections assured citizens of most industrial democracies, Americans elected conservative politicians, supported propositions lowering taxes, and endorsed limiting social programs. At the center of the crisis of the American welfare state was a public that had lost confidence in the effectiveness of government social programs to promote their general welfare. How Americans came to believe that the welfare state was not in the public interest is the question to which we turn in Part Two.

NOTES

1. James O'Connor, *The Fiscal Crisis of the State* (New York: St. Martin's Press, 1973); Ian Gough, *The Political Economy of the Welfare State* (London: Macmillan, 1979); Claus Offe, *Contradictions of the Welfare State* (Cambridge, Mass.: MIT Press, 1984).

2. Ramesh Mishra, *The Welfare State in Crisis* (New York: St. Martin's Press and Sussex, England: Wheatsheaf, 1984).

3. Harold Wilensky and Charles Lebeaux, *Industrial Society and Social Welfare* (New York: Free Press, 1965), p. 42.

4. Harry Cassidy, *Social Security and Reconstruction in Canada* (Boston: Bruce Humphries, 1943), p. 13.

5. Howard Jacob Karger and David Stoesz, *American Social Welfare Policy: A Structural Approach* (White Plains, N.Y.: Longman, 1990).

6. Ramesh Mishra, "Riding the New Wave: Social Work and the Neo-conservative Challenge," *International Social Work* 32 (1989), pp. 171–82; and Joel Blau, "Theories of the Welfare State," *Social Service Review* 63 (March 1989), pp. 226–37.

7. Interview with Stuart Butler by David Stoesz at the Heritage Foundation, October 4, 1984.

8. Philip AuClaire, "Public Attitudes toward Social Welfare Expenditures," *Social Work* 29 (March/April 1984), p. 141.

9. John Doble and Keith Melville, "The Public's Social Welfare Mandate," *Public Opinion* 11 (January/February 1989), p. 59.

10. James Midgley, "The New Christian Right, Social Policy, and the Welfare State," *Journal of Sociology and Social Welfare* 17 (Winter 1990).

11. For a positive treatment of the New Right, see Burton Pines, *Back to Basics* (New York: William Morrow, 1982); for a critical assessment, see Sara Diamond, *Spiritual Warfare: The Politics of the Christian Right* (Boston: South End Press, 1989).

12. Russell Chandler, "Robertson Moves to Fill Christian Right Vacuum," *Los Angeles Times* (May 15, 1990), p. A-5.

13. Celinda Lake and Stanley Greenbert, "What's Left of Liberalism?" *Public Opinion* 11 (March/April 1989), p. 4.

14. Thomas Byrne Edsall, "The Reagan Legacy," in Sidney Blumenthal and Thomas Byrne Edsall (eds.), *The Reagan Legacy* (New York: Pantheon Books, 1988), p. 17.

15. Stanley Greenberg, "Reconstructing the Democratic Vision," *American Prospect* 1 (Spring 1990), p. 83.

16. Phyllis Day, "The New Poor in America: Isolationism in an International Political Economy," *Social Work* 35 (1989), pp. 227–33.

17. Karger and Stoesz, *American Social Welfare Policy.*

18. Ibid. See also Day, "New Poor in America."

19. Harold Wilensky, *The Welfare State and Equality* (Berkeley: University of California Press, 1975).

20. Karger and Stoesz, *American Social Welfare Policy.*

21. Karger and Stoesz, "When Welfare Reform Fails," *Tikkun* (March/April 1989); David Stoesz and Howard Karger, "Welfare Reform: From Illusion to Reality," *Social Work* 35 (March 1990).

22. Center on Budget and Policy Priorities, "Analysis of FY 1990 Budget Proposals and Their Impact on Low Income Programs," Washington, D.C., January 23, 1989, p. 1.

23. Karger and Stoesz, *American Social Welfare Policy.*

24. Samuel Bowles, David M. Gordon, and Thomas E. Weisskopf, *Beyond the Wasteland* (Garden City, N.Y.: Anchor Press, 1983).

25. Lester C. Thurow, *The Zero-sum Solution* (New York: Simon and Schuster, 1985).

26. International Monetary Fund, *Directory of Trade Statistics Yearbook: 1989* (Washington, D.C.: International Monetary Fund, 1989).

27. Charles Magaziner and Robert B. Reich, *Minding America's Business* (New York: Harcourt Brace Jovanovich, 1982).

28. Barry Bluestone and Bennett Harrison, *The Deindustrialization of America* (New York: Basic Books, 1982).

29. Alvin Rabushka and Steven H. Hanke, "Getting Ready for the Global Economy," *Jerusalem Post* 57 (November 8, 1989), p. 9.

30. Oliver Friedrich, "Freed from Greed?" *Time* (January 1, 1990), pp. 58-60.

31. Karger and Stoesz, *American Social Welfare Policy*

32. Robert Kuttner, *The End of Laissez-faire* (New York: Knopf, 1991), pp. 282–83.

33. Karger and Stoesz, *American Social Welfare Policy*

34. N. T. Feather and P. R. Davenport, "Unemployment and Depressive Affect: A Motivational and Attributional Analysis," *Journal of Personality and Social Psychology* 6, 41 (1981), pp. 422–36; S. Platt, "Unemployment and Suicidal Behavior: A Review of the Literature," *Social Science and Medicine* 9 (1984), pp. 93–115; and T. P. Thornberry and R. L. Christenson, "Unemployment and Criminal Involvement," *American Sociological Review* 49 (1984), pp. 398–411.

35. Thomas R. Donahue, "Labor and Social Work Cooperation," paper presented at Hunter College School of Social Work, New York, 1989, p. 6.

36. Bennett Harrison and Barry Bluestone, *The Great U-Turn* (New York: Basic Books, 1988).

37. Bluestone and Harrison, *Deindustrialization of America*, p. 135.

38. Day, "New Poor in America."

39. Ibid.

40. Robert Reich, *The Work of Nations* (New York: Knopf, 1991), pp. 174–80.

41. Quoted in W. Holstein, "The Stateless Corporation," *Business Week* 3159 (1989), p. 98.

42. Kevin Phillips, *The Politics of Rich and Poor* (New York: Random House, 1990), p. 40.

43. Donahue, "Labor and Social Work Cooperation."

44. Kathleen Bradbury, "The Shrinking Middle Class," *New England Economic Review* 16 (September/October 1986), pp. 41–55.

45. Friedrich, "Freed from Greed?"

46. Center on Budget and Policy Priorities, *Analysis of Poverty in 1987* (Washington, D.C.: Center on Budget and Policy Priorities, 1987).

47. Alan Walker, "The Strategy of Inequality: Poverty and Income Distribution in Britain 1979-89," in I. Taylor (ed.), *The Social Effects of Free Market Policies* (Sussex, England: Harvester-Wheatsheaf, 1990).

48. Although the number of families on AFDC decreased slightly from 1975 to 1984 (from 11.4 to 10.7 million families), this drop was due mainly to eligibility changes and program cuts rather than to a drop in those requiring benefits. See Karger and Stoesz, *American Social Welfare Policy*, p. 179.

Part Two

Conservative and Liberal Prescriptions for Welfare

3

Responding to the Crisis: Conservative Prescriptions

David Stoesz

An American welfare state in crisis presented an irresistible target for conservatives who had labored beneath liberal hegemony in social policy for most of the century. During the 1970s when Liberals were confidently fine-tuning the administration of social welfare programs, conservative ideologues created the institutional base for a direct assault on the welfare state. Think tanks of the ideological right flooded Congress and the media with academically respectable rebuttals to liberal orthodoxy in social affairs. With the election of Ronald Reagan to the presidency along with a Republican Senate in 1980, conservatives suddenly commanded the center in the welfare policy debate. During the first Reagan term, budget reductions coupled with tax cuts struck to the heart of liberal social policy. Hostility toward social programs continued into the second Reagan term, resulting in the stagnation of the welfare state. With the election of George Bush to carry out the third term of the Reagan era, contraction of social welfare programs continued, as was most evident in the budget compromise of 1990. Despite rhetorical assurances that the welfare state was not at risk, the conservative initiatives of the 1980s significantly diminished the already inadequate provisions of social welfare programs. Paradoxically, while conservatives exploited the crisis of the American welfare state, they were unable to fashion a pragmatic alternative to the old liberal version.

THE RECONSTRUCTION OF PUBLIC PHILOSOPHY

On June 26, 1986, an ideological obituary appeared in the *Washington Post*.[1] The president of the American Enterprise Institute for Public Policy

43

Research (AEI), William Baroody, Jr., had stepped down, leaving behind one of the most astonishing accomplishments in the annals of contemporary American political thought. Within the remarkably short time of one decade, not only had William Baroody, Sr., and his son elevated AEI from organizational obscurity into the ranks of the nation's premier policy institutes, but they had also masterminded the transformation of the nation's public philosophy.[2]

For a half-century American political thought had been dominated by a liberal philosophy that was often articulated by the policy prescriptions of rival Brookings Institution. The notion that public policy in the United States was the province of well-pedigreed intellectuals who had studied at the nation's most prestigious private universities only to take up residence at Brookings must have chafed Baroody, Sr., who was the son of a Lebanese stonecutter and had worked his way through college, eventually receiving an M.A. degree from the University of New Hampshire. This man who founded AEI as the first conservative think tank in the nation's capital had as keen an appreciation for individual initiative and tenacity as he had contempt for the public policies that seemed so corrosive to personal perseverance and community cohesion. Too often, he observed, public policy conspired to undo the very qualities that marked the genius of the American experience. Too often, this undoing was the result of social welfare policy.

If fault lay in the myriad of liberally inspired social programs, then true conservative reform required dismantling the philosophical consensus from which so many programs had been legislated. Immodestly, Baroody, Sr., marshaled the resources of AEI and took aim at the American welfare state and at the liberal "ideological monopoly" that sustained it.[3] But, mindful that liberal social programs had produced powerful constituencies, he knew that timeworn conservative sniping at government welfare programs would not, by itself, roll back the New Deal. A dual strategy was implemented. Baroody, Sr., directed a steady barrage of reports prepared by academically respectable policy analysts at leaders of business and elected officials. Then, in a dramatic departure from the more staid posture of Brookings, AEI began packaging material especially for the public. By the end of the 1970s, it was difficult to watch a national news program without seeing a commentary from an AEI fellow; the larger metropolitan newspapers routinely published the opinion-editorial pieces that AEI had thoughtfully scripted for them and forwarded at no cost.

How successful was AEI's experiment in shaping public philosophy? Early in the first term of the Reagan presidency, William Baroody, Jr., who had inherited AEI's leadership, could claim much of the credit for the new popularity of conservatism.

The public philosophy that has guided American policy for decades is undergoing change. For more than four decades, the philosophy of Franklin Delano Roosevelt's New Deal prevailed, in essence calling upon government to do whatever individual men and women could not do for themselves. Today we see growing signs of a new public philosophy, one that still seeks to meet fundamental human needs, but to meet them through a better balance between the public and private sectors of society. The American Enterprise Institute has been at the forefront of this change. Many of today's policy initiatives are building on the intellectual foundations partly laid down by the Institute.[4]

To be sure, conservatives such as the Baroodys were not alone in their concern about social policy. Even analysts from liberal policy institutes were having misgivings about the massive infusions of funds that had passed through governmental social programs of the previous decades. In 1977 Charles Schultze, former director of the Bureau of the Budget in the Johnson administration and chairman of the President's Council of Economic Advisors under President Carter, wrote *The Public Use of Private Interest* while working as a fellow at Brookings. In it, Schultze argued that government intervention through higher expenditures and increased regulation was inferior to market strategies in dealing with social problems.[5] The following year Henry Aaron, another Brookings scholar, published a critique of the War on Poverty, concluding that the intellectual basis of poverty programs was inherently flawed.[6] For its part, the liberal Urban Institute contributed *Private Provision of Public Service*, a programmatic evaluation of non-governmental activity in several areas, including social welfare.[7] Thus, as early as the mid-1970s, the American welfare state had come under the scrutiny of analysts representing a range of ideological persuasions. While conservatives would later bask in the anti-welfare legislative triumphs of the early 1980s, few would acknowledge that the dissection of the welfare state had already been begun by liberal scholars almost a decade earlier.

A half-century after the passage of the Social Security Act, which introduced the American welfare state, the consensus about social policy was suddenly subject to redefinition. Liberals who had adhered to precepts that had guided public policy through the New Deal and the War on Poverty were becoming ambivalent about the enterprise. Chronic conservative griping about wasteful welfare programs—so easily dismissed only a decade earlier—had by the 1970s turned to reasoned critique with the presentation of plausible (though still impractical) alternatives. With the election of Ronald Reagan, of course, all this came to a predictable head. The "Great Communicator" enlisted the public in his crusade to cut back welfare programs, claiming that government was the *cause of*—certainly not the *solution to*—many economic and social problems. As conservative anti-welfare sentiment spread through the public, even liberals came to concede the playing field. "Conservative thinking has not only claimed the presidency; it has spread throughout our political and intellectual life and stands poised to become the dominant strain in American public policy," wrote journalist Gregg Easterbrook after Reagan trounced Mondale in the 1984 presidential election. Yet, Easterbrook recognized that the rise of conservative public philosophy had somewhat less to do with the ascendance of Ronald Reagan, and more to do with the increased sophistication of policy institutes on the ideological right. "While the political ascent of conservatism has taken place in full public view, the intellectual transformation has for the most part occurred behind the scenes, in a network of [conservative] think tanks."[8]

THE CONSERVATIVE CASE AGAINST WELFARE

The current debate about social welfare in the United States occurs within a context of policy options largely defined by conservative think tanks. The significance of the policy institutes in shaping the current welfare debate is evident in two books that were prominent in conservative circles during the early 1980s. In 1981 George Gilder's *Wealth and Poverty* appeared, in which he argued that welfare represented a "moral hazard," insuring the poor against the risks inherent in a market economy. As such, not only did social programs interfere with the market, but they handicapped the poor, who needed "the spur of their own poverty"—not welfare—to raise themselves out of destitution.[9] Gilder's pro-business, anti-welfare tract was well received by the business community that funded such policy institutes as the Lehrman Institute, which subsidized *Wealth and Poverty*. Moreover, Gilder's impeccable academic credentials, previously published books, and popularity in conservative circles—not to mention his trenchant prose—made his ideas credible and accessible to a wide audience.

The year after *Wealth and Poverty* was published, an obscure scholar from Iowa was invited to attend a luncheon by William Hammett, president of the conservative Manhattan Institute. Hammett had read the scholar's pamphlet on welfare that had been published by the conservative Heritage Foundation. The author's thesis that welfare actually contributed to dependency appealed to Hammett, who offered to support a book-length treatise—undoubtedly surprising the scholar, who quickly accepted the offer. The instantaneous popularity of the book, published two years later, must have surprised Hammett, too. For a modest $125,000, Hammett had commissioned a book that was to become the subject of dozens of editorials, placed the author on major news programs, and led to a national speaking tour. According to one reviewer, Hammett had bankrolled a conservative equivalent to Michael Harrington's *The Other America*, widely regarded as a catalyst for the War on Poverty.[10] The Reagan-era author was Charles Murray; his book, *Losing Ground*. With the organizational support provided by conservative policy institutes, Murray's ideas vaulted to the top of the policy agenda of the political right, dominating the welfare debate for the remainder of the decade.

Murray's spectacular success spoke more for the power of conservative think tanks than for the originality of his ideas—or their accuracy, for that matter. His proposal of "scrapping the entire federal welfare and income support structure for working-aged persons, including AFDC, Medicaid, Food Stamps, Unemployment Insurance, Worker's Compensation, subsidized housing, disability and the rest"[11] was certainly draconian, but nothing new to an adherent of the far right who had given any thought to welfare. For more seasoned observers, Murray's logic and data were suspect.[12] Nevertheless, throughout the 1980s conservative think tanks set their sights on the American welfare state, and fired away. With the Reagan presidency setting an open season on social programs, conservative think tanks were eager to try out new ideas. Although their first suggestions were often transparently punitive (such as defining catsup as a vegetable in order to reduce the costs of the school lunch program), later proposals on welfare reform were considerably more sound. By the end of the decade, virtually every conservative policy institute had presented to the public its program for reforming welfare.

Unlike the erratic sniping at government welfare programs that characterized conservatives of an earlier generation, the works of intellectuals sponsored by the policy institutes evidenced an important measure of coherence that had been lacking before.[13] In domestic affairs, for example, AEI was able to focus its considerable resources and talent—a budget of $10 million, 77 resident scholars, and 250 affiliated academics—on two projects in its mission of social reform. The first—the "mediating structures" project—enlisted the services of Peter Berger, a sociologist, and Richard Neuhaus, a theologian. In the major publication of the project, *To Empower People*, Berger and Neuhaus stated that the fundamental social problem of our times is the growth of *megastructures*—such as big government, big business, big labor, and professional bureaucracies—and a corresponding diminution in the importance of individuals. The route to the empowerment of people, then, must be to revitalize *mediating* structures, among them the neighborhood, family, church, and voluntary association.[14]

To Empower People proved a readable and lucid work that served AEI well. The project's apparent impartiality, however, was little more than a veneer. An implicit animosity toward government social programs pervaded the mediating structures project, as evident in a modest institute-sponsored study of the Meals on Wheels Program. For AEI's Michael Balzano, governmental support of Meals on Wheels was less a method for expanding essential nutrition to the ill and homebound elderly, and more an attempt to subvert the native altruism of local mediating structures. In *Federalizing Meals on Wheels*, Balzano argued that the Older Americans Act eroded the voluntary impulses of church and community groups by subsidizing nutritional programs for the elderly. "In most cases, common sense and the desire to help one's neighbor are all that are necessary," Balzano concluded. He then took a shot at professionals who were employed in Meals on Wheels: "One does not need a masters degree in social work or gerontology to dish out chow at a nutrition center."[15]

Following the mediating structures project, AEI's project on democratic capitalism endeavored to elevate the role of the corporation in public life. This necessitated a bit of theoretical hanky-panky, since the mediating structures project had portrayed big business as a megastructure and, therefore, inimical to the vitality of mediating structures. The problem was deftly disposed of by Michael Novak, a theologian and director of the project. In *Toward a Theology of the Corporation*, Novak used no more than a footnote to transfer big business from its designation as a megastructure, effectively portraying big government and its parasitic professional associations as institutions of cultural and economic oppression against a corporate sector that had been the genius behind the American experience.[16]

Under the direction of Novak, the project on democratic capitalism intended to reform the national philosophy by portraying the corporation as a promoter of cultural enlightenment rather than a purveyor of vulgar capitalism. "The instrument invented by democratic capitalism to achieve social goals is the private corporation," he proselytized.

> The corporation ... is not merely an economic institution. It is also a moral and a political institution. It depends on and generates certain moral-cultural virtues; it depends upon and generates new political forms. . . . Beyond its economic effects, the corporation changes the ethos and the cultural forms of society.[17]

Under Novak, AEI's "democratic capitalism" became a cultural analysis in which the corporation was part of a three-part system of checks and balances. Society, according to Novak, is a trinity comprised of the economy, the state, and a social culture, each represented by the corporation, government, and mediating structures, respectively. By elevating the concept of pluralism from the political context to the cultural, Novak positively associates the viability of the corporate sector with a free society. Thus anointed, the corporation is less an economic abstraction than a vehicle for social-cultural transformation.

The theoretical work of AEI was complemented by the more pragmatic efforts of analysts associated with other think tanks. According to Martin Anderson of Stanford's Hoover Institution, liberal social programs were no longer necessary. "The war on poverty has been won, except for perhaps a few mopping-up operations," he wrote on the eve of the Reagan presidency. "The combination of strong economic growth and a dramatic increase in government spending on welfare and income transfer programs for more than a decade has virtually wiped out poverty in the United States."[18] Like so many promising conservative intellectuals, Anderson was to have a chance at seeing his platform for social reform put into action when he became domestic advisor to the Reagan administration. For his move to Washington, D.C., Anderson packed a short list for welfare reform:

1. Reaffirm the need-only philosophical approach to welfare, and state it as explicit national policy.

2. Increase efforts to eliminate fraud.

3. Establish a fair, clear work requirement.

4. Remove inappropriate beneficiaries from the welfare rolls.

5. Enforce support of dependents by those who have the responsibility and are shirking it.

6. Improve the efficiency and effectiveness of welfare administration.

7. Shift more responsibility for welfare from the federal government to state and local governments and to private institutions.[19]

While the Hoover Institution pursued a more traditionally conservative approach to social reform, the upstart Heritage Foundation toyed with proposals and alliances that other think tanks of the right had avoided. Although Heritage's endorsement of the "urban enterprise zone" concept seemed sound, its flirting with a "family security plan" through which investments in Individual Retirement Accounts could be substituted for contributions to Social Security verged on political lunacy.[20] Most troubling, though, Heritage began violating intellectual decorum by dallying with militants of the "traditionalist" movement. Heritage bet that its association with fundamentalists would add, rather than detract, from its influence. So important was the traditionalist connection that Heritage Vice-president Burton Pines lauded evangelicals and fundamentalists in his book *Back to Basics*. In this readable account, Pines applauded local conservative activists for their challenge to liberal values and chronicled the offensive launched against programs of the welfare state. "Pro-family" traditionalists had disrupted the Carter White House Conference on Families, effectively precluding any progressive legislation that might have evolved from it. Traditionalists also had enjoined proponents of a domestic-violence bill in protracted debate, blocking its passage. Finally, traditionalists supported the Family Protection Act, a conservative proposal limiting contraception, abortion, children's rights, and sex education, and reducing federal support for programs aiding homosexuals and the divorced.[21] Significantly, Pines noted the pivotal role of conservative think tanks in the traditionalist movement and was quick to acknowledge his debt to AEI, an organization he described as focusing "primarily on the long (sometimes very long) range and fundamental transformation of the climate of opinion." Bringing the Hoover Institution into the fold, Pines portrayed their work as a crusade. "Together," he concluded, "Hoover, AEI and Heritage can today deploy formidable armies on the battlefield of ideas—forces which traditionalist movements previously lacked."[22]

Through AEI, Hoover, and Heritage, conservative intellectuals forged a powerful critique of government social programs and effectively promoted it to the public. The now familiar case against the welfare state posits that governmental domestic policy is hazardous for several reasons. First, social programs are funded through revenues derived from taxes that, if they were not so diverted, could be used for further capitalization of the private sector. Second, social programs invariably grant the state the right to intrude into areas that should be held private, such as the family. Third and finally, social programs are administered through an unresponsive and expensive public bureaucracy. The surest way to make social welfare more cost effective is through assigning its responsibilities to the private sector (i.e., privatization) or, short of that, by eliminating unnecessary red tape (i.e., deregulating the welfare bureaucracy). These think tank criticisms complement the more traditional complaints about social welfare—that benefits erode the work ethic and family solidarity.

By the early 1980s, conservatives were well positioned to rescript social welfare policy. Through a network of policy institutes, scholars had updated conservative ideology so that it more realistically dealt with welfare. With the election of Ronald Reagan and a Republican Senate in 1980, substantial parts of the national government would be receptive. And by being inundated in the electronic and print media with conservative prescriptions for social affairs, the public had been primed for a conservative approach in domestic matters. After decades of liberal social policy, the right was just about ready to contain the welfare state. All that remained was the legislation.

CONTAINING THE WELFARE STATE

During the next eight years, welfare advocates were fed a disconcerting diet of social legislation. Not content with simply reducing federal appropriations for welfare, the Reagan administration sought to contain social programs by enlisting multiple strategies—tax policy, administrative discretion, and deficits—often proceeding on several fronts at once. By the end of the Reagan presidency, liberals surely wondered what had hit them. The expansion of the American welfare state had ground to a halt. Reversing a steady accretion of *liberal* enhancements to public assistance policy, the Family Support Act offered *conservative* welfare reform. Worse, the end of the Reagan administration saw the *repeal* of Catastrophic Health Insurance—the first rollback of a major social program in the history of the American welfare state.

Conservatives were able to contain the welfare state by coining a simple strategy and by applying it ruthlessly. "The originality of the [Reagan] administration lay in its conviction that the way to wealth and national income growth, and out of poverty for the poor, could not be designed by government, or implemented by programs keyed to specific problems," noted Nathan Glazer. "If people could manage by themselves, what would be the need for the hundreds of federal programs directed against specific targets?"[23] Much as a corporation would dispose of an unprofitable subsidiary, conservatives began to divest government of its welfare function.

Within seven months of assuming office, President Reagan showed his hand on welfare by signing the Omnibus Budget Reconciliation Act (OBRA) of 1981. OBRA proceeded on a dual track, cutting public assistance benefits while at the same time combining categorical programs into a Social Services Block Grant. The new AFDC eligibility guidelines were particularly punitive since they were directed at poor families who were participating in the labor force. Suddenly, AFDC family heads who were trying to improve their economic lot found their child care expenses capped at $160 per month per child, the deduction for work expenses limited to $75 per month, and the earned income disregard (the first $30 per month and one-third of income thereafter) eliminated after four months. As if to strangle the welfare bureaucracy in paperwork, OBRA required the welfare department to redetermine *monthly* the eligibility of those on AFDC who insisted on working. These, among other measures, had an immediate impact on the AFDC rolls: 408,000 families lost eligibility altogether, and another 299,000 had their benefits reduced. Federal and state governments realized savings of $1.1 billion in 1983.[24] Significantly, OBRA disentitled working poor families. Five percent of the total AFDC caseload became ineligible due to OBRA, and "about 35 percent of those who were working were terminated by the legislation."[25]

For most of the families made ineligible for AFDC by the provisions of OBRA, loss of benefits submerged them in poverty. Monthly income loss ranged from $229 in Dallas to $115 in Boston. Former AFDC beneficiaries in these cities had also lost Medicaid coverage. In Dallas, 59.2 percent of terminated families could not secure alternative health insurance; in Boston, 27.5 percent.[26] A study of AFDC families in Georgia found that 79 percent fell below the poverty level as a result of OBRA, compared to 70 percent before 1981.[27] An investigation of the quality of life of 129 AFDC families in New Jersey that had lost benefits was Dickensian in its portrayal:

> More than half the families were below the poverty level, 4 out of 10 families did not have enough to eat, 2 out of 10 were spending less than the amount required to provide a minimally adequate diet, almost 3 out of 4 had problems paying rent and utility bills, and most significantly, nearly 8 out of 10 families had to forego or delay medical and/or dental care.[28]

OBRA also functioned to deregulate federal social programs by replacing Title XX categorical grants with a Social Services Block Grant. At the same time, the administration reduced funding approximately 25 percent with the rationale that this represented the savings accrued by consolidating management and devolving program administration from the federal to state governments. Ultimately, expenditures for Title XX were to peak at $2.9 billion in 1979 and plummet to $2.4 billion in 1982. In 1990 dollars, however, federal expenditures showed a constant decline—from $5.3 billion in 1979 to $2.7 billion in 1990, *a drop of almost 50 percent.*[29] Welfare advocates were overwhelmed by this important transition. Speaking on behalf of powerless beneficiaries—the frail elderly, abused children, the mentally incompetent—welfare advocates who had spent decades cultivating relations with federal agencies that funded their programs now found themselves on the defensive. Not only had the focus of activity shifted from Washington, D.C., to state capitals, but welfare advocates were also pitted against one another in a Darwinian scramble over a diminishing pool of funds.

OBRA funding reductions accompanying the creation of the Social Services Block Grant strained an already fragile foundation for a wide variety of programs. Since the 1970s, social activists had built a Rube Goldberg structure of program supports, often matching federal seed money with state funds to supplement whatever existing contributions had been made to local nonprofit agencies. The result was a labyrinth of categorical programs. Yet, for all its duplication, red tape, and sheer confusion, this *non*systemic solution seemed to work. In an analysis of 14 categorical programs between 1971 and 1980, Dan Finnegan found that "funds provided by the categorical grants were positively associated with additional state funding for community services. More important, these funds were positively associated with an increasing proportion of state expenditures being allocated to community programs."[30] With OBRA, not only were there fewer inducements for states to support programs, but funding for local nonprofit agencies fell sharply. Federal funds to programs in which nonprofit agencies had been active (excluding Medicare and Medicaid) were reduced by about $26 *billion* each year (about 25 percent) between 1982 and 1984. Yet, increased fund-raising efforts by nonprofit agencies to compensate for the loss of governmental funds recovered only 7 percent of the loss.[31] In 1977, government funds accounted for 53.5 percent of the funding for social services provided by nonprofits; in 1984, that amount had dropped to 43.9 percent—a reduction of approximately one-fourth.[32] Thus, much of the burden for federal divestiture of its welfare function was left to local nonprofit organizations, which were faced with an increasingly troubled and destitute clientele but with fewer resources to help them. It would not be an exaggeration to conclude that, a decade after the imposition of OBRA, a substantial portion of the response to alarming increases in social need fell to nonprofit agencies, which, in turn, were left holding the bag.

While social activists were left treading water because of OBRA, the Reagan administration turned its attention to the problem of income distribution. For conservatives, the liberal penchant for income distribution eroded the work ethic of the poor by artificially supplementing their income. (It also eroded the "work ethic" of the rich by overtaxing their incomes.) Moreover, theologian Michael Novak had branded as dubious and naive the assumption that "those who have, will better help the poor if they give of their abundance to the poor." Furthermore, "supposing that gaps between poor and rich are immoral, it does not follow that transfer payments are the most practical method of equalizing incomes, or that their use promotes independence and self-sufficiency."[33]

For conservatives who were "eager to defund the welfare state,"[34] simple reductions in welfare benefits failed to get at the heart of the problem. For that reason, the policy entrepreneurs of the ideological right insisted on a dose of preventive medicine—transforming the very tax structure that generated the revenues necessary for redistributive welfare benefits. In the interest of fairness, however, conservatives recognized that it would be necessary to fold the interests of the poor into the argument. If taxes were less progressive, the rich would benefit, but at the expense of the poor. However, if the poor were provided rebates, they would benefit as well. By exempting the poor from the predations of a regressive tax structure, conservatives were able to cut the flow of vital revenues for welfare programs, while at the same time improving the lot of those who were strapped economically. In an elegant shift in intention, tax policy became social welfare policy—but in a manner completely antithetical to the liberal understanding of both tax and welfare policy.

Time and time again, tax policy was substituted for welfare policy during the Reagan administration. Claiming that the burden of inflation disproportionately affected those on limited incomes, Reagan successfully argued for a tax cut soon after taking office. Increasingly, the concept of tax expenditures—indirect payments through tax exemptions, credits, or rebates—appeared in social policy. Granting tax exemptions for health and retirement benefits paid by employers has been standard practice since the 1920s, of course. Such exemptions have been the basis for the very substantial investments made in "occupational welfare" in the United States. In 1991, for example, the tax expenditure due to exemptions granted employers for the provision of health and retirement benefits will exceed $148 billion, as compared to government welfare provisions of $429 billion for comparable purposes.[35] Yet, the idea of using tax expenditures as welfare aid to the poor is a relatively recent concept. In 1975 the Earned Income Tax Credit (EITC) was instituted, whereby low-income taxpayers would be given a rebate. The EITC was just the program that conservatives were looking for, and they used it as a substitute for welfare. During the period that direct public welfare expenditures for the poor were under assault, indirect payments under EITC actually increased, as Table 3.1 shows.

In a related manner, the Economic Recovery and Tax Act of 1981 allowed tax-payers to establish Individual Retirement Accounts (IRAs) that were tax exempt—a provision that continued for lower-income taxpayers under the restrictions imposed by the Tax Reform Act of 1986. In 1985, $1.1 billion had been invested in IRAs by taxpayers reporting income below $10,000, and $9.7 billion for those with incomes from $10,000 to $30,000.[36]

Still, the tax rebates given the poor through tax policy failed to compensate for the losses of benefits through welfare programs. "Low-income families, especially the working poor, lost appreciably more by cuts in government services than they gained in tax reduction," admitted conservative analyst Kevin Phillips.[37] And since the wealthy continued to benefit from less progressive taxation, the income disparity between rich and poor widened. Between 1980 and 1990, the federal tax burden for the richest quintile of tax filers *decreased* 5.5 percent, while taxes of the poorest fifth *increased* 16.1 percent, *despite tax expenditures for the poor*.[38] Predictably, the rich gained a larger portion of the nation's income during the Reagan era (see Table 3.2). Not only was income redistributed *upward* as a result of tax policy, but this occurred to such a degree that the income

Table 3.1 Total Amount of Earned Income Tax Credit Rebates, Selected Years

Year to Which Credit Applies	Total Amount (millions)
1975	$1,250
1980	1,986
1985	2,088
1990	5,858

Source: Adapted from Committee on Ways and Means, U.S. House of Representatives, *Overview of Entitlement Programs* (Washington, D.C.: U.S. Government Printing Office, 1990), p. 837.

gap between rich and poor reached its widest point since the federal government began gathering such data in 1947.

Although the Reagan administration chalked up major victories against means-tested programs in its assault on the American welfare state, the social insurance programs remained resistant to conservative prescriptions. This was not for lack of imagination. Conservative theoreticians fashioned privatized approaches to almost every governmental function (except defense expenditures): Individual Retirement Accounts (IRAs) were viewed as a substitute for Social Security, individual medical accounts for Medicare, and urban enterprise zones as a replacement for federal community development programs. And then—perhaps emboldened by their triumphs in cutting poverty programs—conservative politicians moved to take on even the social insurance programs, despite rhetorical assurances to the contrary. Through more restrictive determinations for disability under Social Security, the Reagan administration sharply reduced the number of beneficiaries. From 1981 to 1984, the number of initial terminations for disability insurance were four times that for the period 1977-80.[39] Between 1978 and 1983, the number of disability beneficiaries declined by more than 1 million—a reduction of 21.7 percent.[40] And conservatives sensed an opportunity from this "field experiment" with Disability Insurance: social insurance was vulnerable if cuts could be targeted at subpopulations. Although more than half of those terminated were to have their benefits restored by 1987, the net result was the termination of 37 percent of cases.[41]

Table 3.2   Change in Distribution of Total U.S. After-tax Income, 1980-1990

Income Quintile	1980	1990
Richest fifth	44.8%	49.9%
Next richest fifth	22.6	21.7
Middle fifth	16.2	14.9
Next poorest fifth	11.4	9.9
Poorest fifth	5.4	4.3

Source: Adapted from Robert Greenstein and Scott Barancik, *Drifting Apart* (Washington, D.C.: Center on Budget and Policy Priorities, 1990), p. 10.

The most important changes in social insurance during the Reagan era were the 1983 amendments to the Social Security Act. Indeed, the social insurances—primarily Social Security and Medicare—did prove troublesome for conservative ideologues. Any attempt to roll back the welfare state required containing—but preferably reducing—the social insurances, because of their enormous revenue consumption. Yet, as the Disability Insurance experiment was already demonstrating, social insurances tended to be well defended because benefits were dispersed across income groups. Nevertheless, with the prospect of the largest social insurance fund—Old Age and Survivors Insurance and Disability Insurance (OASDI)—facing the actuarial equivalent of "Chapter 11," conservatives recognized an opportunity to tackle the mainstay of the American welfare state: Social Security. Both conservative and liberal economists agreed that Social Security would be in receivership sometime in 1983 if major changes were not made in the program. Between 1975 and 1981, the Old Age and Survivors Fund saw a steadily increasing deficit—from $790 million to $4.9 *billion* per year.[42] Through OBRA, therefore, Congress and the administration whittled away at benefits, including elimination of the minimum benefit, elimination of benefits for postsecondary students, and restrictions on payment of the death benefit. For 1983, these reductions were expected to save the program $3.6 billion—an amount insufficient to make up for future shortfalls.[43] But in order to avoid the appearance of ideological tampering, the administration proceeded carefully, empaneling a bipartisan commission to restore the program's integrity. Through the 1983 amendments to the Social Security Act, revenues were increased by requiring newly hired federal employees to contribute and by hiking the payroll tax. Benefits, on the other hand, were decreased by delaying cost-of-living increases and by stabilizing future Cost of Living Allowances (i.e., if trust funds fall below a certain level, future benefits will be keyed to the consumer price index or the average wage increase, whichever is lower), taxing Social Security benefits (i.e., if taxable income plus Social Security benefits exceed $25,000 a year for an individual or $32,000 for a couple), and delaying the retirement age to 67 by the year 2027 for those wanting to collect full benefits.[44] For 1990, these changes added more than $308 billion to the Old Age and Survivors Insurance and Disability Insurance Trust Funds.[45]

Although the result was widely viewed by liberals as a successful salvage operation, less apparent were the major accomplishments that conservatives could claim. By trimming benefits through OBRA, they had reversed decades of steady expansion of the Social Security Program; by increasing the regressive payroll tax through the 1983 amendments, they placed the solvency of the program squarely on the shoulders of middle-income workers. In 1990, Senator Daniel Patrick Moynihan boldly suggested canceling the proposed payroll tax increases, claiming that the surplus—$69.1 billion in 1989—was being used by Republicans to offset the budget deficit. In raising this suggestion, Moynihan challenged the fairness of the 1983 amendments, arguing that an increase in the regressive payroll tax would be used to balance a deficit attributed to earlier tax cuts that had substantially aided the rich.[46] While total annual federal revenue receipts from income tax had fallen from 47 percent to under 45 percent, revenues from Social Security increased from 31 percent to 36 percent. Senator George Mitchell pegged the resulting income redistribution from middle-income workers to the wealthy at $80 billion.[47] This was masterful politics. Conservatives had artfully maneuvered an increase in a regressive tax in order to save a popular social insurance program, the surpluses thus accrued being diverted to alleviate a deficit, the scale of which effectively precluded any new social programs.

For welfare advocates who had not been cowed by the first Reagan term, the second offered little relief. Faced with runaway deficits, the Balanced Budget and Emergency Deficit Control Act (Gramm-Rudman-Hollings) was passed in 1985. Although certain provisions were ruled unconstitutional, congressional leaders used the basic provisions of the act for making appropriations contingent on meeting targets in reducing the deficit. The impact of Gramm-Rudman-Hollings on social programs was immediate. The Title XX Social Services Block Grant was reduced $116 million in 1986 and $37.8 million in 1990 because of deficit restrictions.[48]

The Tax Reform Act of 1986 continued the conservative substitution of indirect payments through tax expenditures in lieu of direct welfare payments. As a result of negotiations with liberals who were concerned about the continuing erosion of income of the working poor, roughly 6 million low-income families were effectively removed from the tax rolls.[49] Instead of paying taxes, these families would be receiving cash payments from the Treasury through the EITC. In a related matter of some philosophical consequence, liberals also agreed to a more regressive tax structure in which the previous 14 income gradations were collapsed into just three. Moreover, tax reform abruptly terminated what had been the increasingly generous deductions allowed to nonitemizers for their contributions to tax-exempt organizations. Thus, another of the weakened supports for the besieged voluntary sector of social welfare agencies fell away.

CONSERVATIVE WELFARE REFORM: THE FAMILY SUPPORT ACT AND CATASTROPHIC HEALTH INSURANCE

Welfare reform has been a heated topic in the United States for several decades. Most presidents since John F. Kennedy have either offered welfare proposals or, at least, given lip service to the need for reform. Until recently, welfare reform had a liberal connotation since reform proposals usually called for major increases in benefits as well as expanding eligibility for welfare programs. Thus, welfare reform often tended to mean some form of a guaranteed annual income for the poor. The liberal orientation to welfare reform was so prevalent that even conservative administrations used it as the basis for welfare reform initiatives. For example, in the 1970s Richard Nixon proposed a massive overhaul of welfare in the form of the Family Assistance Plan (FAP), a guaranteed annual income program.

By the 1980s, however, the liberal orientation to welfare reform was eclipsed by a conservative vision. Welfare reform proposals in the 1980s were shaped within an overall conservative and anti-welfare context. For example, the Low-income Opportunity Act proposed by the Reagan administration would have effectively eliminated a poor mother's entitlement to support from governmental welfare programs. Reagan's proposal, predicated on the belief that state and local governments could best assess the needs of the poor, was designed to give states wide latitude in program design, eligibility guidelines, benefit levels, and the allocation of program resources. Essentially, the Reagan proposal called for a series of state-sponsored welfare experiments with virtually no assistance from the federal government.

Instead of establishing a federal welfare program mandating adequate benefit levels, congressional Democrats followed the conservative trend by proposing welfare reform that allowed states to continue to define need, set their own benefit levels, establish (within federal limitations) income and resource limits, and administer the program. Although the welfare reforms proposed by Congress were more conservative than earlier Democratic plans, the Reagan administration threatened to veto any reform bill that did not include a tough work requirement.

The Family Support Act

In 1988, differences between the moderately conservative Democratic plan and the very conservative Reagan proposal were ironed out in a compromise bill—the Family Support Act—which Thomas Downey, chair of the House Subcommittee on Public Assistance, hailed as the first "significant change in our welfare system in 53 years."[50] Under the Family Support Act, $3.34 billion was allocated for a five year period to establish education and job-seeking opportunities—Job Opportunities and Basic Skills (JOBS)—for AFDC recipients. During 1990 and 1991, states would have to enroll at least 7 percent of AFDC parents in workfare; by 1995, the enrollment will rise to 20 percent. Although two-parent families are covered in the act, beginning in 1997 one parent will be required to work at least 16 hours a week in an unpaid job in exchange for benefits.[51] The more progressive provisions of the bill include the extension of eligibility for daycare grants and Medicaid for one year after a client leaves AFDC for private employment. The bill also mandated the automatic deduction of child support from an absent parent's paycheck. Dan Rostenkowski, chair of the House Ways and Means Committee, estimated that 65,000 more two-parent families would receive benefits, 400,000 people would participate in workfare by 1993, and 475,000 would be eligible for transitional Medicaid benefits.[52]

Apart from the hype, the Family Support Act was anything but major welfare reform. The key to the act was the promise of self-sufficiency for those dependent on AFDC and the corresponding savings to be realized by government once employment in the private sector was secured. Yet the prospect of economic independence proved elusive. For example, the provisions of the act will undoubtedly help parents who are occupationally upwardly mobile; however, the great majority of people on AFDC exhibit a job history in which welfare complements episodic and low-wage employment. In light of this, the new welfare initiative extends important benefits to the working poor, but it is unlikely to boost people off of welfare by itself. In a review of workfare projects, Harvard's David Ellwood calculated increased earnings of $250-$750 per year. According to Ellwood, "most work-welfare programs look like decent investments, but no carefully evaluated work-welfare programs have done more than put a tiny dent in the welfare caseloads, even though they have been received with enthusiasm."[53] Moreover, some provisions of the bill were clearly punitive and unlikely to enhance substantially the self-sufficiency of AFDC recipients. Requiring one parent of two-parent households to do make-work in exchange for benefits is unlikely to increase economic indepen-dence, and may actually impede it if beneficiaries are forced to do make-work when they could be seeking real work in the labor market. Garnish-ing wages is unlikely to increase economic independence, especially if a parent's wages are so low that such a requirement creates incentives to quit work instead of paying child support. Mimi Abramovitz observed that for poor men this provision "may be more like squeezing blood from a stone."[54] Finally, the reliance on states to operate workfare programs that are not adequately funded is likely to result in uneven welfare reform. More progressive states such as Massachusetts and California will expand on generous workfare programs already in place, while poorer states such as Mississippi and New Mexico will be hard pressed to deploy programs that are anything but punitive.

In the context of what *had* been happening to AFDC for more than a decade, the Family Support Act was anything but adequate. From 1970 to 1988, the median AFDC benefit to states had dropped 35 percent in constant dollars as a result of inflation. Had AFDC benefits simply re-mained constant with inflation, beneficiaries in 1988 would have received $5.88 billion *more* than what they got. The 1988 welfare reform initiative proposed to "reallocate" (over five years) only 57 percent ($3.34 billion) of this lost income back to the poor through compulsory workfare.[55] In relation to the provisions of OBRA seven years earlier, the Family Sup-port Act was perverse. OBRA had punished the poor who had demon-strated their adherence to the work ethic despite the red tape of welfare bureaucracy, by terminating their benefits; the Family Support Act in-creased benefits to those *not* in the workforce through a paternalistic workfare program. Of all ideologues, *conservatives* had reconfigured welfare in such a way that the poor were not only dissuaded from work, but also received important benefits if they got on welfare.

Worse still, the promised savings of workfare soon faded. Two years into the JOBS program, the Congressional Budget Office projected that 10,000 families would be off AFDC by 1991, 20,000 by 1993, and 50,000 by end of the five years of the program—only a 1.3-percent reduction in the number of AFDC families. "The effect of the JOBS program on the number of AFDC recipients or on spending on benefits in welfare pro-grams is thus expected to be modest," concluded the House Ways and Means Committee.[56] Nevertheless, with limited exception, the Family Support Act was a conservative triumph. As Mimi Abramovitz wrote in 1988, "By replacing liberal tenets of entitlement, self-determination and Federal responsibility with more conservative notions of contract, com-pulsion, and states' rights . . . welfare reform erodes some of the fundamental principles that support the U.S. welfare state."[57] That the Family Support Act received the almost unanimous endorsement of welfare advocates was perhaps the best measure of how far liberalism had sunk in guiding social policy. Despite its limitations, the Family Support Act embodied three fundamental conservative values: reciprocity, productivity, and familial responsibility.

Reciprocity

Conservatives as well as many liberals argue that welfare programs contribute to dependency and dysfunctional behaviors, especially when benefits are not conditional on reciprocity or, in other words, a standard of conduct expected of recipients. In a convincing argument, Lawrence Mead observed that

> the damage [by welfare programs] seems to be done, not by the benefits, themselves, but by the fact that they are *entitlements*, given regardless of the behavior of clients. They raise the income of recipients, but, more important, free them to behave without accountability to society.[58]

Consequently, a condition of the Family Support Act is that employment—or, in the absence of a job, education or job-finding activities—be considered as a condition for eligibility. Although reciprocity is usually advanced by conservatives as a way to encourage socially desirable behavior by welfare recipients, it has also been used by liberals to promote the credibility of welfare programs. In introducing his ill-fated Family Security Act of 1987, which included a workfare component, Daniel Patrick Moynihan argued,

> Mothers, the custodial parents in most single-parent families, must try to earn income, at least part time, to help support their children. The statistics are a stark testament to the need: 72 percent of all mothers with children between 6 and 18 are in the labor force. Over half of all mothers with children under age 3 are in the labor force. This marks a great change in the position of women in American life. The only women who have not participated in this change are the heads of AFDC families, of whom fewer than 5 percent work part-time or full-time. As a nation, we find a 7 percent unemployment rate barely tolerable. What then are we to think of a system that keeps 95 percent of poor mothers unemployed and out of the labor force?[59]

The concept of reciprocity—or put another way, the social obligation of the poor to conform to generally held social values such as the work ethic, morality, sobriety, and a domestic life rooted in the nuclear family—has been an ongoing issue in social welfare policy. From the beginning, private charities and (later) the state have expected the poor to conform to social norms. For example, during the 1950s and 1960s the notorious "man in the house rule" could result in a female client's expulsion from AFDC if a man was found living in her home. In 1967 new AFDC amendments were added that pressured recipient mothers into working. As part of these new rules, work requirements became mandatory for unemployed fathers, mothers, and certain teenagers. AFDC recipients who were deemed employable and refused to work could be terminated. Within that context, the spirit of reciprocity contained in the Family Support Act represented a resurrection of old values rather than a new perspective on welfare.

The meager funding of the Family Support Act subverted its very purpose of economically freeing the poor from public assistance. A study of five workfare experiments by the Manpower Demonstration Research Corporation generated a surprising finding: the most dependent AFDC recipients—those with no pre-assistance earnings and on public assistance for more than two years—showed the greatest savings from participation in workfare because they customarily consume a greater portion of welfare resources.[60] In other words, workfare focusing on the hard-core welfare dependent can result in greater savings than workfare designed for those AFDC recipients who possess more employment assets and who are, accordingly, more likely to become independent of AFDC. However, social administrators with tight welfare budgets and pressures to succeed will likely target higher functioning welfare clients who possess greater chances for success in the labor market.

Productivity

The emergence of a highly competitive global economy has led to an emphasis on the need for the United States to exploit more fully its productive capacity by more effectively utilizing its labor force. The increasingly competitive global marketplace, severe budgetary restraints, and the apparent hegemony of conservative values have forced social programs to become more congruent with economic productivity. Coupling welfare to productivity has made for some strange bedfellows. For example, in response to the large number of mothers in the labor force, Senator Orrin Hatch—an arch-critic of progressive welfare programs—proposed a $375-million daycare program in 1987.[61]

Many liberals argue that allying welfare with productivity draws social programs closer to the American economic system—a strategy that may be necessary to justify greater expenditures for social welfare in the future. A proposal offered by Senator Edward Kennedy—the Minimum Health Benefits for All Workers Act, which would assure all employees of basic health insurance—is an example of such a strategy.[62] Under the rubric of "industrial policy," both conservatives and liberals have advocated using major governmental initiatives to enhance the competitiveness of the American economy. As a result, many welfare advocates are basing their rationale for new social programs on investments in human capital or in community activities that contribute to the economic vitality of the nation.

Familial Responsibility

Another trend illustrated in the Family Support Act is the belief that the government should abandon its role as the "rescuer of first resort." Retreating to traditional values, this philosophy dictates that biological parents have the ultimate responsibility for support of their offspring. Although since 1981 even impoverished noncustodial parents have been required to pay child support, the Family Support Act calls for even more stringent child-support enforcement. For example, under the provisions of the act, states must contact employers and arrange for child support payments to be withheld automatically from an employee's paycheck after a grant is awarded. In addition, interstate administrative mechanisms expedite the location of a delinquent parent.

The automatic withholding of child support payments clearly has the potential to keep some families off the AFDC rolls, but it has proven to be of limited value when applied to all AFDC families. While available research suggests that the typical child support situation involves a man who is remarried and whose income can provide some economic support for his biological children, the past record for child support enforcement is generally bleak. In 1986 child support collections were successful in only 15.7 percent of AFDC cases.[63] Perhaps more a principle than a fiscal attempt to gain revenue, this policy reinforces a belief in the responsibility of the parent to provide financially for the child.

The Family Support Act is flawed in other ways. In November 1987, there were 7.1 million unemployed workers; 5.5 million part-time workers who could not find full-time work; and several million working poor who, even though they were working full-time, did not earn enough to escape poverty. The number of impoverished working Americans climbed by nearly 2 million, or 23 percent, between 1978 and 1987. According to Harvard economist Robert Reich,

> The number who worked full time and year round but were poor climbed faster, by 43 percent. Nearly 60 percent of the 20 million people who now fall below the Census Bureau's poverty line are from families with at least one member in full-time or part-time work.[64]

If workers are unable to earn enough to be economically self-sufficient, how can welfare recipients be expected to become economically independent of public assistance? Moreover, even though unemployment has been reduced to around 6 percent, it is differentially distributed. Relatively well-off sections of the country experience lower unemployment, while the "Rustbowl" of the industrial Midwest and the farm states experience high rates of unemployment. Furthermore, unemployment rates tend to differ widely even within states. Vigorous promotion of workfare may thus force poor rural families to move to urban areas for job possibilities—a trend that will further impoverish and depopulate already shaky rural areas.

Catastrophic Health Insurance

For all the reversals and disappointments that welfare activists suffered under the Reagan presidency, the worst seems to have been saved for last. The end of the Reagan presidency saw the first repeal of a major social welfare program: Catastrophic Health Insurance. The Medicare Catastrophic Coverage Act of 1988 was intended to protect 32 million beneficiaries from extraordinary health-care costs beyond those already covered under Part A of Medicare. For 1989, 40 percent of program costs were to be borne by a nominal $48-per-year increase in Part B premiums; and the other 60 percent, through an annual surcharge on the wealthy elderly of up to $1,050 per person—an amount only 5 percent of enrollees would have to pay.[65] Altogether, Catastrophic Health Insurance was crafted in the best tradition of the New Deal. First, it was an insurance program that was grafted onto another popular insurance program: Medicare. Second, it had the endorsement of the largest elderly advocacy organization in the nation: the American Association of Retired Persons (AARP). Third, it was financed through a moderately progressive tax. Moreover, Catastrophic Health Insurance met a criterion imposed by Reaganomics: it was to be a self-financing program. Even though the program did not cover long-term nursing care, it did cover many of the costs that were bankrupting the families of elderly Americans. Yet Catastrophic Health Insurance provoked such a fire storm of criticism that a reluctant Congress retracted it the year after it had been enacted.[66] Conservatives could not have been more delighted. Their earlier setback with terminating cases from Disability Insurance had given way to an unexpected triumph: the repeal of a social insurance program. The demise of Catastrophic Health Insurance marked a new stage in the assault on social programs; and rather than be content with swiping at the more vulnerable means-tested programs, conservatives had found a way to cut to the heart of the American welfare state—its previously well-fortified public insurance programs.

THE BUDGET COMPROMISE OF 1990

Welfare advocates were to find no succor as George Bush was elected to carry forward the Reagan tradition. Despite a rhetorical appeal to voluntary charity—"a thousand points of light"—the Bush administration continued to lay siege to the welfare state. In one respect, the administration had little choice; it had been conveniently backed into a corner. As Senator Daniel Patrick Moynihan averred, the budget deficit had effectively straightjacketed domestic policy "for the next two or three presidencies," leaving no room for even marginal increments to social programs.[67] For anti-welfare conservatives, this posed less a problem than an opportunity to snipe further at welfare expenditures, as the 1990 federal budget compromise demonstrated.

In the Omnibus Budget Reconciliation Act (OBRA) of 1990, conservatives found reason to congratulate themselves for having initiated a second act in the deconstruction of the American welfare state. The stage had been set by the tax cuts of the first Reagan term, which contributed to the unprecedented budget deficit. The massive tax cut of the early 1980s not only conformed to supply-side economic ideology, but it also gave conservatives an apparently foolproof strategy for debunking liberal social programs. If on the one hand the tax cuts happened to restore economic vitality, Keynesian theory would be discredited and—along with it—liberal persistence about funding social programs through government expenditures. If on the other hand the tax cuts caused an enormous budget shortfall, the result was also positive insofar as future expenditures for social programs would be precluded. Essentially, the conservatives had it both ways when it came to domestic expenditures for social programs.

While, as it turns out, a massive budget deficit was generated by the tax cuts, the question still remained as to how this would be addressed through subsequent federal budgetary priorities. Throughout the 1980s, Congress and the Reagan, then Bush, administrations postponed the day when the budget would have to be reconciled through the Gramm-Rudman-Hollings Deficit Reduction Act. Reflecting the profound political and ideological consequences of any plausible budget compromise, the initial 1990 budget deal was cut at Andrews Air Force Base—beyond the view of the public, press, and lobbyists. When the budget package failed to get past infuriated liberal Democrats who were being threatened by an elder lobby concerned with Medicare cuts, as well as conservative Republicans who had signed a campaign pledge not to raise taxes, another round of bargaining ensued. That the second compromise was enacted proved less significant, perhaps, than the almost complete absence of detail broadcast to the public on its implications. Buried within the compromise were provisions that could substantially undermine the liberal welfare state.

The primary purpose of the 1990 OBRA was to construct a pay-as-you-go procedure for fiscal years 1992 through 1995 that would address the Gramm-Rudman-Hollings deficit targets. This compromise bill placed expenditure limits on defense and on international and domestic discretionary expenditures through 1995, and required that any "overages" be made up by across-the-board cuts in programs in each respective category.[68] Importantly, savings in one category could not be transferred to another, but must be credited toward the federal deficit. The 1990 OBRA increased income taxes for the wealthy, imposed a 10-percent excise tax on luxury items, and raised taxes on cigarettes, gas, and alcohol. In order to avoid confusion about any particular spending category's going over budget, the Office of Management and Budget was given unilateral authority to determine the deficit status of all programs.

After a decade of punishing program cuts, welfare state liberals greeted the budget compromise with relief. The 1990 OBRA increased domestic expenditures over a five-year period by $22 billion.[69] For 1991, the budget compromise promised much-needed relief for discretionary programs that were still reeling from the cuts made during the previous decade (see Table 3.3). Social entitlements also increased. Additions to Medicare included routine mammography screening; Medicaid was extended to cover children through age 18.[70] Significantly, Social Security was protected from sequestration. According to the House Budget Committee, Social Security was safely "off-budget," guarded by "firewall" procedures in Congress.[71] The most generous provisions of 1990 OBRA, however, were reserved for the working poor through a major expansion of the EITC that would provide credits for low-income health insurance costs and child care expenses totaling $18.3 billion over the next five years.[72]

The long-awaited beneficence of the 1990 OBRA obscured several drawbacks, though. The most prominent of these has altered Medicare; the annual deductible for Part B rose $25, and the monthly premium now increases at a rate that is faster than inflation. Additional Medicare reductions of $32 billion over five years were targeted at doctors and hospitals. The tax changes in the deficit compromise were more progressive, but not of such magnitude that they would directly affect the increasingly skewed income distribution of the nation. "The relative proportions of the total federal tax burden borne by different income groups change only a tiny fraction under the new legislation," noted researchers of the liberal Center on Budget and Policy Priorities.[73] Moreover, a defensive House Budget Committee noted that the total tax increases under the 1990 OBRA—2.2 percent over five years—paled in contrast to the revenues lost in the 1981

Table 3.3   Selected Social Welfare Expenditures for 1991

Selected Programs	Increase (millions)
Head Start	$400
Job Training Partnership Act	143
Child Care Block Grant	732
Community Development Grants	273
WIC Program	224
Substance Abuse, Mental Health	256

Source: House Budget Committee, "Fiscal Year 1991 Budget Agreement," Washington, D.C., October 27, 1990, p. 37.

Reagan tax cut of 16 percent.[74] Also objectionable is the fact that the extension of Medicaid to cover every poor child is phased in over a 12-year period; thus, all poor children will not be assured of health care until October 2002.[75]

Besides, in striking a deal for a budget compromise that included badly needed benefits, Democrats also struck at the heart of welfare state liberalism. Included in the budget compromise were features that altered the very structure of domestic policy, at least as liberals had come to understand it. First and foremost, the budget compromise established that defense and domestic expenditures would be segregated. Future reductions in defense appropriations—the "peace dividend"—would be credited toward the deficit instead of being transferred to domestic programs. Second, any increases in select domestic programs must be met at the expense of other domestic expenditures. As far as social programs were concerned, the federal budget was a zero-sum game. The consequences of the budget compromise could be devastating.

As the economy heads toward recession, unemployment and poverty levels are likely to rise, increasing the number of Americans needing various services. In the years ahead, a variety of domestic needs will be pitted largely against each other— and against existing domestic non-entitlement programs—in a competition for limited resources. Since no funds can be transferred from other budget areas, increases in one domestic non-entitlement program will, to a significant degree, require reductions in another.[76]

The combination of budget deficits and budget compromises provides an unusual opportunity for conservatives to undo important elements of the welfare state. Most of the benefits that the budget compromise allocates to the poor ($13.1 billion out of the $22 billion) are through the EITC. The EITC benefits the working poor who cannot, or prefer not to, qualify for welfare benefits. In funneling benefits through the EITC, conservatives cleverly avoid the stigma associated with welfare, while at the same time targeting benefits for a group that is more likely to be politically active than "welfare" beneficiaries. Not incidentally, the EITC is administered through the Internal Revenue Service of the Treasury Department, thus bypassing altogether the social programs of the Department of Health and Human Services, which are associated with established, liberal professional and client interests. In this respect, a very real question is not *if*, but *when*, the EITC becomes the conservative expression of support for the working poor—a Republican answer to Democratic welfare programs.

A second opportunity emerged in the compromise. No sooner had OBRA been signed by President Bush than his budget director, Richard Darman, announced that he and his staff would be determining whether to advance a proposal limiting Social Security benefits for the rich while increasing benefits to the middle class and working poor.[77] Ultimately, Darman's strategy was targeted not at Social Security, but at Medicare. The administration's proposed 1992 budget not only resurrected the $26-billion cut in Medicare that had stalemated the 1990 budget compromise, but also introduced a $125,000 income cap for Part B—an unprecedented imposition of a means-test in a social insurance program. At this writing, Congress has yet to agree to the means-testing of Medicare. Such authorization notwithstanding, welfare state liberals had been put on notice about conservative intentions regarding social insurance. Put another way: if, through the 1990 budget compromise, social insurance was indeed protected by a firewall, then Richard Darman was an arsonist.

The integrity of the 1990 budget agreement itself was soon tested as the United States led allied nations to war with Iraq. Citing the promises of allies to contribute to the costs of the Gulf War, the administration expected to spend $15 billion in U.S. funds. Conveniently, the administration held the Gulf War off budget, meaning it did not have to meet budget restrictions imposed by the 1990 OBRA.

While President Bush's proposed 1992 budget was not accepted in its entirety by Congress, its contents did give a preview of conservative strategy for the 1990s. Even without factoring in the costs of the Gulf War, the president's proposed 1992 budget reflected the increased competition among domestic needs. Indeed, the most striking feature of the budget summary was the proliferation of negative entries—budget rescissions calculated to keep expenditures within the limits of the 1990 OBRA. In order to present new social initiatives, the administration often cannibalized existing programs. Curiously, President Bush's celebrated appeal to the voluntary sector—"a thousand points of light"—vanished in the 1992 budget. In 1990 the president had signed the National and Community Service Act, Title III of which authorized the Points of Light Foundation. The Points of Light Foundation had been scheduled to receive $7.5 million of the act's 1992 $95.5-million appropriation.[78] In a change of heart, however, the administration's 1992 budget proposal eliminated all funding for the act, including the Points of Light Foundation. Perhaps the most ambitious aspect of the budget was its further devolution of social program responsibility to the states in the form of a $15-billion block grant.[79] All told, the proposed budget reflected conservative priorities in social policy. As the Center for Budget and Policy Priorities concluded, after adjusting for inflation the proposed 1992 budget represented a $1.8-billion reduction in appropriations for low-income programs.[80]

By the end of the 1980s, conservatives had effectively placed boundaries on the liberal welfare state. As a final check against the seemingly infinite expansion of social programs, the budget compromise of 1990 held domestic expenditures static for three to five years. Liberal Democratic veterans of the federal budgetary process discovered that the Budget Enforcement Act (Title XIII of OBRA 1990) eliminated any room for maneuvering even minor increments in support of social programs.[81] The Congressional Budget Office (CBO) reported that the proposed budget "largely conform[s]" to the 1990 budget agreement—a seemingly benign conclusion until one recognizes that the CBO is the accounting arm for a Congress that is predominantly Democratic.[82]

Yet, despite conservative obstructions, scholars and legislators of the right were unable to construct a conservative vision of the common good. For all the criticism leveled at liberal social programs during the 1980s, a coherent vision of welfare failed to emerge. This is somewhat surprising, considering the enormous influence that conservatives enjoyed during the early part of the decade. It is nothing less than astonishing, considering the number of "institutional candidates"—voluntary agencies, independent practitioners, employee benefits, commercial human service providers—that philosophers of the right could have employed to construct a conservative welfare state. During the 1980s conservatives might well have reshaped the American welfare state in a manner that was more congruent with indigenous needs, yet they squandered their political and economic capital on reckless initiatives such as those leading to the Iran-Contra debacle and the savings and loan scandal. Those few who persisted in focusing on poverty drew the epithet "bleeding-heart conservative." After a decade of deconstructing social programs, conservatives had proven their inability to pose a pragmatically plausible alternative to the liberal welfare state.

NOTES

1. Sidney Blumenthal, "Think Tank Adrift in the Center," *Washington Post* (June 26, 1986). That Baroody's resignation was abrupt says much about the strength of the conservative tide at the time. Baroody's departure was tied to plummeting support for AEI on the part of conservative foundations, which, when AEI appeared to be too centrist, diverted support to more doctrinaire think tanks of the right, such as the Cato Institute and the Heritage Foundation.

2. Michael Balzano, Jr., "The Sacking of a Centrist," *Washington Post* (July 6, 1986).

3. James Smith, *The Idea Brokers* (New York: Free Press, 1991), pp. 176-80.

4. William Baroody, Jr., "The President's Review," in the *AEI Annual Report 1981-82* (Washington, D.C.: American Enterprise Institute, 1982), p. 2.

5. Charles Schultze, *The Public Use of Private Interest* (Washington, D.C.: Brookings Institution, 1977).

6. Henry Aaron, *Politics and the Professors* (Washington, D.C.: Brookings Institution, 1978).

7. D. Fisk, H. Kiesling, and T. Muller, *Private Provision of Public Service* (Washington, D.C.: Urban Institute, 1978).

8. Gregg Easterbrook, "Ideas Move Nations," *Atlantic Monthly* (January 1986), p. 66.

9. George Gilder, *Wealth and Poverty* (New York: Basic Books, 1981), p. 118.

10. Chuck Lane, "The Manhattan Project," *New Republic* (March 25, 1985).

11. Charles Murray, *Losing Ground* (New York: Basic Books, 1984), pp. 227-28.

12. Robert Greenstein, "Losing Faith in 'Losing Ground,'" *New Republic* (March 25, 1985).

13. Doubtless, conservative policy institutes benefited from the defection of several prominent former liberals who professed what was to become "neo-conservatism." Peter Steinfels, *The Neoconservatives* (New York: Simon and Schuster, 1979).

14. Peter Berger and Richard Neuhaus, *To Empower People* (Washington, D.C.: American Enterprise Institute, 1977).

15. Michael Balzano, *Federalizing Meals on Wheels* (Washington, D.C.: American Enterprise Institute, 1979), p. 37.

16. Michael Novak, *Toward a Theology of the Corporation* (Washington, D.C.: American Enterprise Institute, 1981), p. 5.

17. Ibid., p. 50. At the same time Novak warned those who considered doing good works through the public sector: "I advise intelligent, ambitious, and morally serious young Christians and Jews to awaken to the growing dangers of statism. They will better serve their souls and serve the Kingdom of God all around the world by restoring the liberty and power of the private sector than by working for the state," p. 28.

18. Martin Anderson, "Welfare Reform," in Peter Duignan and Alvin Rabushka (eds.), *The United States in the 1980s* (Stanford, Calif.: Hoover Institution, 1980), p. 145.

19. Ibid., pp. 171–75.

20. Peter Ferrara, *Social Security Reform* (Washington, D.C.: Heritage Foundation, 1982); and Peter Ferrara, *Rebuilding Social Security* (Washington, D.C.: Heritage Foundation, 1984).

21. Burton Pines, *Back to Basics* (New York: William Morrow, 1982). Although the Family Protection Act was not passed, it effectively diverted the attention of the public toward traditional values, which were portrayed positively, and away from liberal values, which were considered ruinous. For more on the traditionalist movement and the welfare state, see James Midgley, "The New Christian Right, Social Policy, and the Welfare State," *Journal of Sociology and Social Welfare* 17 (Winter 1990).

22. Pines, *Back to Basics* p. 254.

23. Nathan Glazer, "The Social Policy of the Reagan Administration," *Public Interest* (Spring 1984), p. 97.

24. Committee on Ways and Means, U.S. House of Representatives, *Background Material and Data on Programs within the Jurisdiction of the Committee on Ways and Means, 1985 Edition* (Washington, D.C.: U.S. Government Printing Office, 1985), p. 376.

25. Robert Moffitt and Douglas Wolf, "The Effect of the 1981 Omnibus Budget Reconciliation Act on Welfare Recipients and Work Incentives," *Social Service Review* 61 (June 1987), p. 248.

26. Committee on Ways and Means, House, *Background Material and Data, 1985*, p. 377.

27. John Wodarski, et al., "Reagan's AFDC Policy Changes: The Georgia Experience," *Social Work* 31 (July/August 1986), p. 277.

28. Isabel Wolock, et al., "Forced Exit from Welfare: The Impact of Federal Cutbacks on Public Assistance Families," *Journal of Social Service Research* (Winter 1985/Spring 1986), p. 94.

29. Committee on Ways and Means, U.S. House of Representatives, *Overview of Entitlement Programs* (Washington, D.C.: U.S. Government Printing Office, 1990), p. 744.

30. Daniel Finnegan, "Federal Categorical Grants and Social Policies," *Social Service Review* 63 (December 1988), p. 625.

31. Alan Abramson and Lester Salamon, *The Nonprofit Sector and the New Federal Budget* (Washington, D.C.: Urban Institute, 1986), p. xi; Waldemar Nielson, *The Third Sector: Keystone of a Caring Society* (Washington, D.C.: Independent Sector, 1980). To make matters worse for nonprofits, charitable contributions made to nonprofit agencies by nonitemizers were no longer deductible from income taxes as of 1989

32. Virginia Hodgkinson and Murray Weitzman, *Dimensions of the Independent Sector* (Washington, D.C.: Independent Sector, 1986), p. 3.

33. Novak, *Theology of the Corporation*, p. 9.

34. Kevin Phillips, *The Politics of Rich and Poor* (New York: Random House, 1990), p. 87.

35. Committee on Ways and Means, House, *Overview of Entitlement Programs*, p. 806.

36. Ibid., p. 821.

37. Phillips, *Politics of Rich and Poor*, p. 87.

38. Robert Greenstein and Scott Barancik, *Drifting Apart* (Washington, D.C.: Center on Budget and Policy Priorities, 1990), p. 17.

39. Committee on Ways and Means, House, *Overview of Entitlement Programs*, p. 57.

40. Ibid., p. 58.

41. Ibid., p. 62.

42. Howard Karger and David Stoesz, *American Social Welfare Policy* (White Plains, N.Y.: Longman, 1990), p. 171.

43. Committee on Ways and Means, House, *Background Material and Data, 1985*, p. 29.

44. Martha Ozawa, "The 1983 Amendments to the Social Security Act," *Social Work* 29 (March/April 1984).

45. Committee on Ways and Means, House, *Overview of Entitlement Programs*, p. 90.

46. Richard Reeves, "Moynihan Roils the Class War's Losers," *Los Angeles Times* (January 24, 1990), p. B-7; Larry Martz and Rich Thomas, "Fixing Social Security," *Newsweek* (May 7, 1990).

47. Phillips, *Politics of Rich and Poor*, p. 80.

48. Committee on Ways and Means, House, *Overview of Entitlement Programs*, p. 744.

49. Robert Pear, "Congress Has Pulled Back from Tax Code as a Social Policy Lever," *San Diego Union* (October 5, 1986), p. C-1.

50. W. Eaton, "Major Welfare Reform Compromise Reached," *Los Angeles Times* (September 27, 1988), p. 15.

51. Rich, "Panel Clears Welfare Bill," *Washington Post* (September 28, 1988), p. 18.

52. Ibid.

53. David Ellwood, *Poor Support: Poverty in the American Family* (New York: Basic Books, 1988), p. 153.

54. Mimi Abramovitz, "Why Welfare Reform Is a Sham," *Nation* (September 26, 1988), p. 239.

55. David Stoesz and Howard Karger, "Welfare Reform," *Social Work* 35 (March 1990), p. 145.

56. Committee on Ways and Means, House, *Overview of Entitlement Programs*, p. 618.

57. Abramowitz, "Why Welfare Reform Is a Sham," p. 240.

58. Lawrence Mead, *Beyond Entitlement* (New York: Free Press, 1986), p. 65; original emphasis.

59. Daniel Patrick Moynihan, quoted in the *Congressional Record* (October 15, 1987), pp. S10401-2.

60. Daniel Friedlander, *Subgroup Impacts and Performance Indicators for Selected Welfare Employment Programs* (New York: Manpower Demonstration Research Corporation, 1988).

61. Orrin Hatch, quoted in the *Congressional Record* (September 11, 1987), pp. S9001–3.

62. Committee on Labor and Human Resources, U.S. Senate, *Minimum Health Benefits for All Workers Act of 1988* (Washington, D.C.: U.S. Government Printing Office, 1988).

63. M. S. Greene, "Crackdown Vowed on Child Support," *Washington Post* (January 24, 1987).

64. Robert Reich, "As the World Turns," *New Republic* 200 (1989), p. 23.

65. Julie Rovner, "Beneficiaries Balk at Catastrophic Plan Tab," *Albuquerque Journal* (December 24, 1988), p. A9; Committee on Ways and Means, U.S. House of Representatives, *Background Material and Data on Programs within the Jurisdiction of the Committee on Ways and Means, 1989 Edition* (Washington, D.C.: U.S. Government Printing Office, 1989), p. 195.

66. Phillip Longman, "Catastrophic Follies," *New Republic* (August 21, 1989).

67. Daniel Patrick Moynihan, *Came the Revolution* (San Diego: Harcourt Brace Jovanovich, 1988), p. 293.

68. Congressional Budget Office, "Final Sequestration Report for Fiscal Year 1991," Washington, D.C., November 6, 1990, p. 1.

69. Spencer Rich, "A Rare Mood of Benevolence on Capitol Hill," *Washington Post Weekly* (November 12–18, 1990), p. 32.

70. Paul Leonard and Robert Greenstein, *One Step Forward: The Budget Deficit Reduction Package of 1990* (Washington, D.C.: Center on Budget and Policy Priorities, 1990).

71. House Budget Committee, "Fiscal Year 1991 Budget Agreement: Summary Materials," October 27, 1990, p. 38.

72. Leonard and Greenstein, *One Step Forward*, p. 15.

73. Ibid., p. 11.

74. House Budget Committee, "Fiscal Year 1991," p. 24.

75. Leonard and Greenstein, *One Step Forward*, p. 26.

76. Ibid., p. 32.

77. Alan Murray, "Administration Weighs Cutting Benefits of Rich," *Wall Street Journal* (November 15, 1990).

78. "National and Community Service Act of 1990," Conference Report, U.S. House of Representatives, October 17, 1990.

79. *Budget of the United States Government, Fiscal Year 1992* (Washington, D.C.: U.S. Government Printing Office, 1991).

80. Robert Greenstein and Peter Leonard, *Unchanged Priorities: The Fiscal Year 1992 Bush Budget* (Washington, D.C.: Center on Budget and Policy Priorities, 1991).

81. William Eaton, "Budget Agreement Having Positive Effect on Congress," *Los Angeles Times* (April 29, 1991).

82. Congressional Budget Office, *An Analysis of the President's Budgetary Proposals for Fiscal Year 1992* (Washington, D.C.: Congressional Budget Office, 1991), p. 93.

4

Responding to the Crisis: Liberal Prescriptions

Howard Jacob Karger

As the dust settled at the end of the second Reagan term, liberals were in retreat—a direction effectively exploited by George Bush, who was able to indict the Democratic presidential candidate Michael Dukakis for adhering to a philosophy that had guided American public policy for most of the century. Liberalism—a philosophical beacon for progressives who had sought to rid the nation of political corruption and corporate abuse during industrialization—had, within a decade, become no less than a curse. "The American welfare state in the mid-1980s," noted Berkeley welfare philosopher Neil Gilbert, is "adrift in a sea of ideological confusion."[1] Accustomed to hegemony in the social policy debate, liberals and the left were poorly prepared to function as gadflies to the policy initiatives of the more boisterous Reaganauts. In retrospect, this is surprising, given the deceit, duplicity, and just plain bad judgment sometimes demonstrated by conservatives in matters of social policy during the decade. In the face of such a reversal of ideological fortune and in the midst of so much social debris, the 1980s should have provided the stuff for a revitalization of the liberal left. Yet, conservatives romped through the decade virtually unchallenged, only occasionally reprimanded by the aging statesmen of the left, Michael Harrington and John Kenneth Galbraith.

LIBERALS AND THE DECLINE OF THE WELFARE STATE

After the War on Poverty, liberals were gratified to find that entitlements—both social insurances and means-tested programs—were expanding; however, discretionary poverty programs were being reduced, transferred to established agencies, or eliminated altogether. The ambivalence of the

Nixon administration toward social welfare was to be followed by two inconsequential presidencies, leaving liberals with the safe assumption that their most effective strategy in social welfare was an incremental one. Yet, the ideological truce that liberals had all but negotiated with conservatives was soon exploded by the Reagan presidency. By the end of the 1980s, the entire liberal policy edifice was up for reassessment. Indeed, a careful check of the structural integrity of the liberal policy platform would have made a building inspector shudder.

1. *National Economic Planning*—By the end of the 1980s, the United States had no industrial policy to assure that all American communities would benefit from national prosperity. As early as 1975, Ira Sharkansky had likened the United States to a developing nation, drawing parallels between our economic backwaters and those of the Third World.[2] Since then, conditions of American innercities and rural regions such as Indian reservations and Appalachia have worsened. During the 1980s, the United States lost ground internationally, particularly to the highly charged economies of Japan and Germany. This economic shift resulted in the United States' going from the world's largest creditor nation to the largest debtor nation—a status that will probably worsen. A century ago the specter of communism haunted Europe; today, the United States is haunted by the consolidation of the European Economic Community.

2. *Universal Benefits as a Right of Citizenship*—With the exception of public education—and it has taken a drubbing recently—the United States can assure its citizens few essential goods and services as a right of citizenship. This is especially true when U.S. social provisions are compared to those of the European welfare states. In an exhaustive study of the social development of 107 nations, Richard Estes found that the United States ranked nineteenth.[3] More specifically, the liberal "trinity" of American welfare reform has foundered:

i. *Full-employment* has not been achieved despite the Humphrey-Hawkins Full Employment Act, which placed unemployment at a frictional level. Instead, the Comprehensive Employment and Training Act was cut and replaced by the Job Training Partnership Act in 1982. Any subsequent reduction in unemployment was due to a tight labor market, not federal jobs programs.

ii. *National health care*, whether in a national health service or a national insurance format, has been limited to experimental state programs. Proposals such as the Massachusetts health plan will prove to be marginal, even if they are fully implemented. The latest congressional attempt to forge a national plan—the Pepper Commission

Report—was "dead on arrival," according to the Bush administration.[4]

iii. A *guaranteed annual income* has not received serious consideration since Nixon's Family Assistance Plan.

3. *Income Redistribution by a Progressive Tax Structure*—The 1981 tax cut and the 1983 Social Security reforms penalized the poor while giving substantial tax relief to the rich—an upward redistribution of wealth that was not changed by the 1990 Gramm-Rudman budget compromise.[5] As a result, the income disparity between the rich and the poor is now the widest since the Census Bureau began collecting this data in 1947.

4. *Reductions in Defense Spending*—The 1980s saw the largest peace time military buildup in the nation's history, while social programs were comparatively trimmed. Subsequent discussions about what to do with any realizable peace dividend evaporated with the Persian Gulf War. Future shifts of expenditures from military to domestic programs were prohibited through the 1990 Gramm-Rudman budget compromise.

By the end of the 1980s, it appeared that liberalism no longer provided a valid map for developing future social welfare initiatives.

THE LEFT AND THE WELFARE STATE

By 1970 the battle lines that were to continue throughout the 1980s had already been drawn. Liberals who had promoted an expansive vision of equality and empowerment now assumed the rear-guard position of trying to keep the welfare state intact. Conservatives, on the other hand, concentrated on whittling away at social programs. Throughout much of the 1960s and early 1970s, leftists were either conspicuous by their silence or else, in some cases, actually applauded the failure of the Great Society, since it reaffirmed their belief that capitalism could not tolerate anything but a token welfare state.

While the relationship between the left and the welfare state has always been uneasy, the Reagan presidency marked a sharp change in orientation. Prior to the Reagan era, Marxian social thought conflicted with welfare state ideology in several respects. First, many Marxians viewed the welfare state as a mechanism that directed attention toward those members of the society who were experiencing poverty, at the cost of ignoring broader structural problems. Consequently, many pre-Reagan Marxists viewed the welfare state as a palliative; they argued that social welfare programs functioned like junk food for the impoverished, providing just enough subsistence to discourage revolution but not enough to make a real difference in the lives of the poor. According to Jeffry Galper, one of the most articulate critics of welfarism, leftists saw social problems as a logical consequence of an unjust society.[6] Galper maintained that the failure of capitalism led to political movements and that these movements, in turn, pressured institutions to respond with increased social welfare services. For pre-Reagan socialists, social welfare was understood as an ingenious arrangement by business to have the public pay the costs of the social and economic dislocations endemic to capitalism.

Many radicals of the left also saw social welfare as serving the needs of capitalist expansion and production. According to American socialists such as Michael Harrington and Barbara Ehrenreich, social welfare expenditures socialized the costs of capitalist production by making public the costs of private enterprise. Moreover, by socializing the costs of production, capitalism was made stronger and thus less amenable to change. While some radicals believed social welfare programs did respond to human needs, these programs did so in a way that supported an unjust economic system that continued to generate problems requiring social programs. Socialists believed *real* social welfare was structural and could only occur through the redistribution of resources. In a just society—where all goods, resources, and opportunities were equally available to everyone—all but the most specific forms of welfare (health care, rehabilitation, and counseling) would be unnecessary. Given this argument, it is not surprising that radicals viewed welfare state programs as, at best, a puny substitute for social justice and, at worse, an obstacle to real social reform.

Within the radical left framework, poverty was seen as inextricably linked to structural inequality: people required welfare programs because they were exploited and denied access to resources. Radicals rejected a philosophy of equality rooted in individual rather than social terms. Vic George and Paul Wilding, two British socialists, maintained,

> There are many brands of equality. . . . The brand that has been incorporated in social policy is equality of opportunity, i.e., the belief that every individual has a right to such services and circumstances as will enable him to fulfill his abilities. This is a meritocratic view of equality. The emphasis is on equality of competition rather than on equality of results. It is the direct offspring of individualism humanized by the efforts of the Welfare State. As such it is the product of a constellation of values that represents a compromise between laissez-faire and equality of results.[7]

By rejecting *social* equality in favor of *individual* equality, the welfare state in its most benign expression conforms nicely to the requirements of capitalism. However, when social and economic dislocations occur (as in a recession), the welfare state then serves as a potent form of social control.

In their classic book *Regulating the Poor*, Frances Fox Piven and Richard Cloward convincingly argued that the purpose of welfare is not to build a common humanity, but to appease unrest and to regulate the labor supply in accord with the needs of the business cycle. As such, welfare programs support the poor when there are few available jobs, then withdraw aid when business needs menial labor. Piven and Cloward also saw social welfare programs as a tool used by capitalists to control insurgency. When mass protests arise and people demand economic justice, the state (acting as an agent for the capitalists), attempts to buy off discontent with social welfare reforms.[8] The dynamic of social control through relief programs works like this:

> Relief arrangements are ancillary to economic arrangements. Their chief function is to regulate labor, and they do that in two general ways. First, when mass unemployment leads to outbreaks of turmoil, relief programs are ordinarily initiated or expanded to absorb or control enough of the unemployed to restore order; then, as turbulence subsides, the relief system contracts, expelling those who are needed to populate the labor market.[9]

Piven and Cloward contended that "as for relief programs themselves, the historical pattern is clearly not one of progressive liberalization; it is rather a record of periodically expanding and contracting relief rolls as the system performs its two main functions: maintaining civil order and enforcing work."[10]

Pre-Reagan Marxian critiques depicted welfare state programs as a hoax. To achieve real equality the radical vision demanded a major overhaul of the entire social, political, and economic system. For leftist radicals, real welfare reform—a complete redistribution of goods, income, and services—could only occur under socialism.

Despite their disenchantment with the welfare state, many leftists were unprepared for the conservative assault that occurred during the 1980s. Writing the introduction to *Beyond the Welfare State*, on the eve of the 1980 presidential election, Irving Howe made a glaring error when he predicted that "the over-heated reaction against the welfare state . . . [would] . . . prove to be a last gasp of the American right."[11] In fact, the influence of neoconservatives began to increase dramatically by the middle 1970s, and the stability of the post-World War II welfare state (which the left had taken for granted) was seriously challenged during the 1980s.

In spite of early warnings, the election of Margaret Thatcher in 1979 and Ronald Reagan in 1980 sent a shock wave through the international left. Perhaps reflecting upon his own political conundrum, the British Marxian economist Ian Gough observed,

In the 1960s, radicals and Marxists were analyzing the welfare state as a repressive mechanism of social control: social work, the schools, housing departments, the probation service, social security agencies—all were seen as means of controlling and/or adapting rebellious and non-conforming groups in society to the needs of capitalism. Yet in the 1970s . . . these same people were rushing to defend the welfare state against "the cuts" and other attacks on it! . . . There is no doubt . . . [about] . . . the central ambivalence in left-wing attitudes toward state welfare: agency of repression, or a system for enlarging human needs and mitigating the rigors of the free-market economy? An aid to capital accumulation and profits or a "social wage" to be defended and enlarged like the money in your pay packet? Capitalist fraud or working-class victory?[12]

Shortly after Reagan's electoral victory in 1980, the American left adopted Gough's two-step shuffle. In a dramatic turnaround of their own, Piven and Cloward virtually renounced their earlier writing:

The emergence of the welfare state was a momentous development in American history. It meant that people could turn to government to shield them from the insecurities and hardships of an unrestrained market economy. . . . Relief recipients benefit enormously from some of these programs, especially those providing subsidies for food, fuel, and medical care, so that their condition has not worsened on the whole. Public relief, once the sole form of state intervention to ameliorate destitution, has thus come to be embedded in a general structure of income support programs for a wide range of constituencies, from the aged to the disabled to the unemployed. The changes in American society that gave rise to this development lead us to the conclusion that *the cyclical pattern of providing subsistence resources by the state has been replaced by a variety of permanent income maintenance entitlements.*[13]

It did not take long for the left to redefine itself as a defender of the welfare state, rather than a detractor. Throughout the 1980s, once hostile leftists began producing a literature that extolled the virtues of welfare statism.[14] Their opprobrium now focused on neoconservatives. Certainly, the radical and often hyperbolic writing of some New Right thinkers supplied the left with ample ammunition, and (justifiably) it went into orbit in response to the most notorious conservative pronouncements of the decade: Martin Anderson's conclusion that the War on Poverty had been won except for a few mopping-up operations; George Gilder's observation that, to escape destitution, the poor needed most of all the spur of their own poverty; and

Charles Murray's recommendation to scrap the entire welfare and income support structure for working-age persons.

By focusing its energies on the attack against radical neoconservative proposals, the left put itself in the unenviable position of having to defend the status quo of welfare statism—a stance that would have been anathema ten years earlier. By the mid-1980s, leftists were sounding like liberal Democrats, at least on social welfare issues. Assuming a moderate and almost apologist position on the welfare state, however, also meant yielding the intellectual high ground to bold neoconservative proposals. Finding itself aligned with what remained of traditional Democratic party liberals, the left was forced to toe the line and moderate its criticism of inadequate welfare state programs. Hence, it became mute on important issues such as the social incompetence of a growing underclass, and the inability of welfare programs to roll back poverty despite high spending levels; its voice was noticeably absent from discussions about alternative forms of public programs and public spending. In short, the left was straightjacketed by its unqualified defense of liberal social welfare programs. The high cost of defending the welfare state against neoconservative attacks was the loss of intellectual freedom.

THE LEFT SANS SOCIAL CLASS

The most astonishing thing about the left's change of heart toward liberal social programs was that just as leftists took up the defense of the welfare state, social class—the sine qua non of Marxian analysis—reemerged in American culture. As journalist after journalist discovered the "underclass" and brought it to public attention, the left was virtually silent.[15] A victim of ideological lethargy, the American left not only ignored urgent conditions damaging millions of citizens, but failed to exploit what was probably *the* ideological opportunity of the last half of the century: the disparity in life opportunities between a blighted underclass that persevered despite government neglect, and an ostentatious "overclass" whose gluttony seemed endless despite a decade at the public trough.

That the underclass phenomenon warranted attention is unarguable. During the Reagan presidency, federal urban policy failed miserably to address problems associated with the substantial shifts in demography and capital affecting American cities. During the past two decades, millions of Americans have abandoned older industrial cities for the sunbelt. John Kasarda reported that between 1975 and 1985 "the South and West accounted for more than 85 percent of the nation's population growth."[16] The consequence for select cities is depicted in Table 4.1. Most of the explosive growth of southern and western cities was fed by flight from those of the Northeast and Midwest. Residents left behind in older cities tended to be minorities and the impoverished elderly. Between 1975 and 1985, the minority population of northeastern cities increased from 33 percent to 42 percent.[17] As the white population fled urban industrial areas, the economic base of America's cities dramatically changed: blue-collar jobs requiring less education vanished and were replaced by those of the information and services sectors. This particularly penalized the unskilled and poorly educated minority population who were left behind in the industrial cities of the Northeast and Midwest. "Unfortunately, the northern cities that have lost the greatest numbers of jobs with lower educational requisites during the past three decades," concluded Kasarda, "have simultaneously experienced large increases in the number of their minority residents, many of whom are workers whose limited educations preclude their employment in the new urban growth industries."[18] The interaction of white flight and technological transformation was devastating for minorities residing in older industrial cities. If the unemployment rate is combined with the labor force nonparticipation rate, the plight of young blacks is immediately apparent, as shown in Table 4.2. To be young, African American, and out of school was bad enough; the prospects were even worse if you lived in the Northeast, particularly compared to the West. In 1985, 68.0 percent of young blacks living in the Northeast were unemployed, not in school, or not working, compared to 38.9 percent who lived in the West.

The Underclass

The consequence of these developments is illustrated in the spread of an urban underclass. From exploratory investigations of the deterioration of poor urban neighborhoods,[19] social researchers have developed a more sophisticated understanding of factors that contribute to underclass status.[20] In a synthesis of previous studies, Sara McLanahan and her associates identified three factors contributing to underclass status: (1) persistently weak attachment to the labor force; (2) intergenerational dependence; and (3) ghettoization. Of particular interest is the latter—the increased social isolation of the very poor—as shown in Table 4.3. While poverty continued to impact poor neighborhoods (census tracts with 20 percent poor), it worsened considerably the conditions of *poorer* neighborhoods (census tracts with 40 percent poor).

Beginning in the 1970s, a conspiracy of events transformed the industrial city. White flight decimated cities of the Northeast and Midwest, leaving behind larger concentrations of minorities. Technological and economic shifts reduced the demand for unskilled labor, sharply reducing employment opportunities for African Americans. Concomitantly, reduced

Table 4.1   Population Changes of Selected Major
Cities, 1970–1984

City	Population (in thousands) 1970	1984	Percentage Change
St. Louis	622.2	429.3	-31.0
Detroit	1,511.3	1,089.0	-27.9
Cleveland	751.0	546.5	-27.2
Buffalo	462.8	339.0	-26.8
Pittsburgh	520.2	402.6	-22.6
Los Angeles	2,816.1	3,096.7	+10.0
Dallas	844.2	974.2	+15.4
San Antonio	654.3	842.8	+28.8
San Diego	696.6	960.5	+37.9
Houston	1,232.4	1,705.7	+38.4
Phoenix	581.6	853.3	+46.7

Source: Philip Dearborn, "Fiscal Conditions in Large American Cities, 1971–1984," in M. McGeary and L. Lynn (eds.), *Urban Change and Poverty* (Washington, D.C.: National Academy Press, 1988), p. 256.

federal grants to the poor and to cities failed to help those left behind make up for lost ground. As a result, the social and economic circumstances of the poor worsened considerably, further isolating them from the American mainstream. As a result of social and economic deterioration, many urban neighborhoods began to evidence characteristics that were qualitatively different—and more troubling—than those associated with communities that were simply poor. "What distinguishes members of the underclass from those of other economically disadvantaged groups," wrote William Julius Wilson, "is that their marginal economic position or weak attachment to the labor force is uniquely reinforced by the neighborhood or social milieu."[21]

By the 1990s, areas of many industrial cities had virtually imploded.[22] The "wilding" of New York teenagers who savagely beat a female jogger was replicated when a gang of Boston youth raped and murdered a young mother.[23] Gang killings in Los Angeles soared 69 percent during the first eight months of 1990.[24] Gang-related murders in the nation's capital reached a three-year high, leading the police department's spokesperson to ob-

Table 4.2 **Unemployment Rates and Proportion of Male Central City Residents Age 16–24 Who Are Not in School and Not in Labor Force, by Race and Region, 1985**

Region and Race	Unemployment Rate	Percentage Not in School and Not in Labor Force
All regions		
White	13.5	6.1
Black	37.1	14.1
Northeast		
White	16.7	9.4
Black	43.5	24.5
West		
White	11.3	5.5
Black	29.6	9.3

Source: Adapted from John Kasarda, "Jobs, Migration, and Emerging Urban Mismatches," in M. McGeary and L. Lynn (eds.), Urban Change and Poverty (Washington, D.C.: National Academy Press, 1988), p. 187.

serve that "at the rate we're going the next generation is going to be extinct."[25] By the end of the decade, it was increasingly clear that a legacy of the Reagan administration's unwillingness to fashion a coherent urban policy was the emergence of an American underclass.

The Overclass

While industrial urban areas withered, postindustrial citiess expanded dramatically as a result of massive infusions of capital.[26] Rejuvenating the economy had been a primary concern for the Reagan administration, especially after a blistering campaign assault on the "stagflation" that plagued the Carter presidency. More immediately, the severe recession of the early 1980s made it imperative that the administration move swiftly. In short order, Congress agreed to a sizable tax cut that benefited wealthy individuals and corporations, and it stripped much of the regulatory red tape from the financial industry. The latter action would ultimately lead to the greatest financial debacle in the nation's history: the savings and loan (S&L) scandal.

Table 4.3 Trends in Social Conditions of Large Central Cities, 1970–1980 (in percent)

Indicator	Census Tracts with 20 Percent Poor			Census Tracts with 40 Percent Poor		
	1970	1980	Change	1970	1980	Change
Employment rate						
males, age 16+	63.3	56.0	-13	56.5	46.0	-22
AFDC families	19.8	28.0	+40	30.2	42.0	+40
Black persons	27.2	26.5	-3	6.3	8.3	+32
Poor blacks	28.3	30.5	+8	9.4	13.1	+40

Source: Adapted from Sara McLanahan, Irwin Garfinkel, and Dorothy Watson, "Family Structure, Poverty, and the Underclass," in M. McGeary and L. Lynn (eds.), *Urban Change and Poverty* (Washington, D.C.: National Academy Press, 1988), p. 130.

Deregulation of the financial industry had direct implications for social welfare, since poverty programs were funded through public funds. According to supply-side economic theory, government expenditures must be reduced since federal revenues are derived from taxes—monies that the private sector needs for capitalization. In effect, Reaganomics held that government competed with industry for capital by levying taxes on private revenue, starving the goose that lays the golden egg. As regards welfare, eventually an unfettered economy would generate an even greater surplus that could be taxed, thereby compensating for earlier reductions in expenditures for domestic programs. However flawless it may have seemed in theory, in practice Reaganomics proved abrasive to the nation's social fabric. Reagan domestic policy led to a massive shift in wealth from the poor to the wealthy, as discussed in Chapter 3. And through the deregulation of the S&L industry, Reaganomics resulted in an enormous development program—one that ultimately favored the burgeoning cities of the sunbelt at the expense of those of the Rustbowl.

By deregulating the financial industry, the Reagan administration was able to replace a diminished yet enduring government urban policy with a corporate policy that overwhelmed federal programs of the previous half-century. The amount of this "corporate urban policy" is roughly the amount taxpayers will have to fork over to repay depositors (between $300 and $500 billion over the next ten years) for money lost to speculative investments, primarily in real estate. Because S&Ls in conservatorship tend to be located in the sunbelt, the S&L bailout represents an unprecedented intranational transfer of funds. According to economist Edward W. Hill, 37 states will finance the liquidation of the debt incurred in the remaining 13. Of these, several stand to gain substantially: "Texas will receive 43.2% of the gross bailout funds, followed by Arkansas (7%), Florida (6.8%), California (6.7%), New Mexico (5.1%), Louisiana (4.6%), and Arizona (4.2%)."[27] As presently conceived (and assuming a final cost of $300 billion), the bailout will penalize the frostbelt states $123 billion.[28] In presenting his analysis, Hill identified the bailout as an "economic development program in the same sense that debt forgiveness" is offered to Third World nations, except in reverse. Hill argues that "the bulk of the transfer will be coming from the Northeast and Midwest, regions attempting to renew their econo-mies. The recipients are mainly located in regions that have experienced rapid job growth. . . . Money capital is being taken from regions that are attempting to renew their infrastructure, or physical capital, and given to regions with the newest physical capital."[29]

While the S&L scandal has substantial implications for urban policy, it also affects the national culture. If one aspect of the Reagan legacy in urban policy is the rise of the underclass, its corollary is the rise of the overclass. Here, Sidney Blumenthal's acerbic portrayal is worth reprint-ing.

> The overclass is the distorted mirror image of a caricature of the underclass. It is not the old establishment of Prescott Bush, George's father; it is, rather, the demimonde of rentiers who, under Reagan, elbowed their way to the top, where they hastily built mahogany-paneled offices to create an aura of settled legitimacy. This overclass piled up vast wealth shuffling junk bonds, paper assets, and real estate. Its monuments are not factories but Atlantic City casinos and boarded-up department stores. The overclass battened under Reagan; under Bush it sought to consolidate its respectability.[30]

Kevin Phillips provided a statistical profile of the American "plutoc-racy" that emerged during the 1980s. In 1979 the typical CEO made 29 times the income of the typical manufacturing worker; six years later CEOs had increased that differential to 40 times. "Corporate executives and investors were the prime 1980s beneficiaries," Phillips concluded.[31]

While the contradictions posed by an ostentatious overclass lording it over a stricken underclass are not so facilely reconciled in the United States, few of the left found this fertile ground for cultivation. That the Reagan era would not galvanize a dormant American left is surprising, especially considering that the $1 billion in indiscretions of Silverado Savings and Loan—in which President Bush's son Neil is implicated—easily exceeded the $691 million proposed by his father in aid for the homeless for 1991.

Or that the amount by which taxpayers will absolve Lincoln Savings and Loan's Charles H. Keating, Jr.—$2.5 billion—eclipsed what the Bush administration proposed for the Women, Infants, and Children Supplemental Food Program (WIC) for 1991.[32] As journalists are quick to point out, this is the stuff that makes for public indignation, yet the left has exploited little of it.

In fact, during the 1980s, leftist offerings to the public were noteworthy for their lack of inspiration. *The New Class War* by Frances Fox Piven and Richard Cloward, as noted earlier, was significant for its embrace—as opposed to critique—of the welfare state. Not long after, Fred Block collaborated with Piven and Cloward and Barbara Ehrenreich for an anthology, *The Mean Season: The Attack on the Welfare State*—an awkward synthesis of left polemic directed at capitalism, of liberal rationalization of the welfare state, and of defensiveness toward the New Right.[33] Appropriately, *The Mean Season* drew a lashing from Lawrence Mead. "The best-known radicals in social policy . . . lost authority because they are no longer doing much research," he wrote in a comprehensive critique of welfare reform. "The Left is represented by irresolute liberals who grudgingly recognize the problems of welfare but who can imagine no new response."[34]

The most significant book from the left during the 1980s was William Julius Wilson's *The Truly Disadvantaged*.[35] Wilson maintained that one consequence of race-focused social policy such as affirmative action was the upward mobility of minority individuals who abandoned poor communities to their less aspiring neighbors. As middle-class minorities left inner cities, an essential degree of community stabilization went with them, leaving many disadvantaged neighborhoods to economic destitution and social anarchy. In being frank about the social disintegration of inner cities, while noting the insidious effects of public assistance on minority family life, Wilson departed from the welfare state orthodoxy of the liberal left. Wilson's solution to the demise of the African American community was "a comprehensive program that combines employment policies with social welfare policies and that features universal as opposed to race- or group-specific strategies."[36] The means to providing benefits for the underclass was to subsume it in a blanket of universal provisions to a wider population. The strategy *"is to improve the life chances of truly disadvantaged groups such as the ghetto underclass by emphasizing programs to which the more advantaged groups of all races and class backgrounds can positively relate."*[37]

Yet, while Wilson's analysis was profound, his prescriptions were less so. His list of universal benefits bore no small resemblance to the liberal laundry list of welfare state objectives, and his call for a tight labor market to make underclass males more employable had already been achieved (albeit by demographic changes instead of government programs). Equally unfortunate was Wilson's unwillingness to step forward boldly and frame his prescriptions—whatever their merits—as a policy departure fashioned by the left. Instead, Wilson closeted his recommendations away from their public implications as, in his words, *"a hidden agenda."*[38]

The American left entered the 1990s seemingly unpersuaded that much mileage could be gotten from renovating a class analysis to describe and explain what had transpired in social welfare. Unwilling to discipline the social chaos of the underclass and the economic excess of the overclass, the left proceeded halfheartedly and was unable to marshal the allegiance of disenfranchised citizens. Directionless in its prescriptions and irrelevant to the daily frustrations of fellow citizens, the left receded from public attention. When it came time to sum up the Reagan revolution—a legacy eminently suited to leftists who had once flayed liberals for the inadequacy of the American welfare state—the left was not up to the task. The most prescient critique of the Reagan era was to be written not by a leftist, but by a Nixon conservative: Kevin Phillips.

The abandonment of the left's historic emphasis on equality and social revolution was replaced by a focus on rationalizing social welfare programs, including the dependence of recipients on minimal welfare state benefits. Thus, leftist arguments became almost indistinguishable from those of mainstream liberals, except for their shrill cry for higher benefits and more comprehensive welfare programs. In moving closer to the political center and thus abandoning its gadfly role, the left created a disturbing lacuna in the American political spectrum. The abandonment of the left's critique of welfare allowed neoconservative intellectuals quickly to usurp the role of welfare critic, thereby leaving the left in a position where it could only react to neoconservative proposals. With no serious welfare proposals coming from the left, neoconservatives were able to control the welfare debate unilaterally throughout the 1980s. The failure of the left to propose fresh alternatives to the welfare state seems all the more regrettable given the inherent contradictions in neoconservative political and social thought.

While it is possible that a postmortem of the left is premature and that in the coming decade it may move farther from the center and take its case directly to the people, the ability to inject itself into American social life with the same success it enjoyed in the 1960s seems unlikely. As Russell Jacoby has pointed out, many radical-progressive-left intellectuals have abandoned the public arena for an academic life where they communicate more with each other than with the public.[39] Tied to the university, left intellectuals have little recourse but to rely on public officials to serve as conduits for their ideas. Unfortunately, since many likely candidates for this function—Democratic politicians—have abandoned the social programs associated with the New Deal, the plausibility of this option seems doubtful.

INDUSTRIAL POLICY

One of the few bright spots in the otherwise dreary intellectual landscape of the 1980s was the call for the establishment of a national industrial policy. Promoted by liberals during the late 1970s and early 1980s, a national industrial policy would require the federal government to create policies that promote the development (or maintenance) of particular industries rather than be exclusively concerned with macroeconomic policies and inflation.[40] Within the industrial policy camp, this debate focused around whether high-tech "sunrise" industries should be encouraged or whether the declining mass-production (e.g., cars and steel) "sunset" industries should be bolstered. The emphasis on sunrise industries was based on a concern for future employment possibilities, while aid for the sunset industries was rooted in current employment concerns.[41]

The argument for an industrial policy focused on two propositions: (1) the creation of a government-run development bank to provide industrial capital; (2) and the conscious choice by government to pick viable industries and support them accordingly. A national industrial policy would supposedly direct the rebuilding of American industry and infrastructure in a planned manner. This would include the modernization of plants, the retooling of basic industries, the retraining of the labor force, and the construction of highways, schools, bridges, communications, and urban housing. National economic growth plans would be developed by business, the federal government, and labor unions, with the government providing the necessary resources.

Proponents of a national industrial policy argued that it held great promise for a beleaguered American industry. Operating in a manner similar to Japan's Ministry of International Trade and Industry (MITI), American industrial policy would be guided by a vision of a balanced economy. The government would provide the private sector with information about how technology and human needs are expected to alter the industrial structure; and labor, business, and government would then formulate plans to meet the global competition. Comprehensive plans would be developed to deal not only with healthy and weak industries, but also with the social dislocation resulting from economic changes. Moreover, economic plans would be developed to increase the productivity of American industry and its workforce.

Apart from its economic benefits, however, any national industrial policy is also bound to include negative side effects. As "sick" industries are phased out, large numbers of workers would become dislocated. Moreover, as productivity and capitalization increase, firms tend to become more automated and thus require fewer employees, with many workers in previously well paid industrial jobs being forced to find employment in lower-wage service industries. Especially where formal education was once necessary, workers in these jobs would find themselves employable only in the poorly paid service sector.

All in all, the development of a national industrial policy would have significant implications for the American welfare state. For one, a revitalized American industry would require a substantial commitment to increasing human capital, especially in health and education. For another, the rebuilding of American industry would demand a substantial renovation of physical infrastructures, including roads, communications, and educational institutions. This economic activity would undoubtedly produce many well-paying jobs both within and outside of the public sector. In short, the rebuilding of American infrastructure and industry would require massive transfusions of both capital and purpose into welfare state programs.

Despite its good intentions, then, the argument for a national industrial policy suffered from at least two major problems: (1) How would the federal government overcome the paralysis of a $3-trillion debt to initiate aggressive new development strategies? (2) How would welfare state managers incorporate the underclass into an economic plan that called for a disciplined and highly productive workforce? Moreover, most proposals did not even specifically address the role played by the welfare state in any new economic plan. And those economic revitalization arguments that *did* address the issue of the poor were flawed in that they spoke only in a generic sense. Failure to disaggregate the poor into subgroups—the working poor, the underclass, the transitional poor, and long-term welfare dependents—meant that broad plans to assimilate the poor into the economic mainstream would be problematic. Specifically, policies designed to help the working poor in securing economic mobility might not be effective for an underclass that has little notion of a work ethic or workplace discipline. Thus, poverty policies in any national economic plan have to address the diverse needs and characteristics of the disparate subpopulations of the poor if they are to have any chance of success.

NEOLIBERALISM

Traditional liberals tended to view government as the only institution that could bring a measure of social justice to the millions of Americans who could not participate in the social mainstream because of societal obstacles—racism, poverty, sexism, and so forth. However, as a result of the defeat of Jimmy Carter, coupled with the loss of the Senate to the Republican party in 1980, many liberal Democrats began to reevaluate their adherence to liberal positions in domestic policy. This reexamination—christened "neoliberalism" by journalist Charles Peters to differentiate the new ideology from liberalism and neoconservatism—attracted a small following in the early 1980s. Then in 1984, with the resounding defeat of Walter Mondale—a candidate who symbolized liberal social policy—neoliberalism moved to stage center of Democratic party politics. By the late 1980s, several leading Democrats identified as neoliberal—Paul Tsongas, Richard Gephardt, Charles Robb, Albert Gore, Jr., Sam Nunn, Bill Bradley, and Tim Wirth—had founded the Democratic Leadership Council (DLC). Randall Rothenberg charted the influence of neoliberalism on social policy, as evident in changes made in the Democratic party platform even early in the decade.

> The party's June 1982 midterm convention in Philadelphia did not endorse a large-scale federal jobs program, in spite of more than 9 million unemployed. It did not re-propose national health insurance, even though medical costs were still soaring. It did not submit yet again a plan for a guaranteed annual income, although the American welfare system was still not operating efficiently.[42]

The Democratic party was clearly divesting itself of its New Deal legacy.

Neoliberals were essentially liberals who had second thoughts about some basic assumptions of liberalism, such as expensive social programs, government regulation of the economy, and the reallocation of defense expenditures for domestic purposes. For neoliberals the New Deal was too expensive and too unpopular to address current problems. To reestablish credibility in an increasingly conservative political climate, neoliberals distanced themselves from the large-scale government welfare programs with which Democrats had been associated since the New Deal. In their place, neoliberals called for a reliance on personal responsibility, work, and thrift. Accordingly, proposals for welfare reform advanced by neoliberal Democrats emphasized participation in the labor market (workfare), meeting family obligations (child support enforcement), and fiscal frugality (modest budget appropriations).

In place of expensive liberal proposals for welfare reform, neoliberal proposals have tended to reduce governmental costs while encouraging businesses to assume more responsibility for the welfare of the population. For example, Charles Peters, editor of the *Washington Monthly*, advocated means-testing all welfare programs. "We still believe in liberty and justice and a fair chance for all, in mercy for the afflicted, and help for the down and out," explained Peters, "but we no longer automatically favor unions and big government or oppose the military and big business."[43] In reviewing income maintenance programs like Social Security, welfare, veterans' pensions, and unemployment compensation, Peters outlined the neoliberal position:

> We want to eliminate duplication and apply a means-test to these programs. As a practical matter the country can't afford to spend money on people who don't need it. . . . [A]s liberal idealists, we don't think the well-off should be getting money from those programs anyway—every cent we can afford should go to helping those in real need. Social Security for those totally dependent on it is miserably inadequate, as is welfare in many states.[44]

For Robert Reich, a Harvard professor and advisor to the Democratic party, a post-liberal formulation meant abandoning entitlements of social welfare in favor of investments in human capital. In advocating a restructuring of the current welfare apparatus by substituting human capital investment, Reich's position is essentially neoliberal:

> For example, we can expect that a significant part of the present welfare system will be replaced by government grants to businesses that agree to hire the chronically unemployed. . . . Other social services—health care, social security, day care, disability benefits, unemployment benefits, relocation assistance—will become part of the process of structural adjustment. Public funds now spent directly on these services will instead be made available to businesses, according to the number of people they agree to hire. Government bureaucracies that now administer these programs to individuals will be supplanted, to a large extent, by companies that administer them to their employees. . . . *Companies, rather than state and local governments, will be the agents and intermediaries through which such assistance is provided.*[45]

Despite the defeat of Michael Dukakis in the 1988 presidential campaign, neoliberalism remains central to the thinking of the emerging leadership of the Democratic party.[46] In March 1990, the Democratic Leadership Council presented a preliminary draft of its manifesto, *The New Orleans Declaration: A Democratic Agenda for the 1990s*. In clear reference to the New Deal and the War on Poverty, the *New Orleans Declaration* stated that "the political ideas and passions of the 1930s and 1960s cannot guide us in the 1990s." In promoting economic growth and restraining government spending, the *New Orleans Declaration* moved Democratic party politics toward a middle ground—an orientation reflected in social policy. To quote the *New Orleans Declaration*: "We believe the purpose of social welfare is to bring the poor into the nation's economic mainstream, not maintain them in dependence."[47] By 1990, the DLC had established a Washington think tank—the Progressive Policy Institute (PPI)—to formulate legislative proposals in social policy.

WELFARE LIBERALISM IN DISARRAY

Without a tether to the Democratic party, the liberal left orbited irrelevantly above the social policy debates of the 1980s. Increasingly detached from the political process, the proposals of the liberal left seemed imitative at best, and cobbled together at worst. Recognizing the obstacles to a broad reform effort, Robert Morris—a champion of liberal social policy—suggested prioritizing objectives, building consensus around selected goals (e.g., national health insurance and a national employment program), and leaving other goals as optional.[48] The retreat from a liberal vision of the welfare state also led to a sense of resignation for some policy analysts. Robert Kuttner—a prominent liberal economist who during the early 1980s had insisted that an economics of equality could be the basis for universalistic social programs—was forced to concede that the political, economic, and ideological direction of the nation under Reagan made a replication of the European model of the welfare state unlikely.[49] Seven years of Reaganomics had taken a toll on Kuttner's progressive orientation to social policy. In a review of welfare reform proposals, Kuttner eventually backed a modest $2-3 billion incremental restructuring of welfare, noting that "most liberals and conservatives now agree that the welfare system encourages dependency, promotes the breakup of families, legitimizes a culture of illegitimacy, and offers too few opportunities to escape from poverty."[50] Two well-credentialed senior scholars from the liberal Brookings Institution—Alice Rivlin and Robert Reischauer—helped the conservative AEI's Michael Novak compose *The New Consensus on Family and Welfare*. According to the new "consensus," welfare benefits were "toxic," and an optimal welfare policy consisted of minimizing the deleterious effects of poverty and accepting it as inevitable in American society.[51]

As liberalism became a philosophical epithet, Democrats voiced ambivalence about welfare programs. Harvard's Michael Sandel noted that "the alternatives [liberalism] posed lost their capacity to inspire the electorate or animate meaningful debate. . . . By the 1970s, the New Deal agenda had become obsolete."[52] Liberalism "no longer embodies a story in which most Americans can believe," complained Robert Reich.[53] "The values and ideas associated with the New Deal and the Great Society still float about in public discourse," echoed Democratic pollster Stanley Greenberg, "but they are no longer embedded in a common historic experience or a convincing story."[54] Even boiler-plate liberals had begun to reassess their commitment to the American welfare state. "We now stand between two Americas, the one we have known and the one toward which we are heading," a prominent liberal Democrat said in a speech before the Women's National Democratic Club. "The New Deal will live in American history as a supreme example of government responsiveness to the times. *But it is no answer to the problems of today.*"[55] The speaker was Senator Edward Kennedy.

One inclusive reassessment of the American welfare state—*The Common Good: Social Welfare and the American Future,* funded by the Ford Foundation—stuck to traditional liberal precepts and failed to endorse a fundamental restructuring of social welfare. For one thing, the Ford Foundation report omitted the knotty issues of the underclass, welfare dependency, the fiscal paralysis of the state, and the need to adopt a set of realistic expectations for social programs. Furthermore, *The Common Good* failed to provide bold alternatives for a deeply troubled welfare system. Instead of taking stock of the welfare state and trying to find more effective solutions, the Ford Foundation report recommended more of the same, except in larger doses.

The failure to provide an alternative liberal view of welfare contributed to the intellectual poverty that characterized the welfare debate in the 1980s.[56] Yet it would be unfair to place all of the blame for such failure on the liberal intelligentsia. As the consequences of Reaganomics became painfully clear, the left failed to rebut the conservative attack on welfare with pragmatic prescriptions of its own. Well into the second Reagan term, four prominent American leftists—Fred Block, Richard Cloward, Barbara Ehrenreich, and Frances Piven—assessed the conservative "attack on the welfare state" (as mentioned earlier in the chapter). Yet, instead of using the opportunity to promote new initiatives, the authors preferred the security of ideological orthodoxy to the unsafe currents of public opinion and neglected to "lay out a program for the reconstruction of the welfare state."[57]

When traditionally liberal institutions such as universities and policy institutes failed to speak forcefully against conservative initiatives, some welfare activists worked through independent organizations to advance the cause. Begun by Marian Wright Edelman, the Children's Defense Fund (CDF) sought to address the health, educational, and income needs of the nation's children. By the mid-1980s, CDF had become a major voice in children's policy, successfully advocating programs at the federal and state levels. CDF advocated for the Child Health Assurance Program, which expanded Medicaid eligibility to poor pregnant women and children; and it aggressively fought for an expansive child-daycare proposal throughout the decade. The Center on Budget and Policy Priorities (CBPP)—established in 1981 by Robert Greenstein, former administrator of the Food and Nutrition Service of the Agriculture Department—has also fought to defend social programs for low-income beneficiaries. CBPP provided much of the program analysis used to refute arguments presented by the Reaganauts in their campaign to cut means-tested welfare programs. Laudably, CBPP has in fact crunched most of the numbers that welfare advocacy groups needed to rebut the conservative critics of social programs.

For their part, more mainstream progressives began to consider social policy in what might fairly be called a post-welfare state context. PPI began to assemble position papers relating to a range of welfare issues: family policy, individual development accounts, an EITC supplement to wages of the working poor, a youth apprenticeship program, and a national service corps. Notably absent were calls for new expensive entitlements. PPI played its policy cards close to the vest, opting for social programs that reinforced the work ethic and fostered the community responsibility of citizens. Eventually, the liberal left and mainstream progressives began to find a common ground in their positions regarding social policy. In the late 1980s, three impeccably credentialed liberals—Paul Starr, Robert Kuttner, and Robert Reich—founded *The American Prospect*, a journal of contemporary issues designed to revitalize liberal philosophy. Significantly, the lead article of the first issue concerned welfare. In "The Real Welfare Problem," Christopher Jencks and Kathryn Edin acknowledged that most AFDC mothers cheat by failing to report earnings, in order to supplement low welfare grants. Instead of making AFDC more generous, Jencks and Edin recommended that liberals advocate "a new system that focuses explicitly on helping all parents who work in low-wage jobs."[58]

Predictably, conservatives continued to pommel the welfare state. In the spring of 1990, the *Wall Street Journal* recounted the plight of Grace Capetillo, a 36-year-old AFDC recipient who had frugally saved $3,000 for a washing machine and college tuition for her daughter. That Ms. Capetillo was prosecuted for fraud brought forth a torrent of angry letters to the editor, virtually all of which attacked the illogic of the AFDC program.[59] Meanwhile, the conservative superstar Charles Murray—always on the lookout for new material—accepted an invitation by the *London Times* to determine if an underclass existed in Britain. With somewhat more care than that with which he had dispatched U.S. welfare programs in *Losing Ground*, Murray did—to no one's surprise—identify an emerging underclass in England. The burden of responsibility for the British underclass fell, as it had in the United States, on wrongheaded liberals. "When meaningful reforms finally do occur," Murray concluded with characteristic panache, "they will happen not because stingy people have won, but because generous people have stopped kidding themselves."[60]

In fact, momentum was gathering to reconstruct social welfare in the United States—to fashion a formulation of social policy that was as post-Reagan as it was post-New Deal. Liberals and progressives were beginning to recognize the successes of the New Deal, the inadequacies of the War on Poverty, and the failures of the Reagan era, and were beginning to conceive of another generation of American social policy. For those who had watched with regret the plunge in life opportunities for the young, the poor, the old, and the sick, such an assessment was long overdue. Clearly, the right had succeeded in punishing programs of the welfare state, yet it had failed to deploy an alternative to liberally inspired social programs. The conservative response to the crisis of the welfare state was to exploit it. Just as obviously, the liberal left had castigated Reaganauts for their preference for fiscal over human concerns; yet, instead of accepting the challenge to structure a more plausible basis for social welfare policy, the liberal left focused on defending or incrementally expanding often-discredited programs. The liberal response to the crisis of the welfare state was to ignore it. As doctrinaire solutions to social welfare seemed less and less effective, pressure built for a radically pragmatic approach to social welfare—one that aimed to reconstruct the welfare state.

NOTES

1.   Neil Gilbert, "The Welfare State Adrift," *Social Work* 31 (July/August, 1986), p. 251.

2.   Ira Sharkansky, *The United States: A Study of a Developing Country* (New York: Longman, 1975).

3.   Richard Estes, *Trends in World Social Development: The Social Development of Nations, 1970–1987* (New York: Praeger, 1988), p. 107.

4.   Robert Rosenblatt, "Divided Panel Presents a $66-billion Medical-care Plan," *Los Angeles Times* (March 3, 1990), p. A-23.

5.   Lester Thurow, "A Surge in Inequality," *Scientific American* 256 (May 1987); Robert Greenstein, "Poverty Rate and Household Income Stagnate as Rich-Poor Gap Hits Post-war High," Washington, D.C., Center on Budget and Policy Priorities, 1989; Kevin Phillips, *The Politics of Rich and Poor* (New York: Random House, 1990).

6.   Jeffry Galper, "Introduction of Radical Theory and Practice in Social Work Education: Social Policy," mimeographed paper, Michigan State University School of Social Work, circa 1978.

7.   Vic George and Paul Wilding, *Ideology and Social Welfare* (London: Routledge and Kegan Paul, 1976), p. 129.

8. Frances Fox Piven and Richard Cloward, *Regulating the Poor* (New York: Vintage Books, 1971).

9. Ibid., p. 15.

10. Ibid., p. 3.

11. Irving Howe, *Beyond the Welfare State* (New York: Schocken Books, 1982), p. 10.

12. Ian Gough, *The Political Economy of the Welfare State* (London: Macmillan Press, 1979), p. 11.

13. Frances Fox Piven and Richard Cloward, *The New Class War* (New York: Pantheon Books, 1982), pp. ix-xi; emphasis added.

14. See for example, Fred Block, et al. (eds.), *The Mean Season: The Attack on the Welfare State* (New York: Pantheon, 1987); Michael Harrington, *The New American Poverty* (New York: Pantheon, 1984); and Michael Katz, *In the Shadow of the Poorhouse* (New York: Basic Books, 1986).

15. This omission is addressed in detail in Robert Kuttner, "Notes from Underground," *Dissent* (Spring 1991).

16. John Kasarda, "Jobs, Migration, and Emerging Urban Mismatches," in M. McGeary and L. Lynn (eds.), *Urban Change and Poverty* (Washington, D.C.: National Academy Press, 1988), p. 154.

17. Kasarda, "Jobs, Migration, and Emerging Urban Mismatches," p. 156.

18. Ibid., p. 178.

19. Douglas Glasgow, *The Black Underclass* (New York: Vintage, 1981); Ken Auletta, *The Underclass* (New York: Random House, 1982); Nicholas Lemann, "The Origins of the Underclass," *Atlantic Monthly* (June/July 1986).

20. William Julius Wilson, *The Truly Disadvantaged* (Chicago: University of Chicago Press, 1987); Sara McLanahan, Irwin Garfinkel, and Dorothy Watson, "Family Structure, Poverty, and the Underclass," in M. McGeary and L. Lynn (eds.), *Urban Change and Poverty* (Washington, D.C.: National Academy Press, 1988).

21. William Julius Wilson, "Research and *The Truly Disadvantaged*," in Christopher Jencks and Paul Peterson, (eds.) *The Urban Underclass* (Washington, D.C.: Brookings Institution, 1991), p. 474.

22. Christopher Jencks, "Deadly Neighborhoods," *New Republic* (June 13, 1988); Juan Williams, "Hard Times, Harder Hearts," *Washington Post* (October 2, 1988).

23. "Eight Boston Teenagers Charged in Savage Slaying of Young Mother," *Los Angeles Times* (November 21, 1990), p. A-4.

24. Louis Sahagun, "Gang Killings Increase 69%, Violent Crime up 20% in L.A. County Areas," *Los Angeles Times* (August 21, 1990), p. B-8.

25. Gabriel Escobar, "Slayings in Washington Hit New High, 436, for 3rd Year," *Los Angeles Times* (November 24, 1990), p. A-26.

26. Richard Louv, *America II* (New York: Penguin, 1985).

27. Edward W. Hill, "The S&L Bailout," *Challenge* (May/June 1990), p. 42.

28. For this calculation, a ratio used by Hill (ibid.) was employed. Hill's penalty for the frostbelt states was placed at $51.6 billion, but this was based on an earlier low assessment of total bailout costs.

29.   Ibid., p. 44.

30.   Sidney Blumenthal, "Chapped Lips," *New Republic* (July 30 and August 6, 1990), p. 20.

31.   Phillips, *The Politics of Rich and Poor* (New York: Random House, 1990), pp. 179–80, 166.

32.   Detail on Neil Bush's activities can be found in K. Day, "Going after Neil Bush," *Washington Post Weekly* (July 23-29, 1990); those on Keating, in J. R. Adams, *The Big Fix: Inside the S&L Scandal* (New York: Wiley, 1990). Budget figures are from Robert Greenstein and Paul Leonard, *Bush Administration Budget* (Washington, D.C.: Center on Budget and Policy Priorities, 1990).

33.   Block, et al. *Mean Season.*

34.   Lawrence Mead, "The New Welfare Debate," *Commentary* (March 1988), pp. 46, 50.

35.   Wilson, *Truly Disadvantaged.*

36.   William Julius Wilson, "American Social Policy and the Ghetto Underclass," *Dissent* (Winter 1988), p. 63.

37.   Ibid., p. 62; emphasis original.

38.   Ibid., emphasis original.

39.   Russell Jacoby, *The Last Intellectuals* (New York: Basic Books, 1987).

40.   See for example Gar Alperovitz and Jeff Faux, *Rebuilding America* (New York: Pantheon, 1984); Barry Bluestone and Bennett Harrison, *The Deindustrialization of America* (New York: Basic Books, 1982); Samuel Bowles, David M. Gordon, and Thomas E. Weisskopf, *Beyond the Wasteland* (Garden City, N.Y.: Anchor Press, 1983); and Bennett Harrison and Barry Bluestone, *The Great U-Turn* (New York: Basic Books, 1988).

41.   S. M. Miller, "Notes toward the Re-formulation of the Welfare State," in Helga Nowotny (ed.), *Thought and Action in Social Policy: Social Concerns for the 1980s* (Vienna: European Centre for Social Welfare Training and Research, 1984), pp. 69–74.

42.   Randall Rothenberg, *The Neoliberals* (New York: Simon and Schuster, 1984), pp. 244–45.

43.   Charles Peters, "A New Politics," *Public Welfare* 18 (1983), p. 34.

44.   Ibid., p. 36.

45.   Robert Reich, *The Next American Frontier* (New York: Times Books, 1983), p. 248; emphasis added.

46.   W. Schneider, "JFK's Children: The Class of '74," *Atlantic Monthly* 263 (1989), pp. 35-58.

47.   *The New Orleans Declaration: A Democratic Agenda for the 1990s* (Washington, D.C.: Democratic Leadership Council, 1990), p. 3.

48.   Robert Morris, *Rethinking Social Welfare* (White Plains, N.Y.: Longman, 1987).

49.   Robert Kuttner, *The Economic Illusion* (Boston: Houghton Mifflin, 1984).

50.   Robert Kuttner, "The Welfare Strait," *New Republic* (July 6, 1987), p. 20.

51.   Michael Novak (ed.), *The New Consensus on Family and Welfare* (Washington, D.C.: American Enterprise Institute, 1987).

52. Michael Sandel, "Democrats and Community," *New Republic* (February 22, 1988), p. 21.

53. Robert Reich, *The Insurgent Liberal* (New York: Times Books, 1989), p. 278.

54. Stanley Greenberg, "Reconstructing the Democratic Vision," *American Prospect* 1 (Spring 1990), p. 83.

55. Quoted in David Broder, "Reagan's Policies Are Standard for Would-be Successors," *Omaha World-Herald* (January 24, 1988), p. 25A; emphasis original.

56. Ford Foundation Project on Social Welfare and the American Future, *The Common Good: Social Welfare and the American Future* (New York: Ford Foundation, 1989), pp. 87–92.

57. Block, et al., *Mean Season*, p. xv.

58. Christopher Jencks and Kathryn Edin, "The Real Welfare Problem," *American Prospect* 1 (Spring 1990), p. 49.

59. Robert Rose, "For Welfare Parents, Scrimping Is Legal, but Saving Is Out," *Wall Street Journal* (February 6, 1990).

60. Charles Murray, "The British Underclass," *Public Interest* 99 (Spring 1990), p. 28.

Part Three

Reconstructing the Welfare State: Pragmatic Responses to the Welfare Crisis

5

Reconstructing the Welfare State

David Stoesz

As presently constituted, the American welfare state faces a protracted crisis that threatens not only its current stability, but also the future viability of social programs. Enmeshed within a fiscally strapped federal and state political structure, welfare state programs face an uncertain future where, at best, growth of welfare programs will be arrested and, at worst, social benefits will be pared back even further. Robert Reich has scripted how federal reductions in social investments contribute to "the vicious circle," an ever accelerating downward spiral in which local governments are left bidding against each other—offering tax concessions and other inducements—to lure business. "These enticements in turn make it more difficult for the nation to finance adequate education and infrastructure in the future," Reich observed. "The resulting jobs provide little or no on-the-job training and experience pertinent to more complex jobs in the future, and so on."[1]

As corporations transfer production units abroad, communities are left to fend for themselves, struggling to finance essential services from a deteriorating tax base. The result—described by the *Wall Street Journal* as a "bloody-brawl"—has become a Darwinian scramble for survival.[2] Formerly proud and prosperous communities in America's heartland often resemble husks, empty of the sustenance necessary to grow healthy families and communities. Indeed, we are beginning to see regions of America that resemble Third World nations—areas structurally incapable of regaining any semblance of self-sufficiency. Once the powerhouse of the American economy, the industrial Midwest has become the nation's Rustbowl.

Even the most optimistic scenarios call for a no-growth welfare state that is merely holding its own. This scenario is juxtaposed to a paralyzed welfare state facing a series of profound social problems, including in-

creases in teenage pregnancies, an escalation in the use of highly addictive drugs such as cocaine and its notorious derivative crack, and the economic
and social dislocation that is attendant with recession. Not surprisingly,
minority communities are the most ravaged. The true consequences of this
for minority families is only hinted at by casual academic references to
the appellation "underclass"—replete with statistics that only obscure the
significance of the term. Good journalism (such as Stanley Kotlowitz's
disturbing account of the bleak future faced by two brothers, *There Are
No Children Here*)[3] comes closer to understanding the real violence per-
petrated against inner-city families than do dry academic accounts. After
plotting the black diaspora from the South to the northern cities—a migration girded by little more than sharecroppers' simple faith in opportunity—writer Nicholas Lemann surveyed the devastation surrounding Chicago's
poor. "To be born into a ghetto is to be consigned to a fate that no American
should have to suffer," he concluded.[4]

The failure of the welfare state to meet the needs of the poor is replicated by its failure to meet the needs of the middle class. For one, welfare
state programs have failed to arrest the erosion of middle- and lower-
middle-class earnings by more adequately redistributing incomes. Welfare state programs have also frustrated middle-class expectations by not
helping to keep housing, health, and education costs down. The welfare
state has also failed to maintain a decent public school system in many
working class communities. In addition, many middle class people are
losing faith in the ability of the welfare state to rescue them should they
fall from economic grace. This same skepticism also holds true for social
insurance programs; many Americans are no longer certain that there will
be a Social Security program in place when they retire. In short, middle-
class Americans lack faith in the capacity of welfare state programs to
form a safety net under them.

As welfare state programs became incapable of arresting the growth of
social problems, the confidence of the public in the remediative effects of
welfare diminished, which in turn led to a legitimation crisis for the welfare
state. Unconvinced that increased expenditures for social programs resulted in desirable outcomes, the public pulled the plug on taxation. Proposition
13 in California served as a prototype—a barometer of public indigna-
tion—putting civil servants on notice that the apparently limitless growth
of social programs would be capped. Impatient with technical explanations about the lack of progress of social programs, the American polity
became reluctant to fund welfare programs that they perceived as a failure.[5] If professionals retained faith in the logic of the American welfare
state—insisting that it was "on solid ground"[6]—the public was less certain. Tax revolts reflected the public's skepticism about social programs;
for many, governmental social programs were not worth further invest-

ments. The public attitude was clearly reflecting a legitimacy crisis for social welfare policy.

Despite the current welfare crisis, both the left and the right have not offered viable proposals for welfare reform. Although conservatives have promoted a series of welfare proposals that range from the practical to the lunatic, they have not provided an integrated series of reform measures that are workable, humane, and rooted in the real conditions faced by ever greater numbers of Americans. Guided by an ideological perspective grounded in free markets and in the capitalist value of self-reliance, most conservative welfare initiatives have been marked by less than compassionate—if not outrightly punitive—assumptions. Despite evidence to the contrary, the conservative view of welfare contains an implicit assumption that the labor market is capable of providing the necessary high-paying jobs that will allow recipients to leave the welfare rolls permanently. Thus, the major problem seen by conservatives is not the inadequacy of the labor market, but the lack of initiative on the part of welfare recipients in training for and finding well-paying jobs.

On the other hand, the left and liberals failed to capture the intellectual and social opportunities that emerged during the 1980s. Wedded to a welfare state grounded in another political and social era, progressives were unable to offer bold counterproposals to the myriad welfare initiatives that emerged from conservative think tanks in the 1980s. The response of progressives to neoconservative welfare proposals ran the gamut from creating an apologia for the current welfare state to engaging in a battle of polemics. Rarely did the liberal left rebut the anti-welfare offensive of the right with viable policy options. Often, welfare advocates found themselves defending means-tested poverty programs that conservatives had associated with welfare dependency. Robert Kuttner noted that a legacy of the Great Society was liberal Democrats' "fatal mistake of concentrating on 'poverty programs' that isolated the poor as a distinct category, which invited a backlash against broad, universal programs in key areas such as health, housing, and employment, rather working to expand them."[7]

The association of social programs with poverty dogged liberals throughout the 1980s. In one of the few rebuttals to conservative diatribes against social programs, Theodore Marmor, Jerry Mashaw, and Philip Harvey admitted that the right had the public's ear on welfare: "American social welfare policy became regularly a topic of castigation and condescending scorn," they conceded. "Liberal defenders of the welfare state seemed tired, overwhelmed by American conservatism's newly amplified voice."[8] Public antipathy could be attributed to confusion about social insurance programs such as Social Security and Medicare, which enjoyed broad support, and means-tested poverty programs such as AFDC and Food Stamps, which the public disliked. By the end of the 1980s, liberals could fairly claim that the conservative tide had left the most important welfare programs intact, yet the continued expansion of the American welfare state was doubtful. "The public has made it clear that it does not wish to roll back the clock, but the welfare state shows no signs of experiencing a renaissance either. Public confidence in the durability of welfare state institutions remains low."[9]

By the end of the decade, the resurgent liberalism that had propelled social policy at predictable intervals through the twentieth century seemed less and less likely to make an appearance. The response of progressives to conservative welfare propositions was not innovative counterproposals, but highly charged rhetoric. In 1991 *Dissent* saw fit to print a special issue on "social breakdown" to underscore the consequences of a decade of conservatism. Nicolaus Mills concluded that a new social contract had been put in place: "The essence of *caveat civis* was that the government no longer had to defend itself for failing to defend those most in need. It was free to make its overriding goal the entrepreneurial one of promoting the interests of those most capable of creating wealth."[10] Despite the magnitude of changes during the decade, the window of opportunity presented to liberals by the opening up of the welfare debate by conservatives was lost because of liberals' need to defend a welfare structure that was unacceptable to most parties, including recipients. With the 1990 budget compromise, the welfare crisis had reached an impasse. Despite increasing need and demand for social programs, the Budget Enforcement Act effectively precluded new initiatives for the next several years. For many welfare advocates, these events signaled the need to consider a set of pragmatic alternatives for the American welfare state. If the liberal orientation to social welfare was no longer credible, if conservatives had been unable to deploy an alternative version of the welfare state, if escalating social problems warranted new initiatives, was it not time to reconstruct the American welfare state?

IDEOLOGICAL CYCLES AND SOCIAL WELFARE

During periods of uncertainty, people look to metaphors as a guide to the future—no less so, liberal activists who have seen their social credibility crumble over the past quarter-century. According to liberal conventional wisdom, the public would eventually recognize conservative excesses and demand liberally inspired solutions to a host of worsening social problems. Such swings in public sentiment appear periodically, asserted proponents of "the pendulum theory,"[11] an explanation of social change to which welfare advocates have quite naturally gravitated during this mean period of American history. After all, cyclical explanations of social change have been endorsed by noted scholars. Economist Albert O. Hirschman charted the "long periods of privatization during which [Western societies] live through an impoverishing 'atrophy of public meanings,' followed by spasmodic outbursts of 'publicness.'"[12] Historian Arthur Schlesinger, Jr., was more specific, predicting that shortly before or after the year 1990 there should come a sharp change in the national mood and direction— a change comparable to those explosions of innovation that marked the major expansions of social welfare in the United States.[13] Of course, Schlesinger's prophecy was made without knowing that the Reagan era would continue via the presidency of George Bush. Still, the swing of the pendulum continues to beguile welfare advocates. "The conservative view of the welfare state has lost its power," comforted Joel Blau, "and there are signs we are approaching the threshold of a new conception that calls for increasing public responsibility."[14]

Conservatives, predictably, scored a different cadence. After examining the record of economic expansion and political ascendance going back to the Jeffersonian era, Kevin Phillips proposed an ideological cycle of 40–50 years. If Phillips's inception of the present Republican era (beginning in 1968) is conceded, a stridently liberal Democratic administration would not assume the presidency until well into the next century.[15] Taking an international view, Milton and Rose Friedman posited three "tides" of political-economic events that have swept over entire nations: (1) the rise of laissez-faire (the Adam Smith tide); the rise of the welfare state (the Fabian tide); (3) and the resurgence of free markets (the Hayek tide). Much of the credence in the Friedman's schedule rests with the emergence and continuation of conservative governments in the United States and the United Kingdom, as well as the collapse of international communism— pretty easy guesses since both nations have been featuring ardently conservative governments for more than a decade and both are gloating over the implosion of the Soviet bloc. The Friedman's schedule of change would leave an American welfare statist gasping for air. The broad strokes with which they paint suggest that the democratic-capitalist nations are just beginning a romance with international capitalism, which will last a century before it has run its course.[16]

Yet, signposts have also begun to appear that suggest another direction for social policy. In one provocative analysis, David Osborne trailed six governors who were contending with the social and economic dislocations of the 1980s. Regarding social policy, Osborne concluded that, if the experience of several states could be taken as prophetic, the United States was entering a postindustrial era. "The traditional liberal and conservative ideologies that competed within the New Deal paradigm [have] simply outlived their usefulness. They evolved in response to the realities of the industrial age, and that era is over."[17] In synthesizing a paradigm for the next generation of social policies, Osborne proposed five goals: (1) economic growth closely conditioned by other social goals, such as equity and environmental protection; (2) a change in the structure of the marketplace; (3) the deployment of "nonbureaucratic solutions" to social problems; (4) a recognition of fiscal limits; and (5) the investment—not consumption—of resources.[18]

Significantly, Osborne's postindustrial domestic policy drew on native experiences, rather than on European prototypes. In so doing, his exploration of indigenous options for social programs suggested the emergence of a new era in public philosophy. For some time the liberal orientation to public policy had presupposed conflict between the governmental and corporate sectors.[19] Following this convention, to be pro-welfare was to be pro-government, but anti-business. Liberal policy prescriptions based on this relatively simple understanding of political economy tended to be transparent, predictable, and unimaginative. The old formula of taxing the wealthy and business to provide unconditional assistance to the poor, for example, was so timeworn that conservatives had found it easy to anticipate and neutralize. As Osborne's research indicated, those political leaders who had fielded effective initiatives had departed from ideological orthodoxy in favor of what might be called a "radical pragmatism" that guided their thinking.[20] Pushing the frontiers of the plausible, this radical pragmatism allowed progressives to pursue any relevant means, exploit all relevant institutions, and draw on a variety of resources to advance the interests of the multiple publics that comprise American culture.

REDEFINING THE WELFARE STATE:
FIVE PRINCIPLES FOR SOCIAL POLICY

Radical pragmatism provides the philosophical basis for an American social policy that is relevant to the nation's needs during the postindustrial era. Such a social policy would focus on five principles: (1) productivity, (2) the family, (3) social cohesion, (4) the community, and (5) social choice. By reconstructing social programs around these benchmarks, the American welfare state can be made more congruent with domestic demands as well as international events.

The development of the post-World War II American welfare state was predicated on the twin premises of economic growth and low unemployment—a situation that existed in America until the mid-1970s. Given recent developments in the global economy, however, it has become clear that the foundation on which the welfare state was built will have to undergo significant modification. For one, the situation of unlimited economic growth and the domination of world markets by American goods and corporations is no longer a reality. American products are less competitive in world markets, and many American corporations are now wholly or partially owned by foreign investors. Since American economic mastery of the world marketplace can no longer be taken for granted, realistic welfare programs will have to be designed that are not based on unlimited economic growth, abundant chances for upward mobility, and low unemployment.

Thus, a nonideological view of the inability of the labor market to produce the high-paying jobs necessary to move everyone out of poverty must be considered. The number of working individuals (ages 22–64) who are poor has escalated sharply, increasing more than 60 percent since 1978. Forty-nine percent of all poor people heading families now work sometime during the year. Moreover, the number of poor people who are employed full-time on a year-round basis stands at 2 million—an increase of more than two-thirds since 1978. This rise in the number of the working poor is attributable to several factors, chief among them being the replacement of high-paying industrial jobs with low-paying service jobs. Almost 20 percent of jobs will not support a worker and two dependents. In 1986, 34.9 percent of all people who worked part- and full-time earned less than $8,500 a year. Moreover, according to the Joint Economic Committee, about 44 percent of the new jobs created between 1979 and 1985 paid less than $7,400 a year.[21]

The dwindling value of the minimum wage is also related to the increase in poverty rates for the working poor. Throughout the 1960s and 1970s, a three-person family in which one person worked full-time at the minimum wage realized enough income to raise his or her family to the poverty line. However, since 1981 the minimum wage has either been frozen or minimally increased, while at the same time the cost of living has increased 27 percent. Consequently, that same family in 1988 earned only enough income to raise themselves to 77 percent of the poverty line.[22]

Another factor contributing to poverty is under- and unemployment. Between 1981 and 1986, 10.8 million workers lost their jobs because of plant shutdowns, layoffs, or other forms of job terminations. Five million of those workers had been at their jobs for at least three years.[23] From 1979 to 1984, the Department of Labor conducted a special study of 5.1 million workers whose jobs were abolished between January 1979 and January 1984. The study reported that 40 percent of these workers were still unemployed or out of the workforce in 1984. Of the remainder, close to half were employed at either part-time jobs or jobs with lower weekly earnings. The majority of workers studied experienced significant economic losses for a lengthy time after their jobs were terminated.[24] It thus becomes clear that the marketplace alone cannot produce the necessary

s to lift everyone into a secure middle-class standard of living. There-
re, the government must create income/benefit packages that are ongo-
ng and flexible rather than rigid and short term.

A post-New Deal welfare strategy must also demythologize socially
held beliefs about human nature and welfare. For example, many liberals
believe that if given a chance all poor people will choose to work. Some
conservatives such as George Gilder (cited in Chapter 3) maintain that, in
order to get ahead, poor people "need the spur of their own poverty."
Moreover, some liberals argue that the underclass has the same values as
the middle class, except that they are poor. These notions are too simplistic to be a sound basis for social policy. Those in poverty differ as much
as nonwelfare populations; some of the poor will eagerly exploit opportunities to raise themselves out of poverty, while others will not. Any
welfare philosophy that attempts to establish one policy for *all* people in
poverty will prove unsuccessful. Therefore, welfare policies must be developed that consider the differences in human nature and, where appropriate, provide positive incentives. In other cases, some form of coercion
must be instituted to assure compliance with the reciprocal requirements
of welfare programs. In short, a post-New Deal welfare philosophy must
strive for a nonideological view of the capacity of the labor market to
provide a sufficient number of high-paying jobs, while at the same time
it must demythologize socially held beliefs about welfare and human nature.
As part of that reexamination, realistic expectations about the welfare
state must be developed as well as valid benchmarks for measuring the
success of welfare state programs.

Productivity

To reestablish the legitimacy of the welfare state, it is essential to
demonstrate how social programs contribute to the nation's productivity
rather than drag it down. In the early decades of the New Deal, the federal
government grew dramatically, making it a significant player in the national economy. However, government receipts as a percentage of gross
national product have slowed to zero during the past two decades.[25] Continued
demands for benefits and services that are guaranteed through social entitlement
programs have outstripped the fiscal capacity of government. Thus, government borrows heavily in competition with private corporations. As a
result, government social programs are portrayed as stifling private investment and draining the economy of new capital and technology. This
process may be partly responsible for the nation's losing ground to international competitors.

Social advocates have recognized that the expansion of social programs requires a robust economy, but they have yet to integrate social programs fully with the nation's economic requirements. After decades of aversion to reciprocal welfare arrangements, liberals are no longer treating "work" as if it were a four-letter word, but they need to go well beyond workfare in reconstructing social welfare. The Family Support Act of 1988 marked new ground by including "transitional benefits"—child care, Medicaid, transportation allowances—for a year after a welfare mother gains employment. But why should poor women—or men, for that matter—have to be on AFDC in order to obtain benefits that most of the workforce takes for granted? Assuring the working poor of basic benefits should be a priority of social welfare policy. For example, the implementation of a "minimum benefit package" to complement the minimum wage would demonstrate how social programs are investments in the nation's productivity. Universalizing benefits such as health care and child care for all who participate in the labor market is not only justifiable, but also shows middle-income workers that social programs enhance the nation's economic standing.

Technological advantages or their equivalent are translated into positive productivity differences. It is this differential that allows for competitiveness in international trade. Moreover, this dividend also permits the social subsidization of a portion of the potential workforce. Because of America's need to survive in a competitive global economy, and because it can no longer count on its technological advantage to compensate for deficits in productivity, the nation cannot afford to idle a large number of its workforce. Welfare programs that idle 10–15 percent of a potentially productive population are possible only when a nation has such an overwhelming technological edge over competitors that its technology can compensate for deficits in individual productivity. In this scenario—enjoyed for much of the 1950s and 1960s—America could afford to subsidize a significant portion of its potential workforce because of its *overall* productivity. However, this keen technological edge has been reduced, and with it the capacity of the American economy to absorb a large number of nonproductive citizens. To reassert welfare state legitimacy, policymakers must create welfare programs that complement productivity rather than encourage dependency. Moreover, the resentment of a hardworking and financially strapped middle class toward those it sees as being subsidized by their labor can only be overcome when welfare recipients are also seen as being economically productive. In general, the middle class is more sympathetic toward the working poor than the nonworking poor. The categorizing of "ablebodied" and "non-ablebodied" poor remains a potent symbol in the American psyche.

The Family

The American family is undergoing enormous stress as a result of changing economic and social conditions. For example, dual-income families are becoming necessary to ensure middle-class status, while good quality daycare is often difficult to acquire. The fear of drug and alcohol abuse, teenage pregnancy, and high dropout rates add to the difficulties experienced by American families. Yet, when vulnerable families turn to social programs, essential benefits are not there.

Social welfare policy must support the American family, rather than pull it apart. Since its inception in the Social Security Act as a widows' and dependents' assistance program, the AFDC program has become a primary means of support for single-parent families.[26] Indeed, some critics—both liberal and conservative—argue that AFDC contributes to family disintegration. The percentage of unmarried teenage mothers has risen so rapidly that by 1984 it was triple what it had been 25 years before.[27] Tragically, the relationship between public assistance and family breakup is most clearly evident in minority communities, where single-parent households predominate and welfare has replaced a wage earner as a source of family income. Lisbeth Schorr noted that, "of all mothers under the age of thirty receiving AFDC, 71 percent began their childbearing as teenagers."[28]

Liberals have had difficulty establishing a national family policy because of the conservative fear that it would lead to governmental intrusion in family life.[29] Moreover, problems in the very definition of "family" have plagued liberal attempts to develop a family policy, as evidenced by the political fiasco surrounding former President Jimmy Carter's call for a White House Conference on the Family. By the second Reagan term, Daniel Patrick Moynihan conceded that "the long liberal hegemony in the world of social policy has collapsed,"[30] and with it presumably the prospect of a progressive policy toward family. In a dramatically changing social landscape, an exact configuration of family policy is hard to come by. Richard Louv has provided a useful perspective on this dilemma. For Louv, family policy should seek to support the "web" that keeps families from falling into the safety net of government welfare programs. Some of these family supports must include more generous maternity and sick leave, an increase in high quality and affordable daycare, full medical coverage for all families, an increase in after-school and latchkey programs, and adequate Unemployment Compensation benefits. By carefully reinforcing profamily policies in the workplace, schools, and the community, much can be done for families without relying on what have become onerous "welfare programs."[31]

The failure to reinforce related institutions has meant increased stress on American families, to the point that even conservative politicians have endorsed child-daycare and parental-leave legislation.[32] The loss of intact families affects social services directly, as well. As families deploy both parents to the labor market, there are fewer families to provide foster care for abused and neglected children; and family disorganization leaves child welfare workers with a smaller pool of good candidates for adoption.[33] If social advocates are to promote family preservation, they must move away from policies that benefit the individual exclusively and toward those that favor the family. For intact families, basic needs such as shelter can no longer be ignored. Home ownership has become a dim prospect for millions of American families during the past decades as skyrocketing home values outpaced income.[34] For poor families unable to purchase housing, the prospect is bleak. The Congressional Budget Office reported in 1988 that 84 percent of low-income renter families—more than 11 million households—reported problems of high cost, substandard, or overcrowding housing.[35] Thus, it comes as no surprise that an increasing number of the homeless are not single aberrant men and women, but intact families with children. Clearly, basic supports for vulnerable families must be a priority for social policy.

Social Cohesion

Since Lawrence Mead's *Beyond Entitlement*,[36] the idea that welfare beneficiaries owe a standard of conduct in exchange for receipt of public assistance has become a basis for welfare policy. With the enactment of the Family Support Act of 1988, certain beneficiaries of the AFDC program are required to engage in work-related activities or face the loss of benefits. Even though AFDC benefits are significantly below the poverty level nationally, many beneficiaries have accepted the requirement, appreciative of the opportunities presented and recognizing the long-term value of participating in workfare.

The increased interaction between social classes that occurred during the late 1960s has deteriorated since the ebbing of the civil rights movement and the elimination of the compulsory military draft. Moreover, the notion of a collective social entity, in which groups understand their interdependence on each other and on society, has also weakened. In effect, the narcissistic pursuit of self-interest that characterized the Reagan years has come to symbolize the loss of direction prevalent in a highly material, consumption-driven culture. Robert Reich has gone so far as to argue that technically well trained and affluent professionals are "seceding" from their economic, political, and social obligations to American society.[37]

This lack of social integration and the increased separation of the classes is almost certainly a contributing factor in the reemergence of racism as a potent force in American political life.

It is time to expand the idea of social obligation between social classes to include those who are better off. Upper- and middle-income groups should be encouraged, through economic incentives or appeals to altruism, to fulfill their social obligation toward the less-fortunate in more meaningful ways than simply paying taxes. Traditionally, the "progressive" part of progressivism has referred to the expectation that the wealthy, in being better *off*, are also better *able* to pay for public services—hence the origin of progressive taxation. But leaving the obligation at taxes alone is inadequate, and particularly so when the rich dodge their responsibility to pay their share of taxes. Even if the wealthy paid a greater portion of income in taxes, that would only address the economic integration of society. Public policy must also reinforce *social* integration. The civic-mindedness of both the poor and the well-to-do is essential to both democratic government and a free society. Recent proposals for a voluntary national service reflect the concern of many that social obligation not be a responsibility of the poor alone.[38]

Community

The deterioration of America's inner-city communities is obvious even to the casual observer. The decay in physical infrastructures such as schools, roads, housing, and communications has reached crisis proportions in many American cities. The disintegration in the physical infrastructure has corresponded to a decay in the human capital of inner-city communities. High crime rates (committed by increasingly younger professional criminals), epidemic rates of drug and alcohol abuse, the proliferation of crack houses, the high incidence of teenage pregnancies, and a dramatic growth in the number of long-term unemployables characterize much of America's urban landscape. These problems have resulted in many inner-city areas becoming a no-man's land, where even the police are afraid to patrol. Not surprisingly, the communities hit hardest by these problems are the ones with the least resources to combat them.

Despite such promising initiatives as the "mediating structures project" (discussed in Chapter 3),[39] conservatives have done little to enhance social institutions in the nation's backwaters. Because we are a nation that rarely appreciates the value of organizational biography, the institutional costs of this neglect tend to register only impressionistically. Yet, there is little question that social policy of the past decade has extracted a dreadful toll on basic institutions in poor communities. The failure of the Reagan administration—and the inability of its successor—to convince Congress to approve an urban enterprise initiative, while gutting Urban/Community Action Grant programs, has left a vacuum in community development policy.

Many states and cities have attempted to compensate for the absence of federal leadership by establishing their own programs, often with the assistance of nonprofit groups.[40] Unfortunately, these preliminary excursions into community development are inadequately supported by virtue of the social and economic characteristics of many disadvantaged communities. The deterioration of poor communities has been so profound that the term "underclass" is employed with increasing frequency by social commentators. A consensus is emerging around the realization that efforts to combat chronic unemployment, welfare dependency, family disintegration, and social disorganization will be ineffectual without a comprehensive approach that reinforces community institutions.[41] The restoration of social institutions in poor communities must be a priority of future social policy.

To restore the institutional base of poor communities, social policy must enhance nonprofit agencies of the voluntary sector. Since Alexis de Tocqueville, much of what we identify as unique about America—from metropolitan museums to the civil rights movement—has been attributed to the voluntary initiatives of private groups of individuals.[42] Today, many of the pioneering projects that address social problems too controversial to attract broad public support—or that serve those who do not represent profit margins (persons with AIDS, the homeless, refugees)—are managed under private, nonprofit auspices.

Social Choice

Since World War II, we have seen a slow progression in the choices available to populations often associated with welfare programs. The GI Bill offered returning veterans a choice of educational providers. Significantly, African Americans used their GI benefits more than other groups.[43] Medicaid, enacted during the War on Poverty, provided poor people with access to health care they had not had before.[44] By the 1980s, Medicaid recipients were, for the first time, using health services at the same rate as their middle-class compatriots. Section 8 of the 1974 Housing and Community Development Act offered thousands of poor people the opportunity to escape the gulags of public housing.[45]

Citing benefits such as cost-effectiveness, social integration, and geographic mobility, the President's Commission on Privatization concluded that "vouchers are a workable and preferable means of assisting low-in-

come households to obtain housing."[46] Vouchers have been advanced as
a way to make public education more responsive to parents of disadvantaged children,[47] with Wisconsin initiating a demonstration program for
poor Milwaukee children in 1990. Yet, despite these applications, the
promise of vouchers in social services has not been realized, and less than
10 percent of cities and counties have used vouchers for this purpose.[48]

If the poor are to be mainstreamed into the life of the nation, it is essential
to give them a range of choices similar to that available to their more well
off compatriots. Too often, the poor are given no choice but to rely on a
governmental monopoly for services—one that is laden with red tape and
is unresponsive to client needs, and that offers inferior service. Any government
monopoly of service in a democratic-capitalist society makes the presumption
that clients are unable to make wise decisions about their needs. While
such paternalism may be warranted in select cases, it is unwarranted when
applied to *all* of the poor, who are just as capable in decision-making as
their middle-income fellow citizens—if not more resourceful.

Creatively developed, these strategies for promoting productivity, the
family, social cohesion, the community, and social choice can serve as the
principles through which the American welfare state may be reorganized.
While these may seem conservative—indeed, conservatives have frequently
used these categories to retract public policy—there is no reason they cannot
be used to achieve progressive ends. Students of those industrial nations
that have made greater investments in public programs than has the United
States will find these values reflected in their social policies.

The challenge to American welfare advocates, then, is to integrate these
values into public policy so that the public itself can appreciate how social
programs *contribute* to the United States. Specific policies that would make
the welfare state more consonant with the American experience are discussed in the next chapter.

NOTES

1.   Robert Reich, *The Work of Nations* (New York: Alfred A. Knopf, 1991),
p. 265.

2.   H. Lancaster, "Competition by States to Lure Firms Turns into a Fierce
Struggle," *Wall Street Journal* (November 28, 1983), p. 1.

3.   Stanley Kotlowitz, *There Are No Children Here* (New York: Doubleday,
1991).

4.   Nicholas Lemann, *The Promised Land* (New York: Knopf, 1991), p.
353.

5.   Henry Aaron, *Politics and the Professors* (Washington, D.C.: Brookings
Institution, 1978).

6. Charles Atherton, "The Welfare State: Still on Solid Ground," *Social Service Review* 63 (Fall 1989).

7. Robert Kuttner, *The Life of the Party* (New York: Viking, 1987), p. 225.

8. Theodore Marmor, Jerry Mashaw, and Philip Harvey, *America's Misunderstood Welfare State* (New York: Basic Books, 1990), p. 16.

9. Ibid., p. 57.

10. Nicolaus Mills, "*Caveat Civis* and the Reagan Legacy," *Dissent* (Spring 1991), pp. 170–71.

11. Marc Miringoff and Sandra Opdycke, *American Social Welfare: Reassessment and Reform* (Englewood Cliffs, N.J.: Prentice-Hall, 1986), p. 10.

12. Albert O. Hirschman, *Shifting Involvements: Private Interest and Public Action* (Princeton, N.J.: Princeton University Press, 1982), p. 132.

13. Arthur Schlesinger, Jr., *The Cycles of American History* (Boston: Houghton Mifflin, 1986), p. 47.

14. Joel Blau, "Theories of the Welfare State," *Social Service Review* 63 (March 1989), p. 26. The left has finally begun to reconsider the possibility that a resurgence of liberalism is unlikely in the foreseeable future. See Fred Siegel, "Waiting for Lefty," *Dissent* (Spring 1991).

15. Kevin Phillips, *The Politics of Rich and Poor* (New York: Random House, 1990), pp. 245–46.

16. Milton and Rose Friedman, "The Tide in the Affairs of Men," in Annelise Anderson and Dennis Bark (eds.), *Thinking about America: The United States in the 1990s* (Stanford, Calif.: Hoover Institution, 1988).

17. David Osborne, *Laboratories of Democracy* (Boston: Harvard Business School Press, 1988), p. 321.

18. Ibid., pp. 327–28.

19. Robert Reich, *The Next American Frontier* (New York: Times Books, 1983).

20. This term has been used to describe the philosophy of C. Wright Mills. See Irving Horowitz, *C. Wright Mills: An American Utopian* (New York: Free Press, 1983). Rick Tilman, however, provides a more complete description of the origins of Mills's pragmatism. See Rick Tilman, *C. Wright Mills: A Native Radical and His American Intellectual Roots* (University Park: Pennsylvania State University Press, 1984).

21. Michael Harrington, with the assistance of Robert Greenstein and Eleanor Holmes Norton, *Who Are the Poor?* (Washington, D.C.: Justice for All, 1987), p. 10.

22. Ibid., p. 11.

23. Ibid., p. 10.

24. Center on Budget and Policy Priorities, *Smaller Pieces of the Pie* (Washington, D.C.: Center on Budget and Policy Priorities, 1987).

25. John Kirlin and Dale Marshall, "The New Politics of Entrepreneurship," in Lawrence Lynn, Jr. (chair), *Urban Change and Poverty* (Washington, D.C.: National Academy Press, 1988), p. 354.

26. Michael Novak (ed.), *The New Consensus on Family and Welfare* (Washington, D.C.: American Enterprise Institute, 1987), p. 47.

27.   Lisbeth Schorr, *Within Our Reach* (New York: Anchor, 1988), p. 13.

28.   Ibid., p. 12.

29.   Brigitte Berger and Peter Berger, *The War over the Family* (New York: Anchor, 1983), p. 210.

30.   Daniel Patrick Moynihan, *Family and Nation* (New York: Harcourt Brace Jovanovich, 1986), p. 189.

31.   Richard Louv, *Childhood's Future* (Boston: Houghton Mifflin, 1990), pp. 370–74.

32.   None other than arch-conservative Orrin Hatch sponsored a major child-daycare proposal to the One-hundredth Congress.

33.   Howard Karger and David Stoesz, *American Social Welfare Policy* (White Plains, N.Y.: Longman, 1990), pp. 237–38.

34.   Ibid., p. 246.

35.   Congressional Budget Office, *Current Housing Problems and Possible Federal Responses* (Washington, D.C.: U.S. Government Printing Office, 1988), p. xii.

36.   Lawrece Mead, *Beyond Entitlement* (New York: Free Press, 1986).

37.   Reich, *Work of Nations*, pp. 282–300.

38.   Timothy Noah, "We Need You: National Service, An Idea Whose Time Has Come," *Washington Monthly* (November 1986); Charles Moskos, *A Call to National Service* (New York: Free Press, 1988).

39.   Peter Berger and Richard Neuhaus, *To Empower People* (Washington, D.C.: American Enterprise Institute, 1977).

40.   Osborne, *Laboratories of Democracy*.

41.   For a structural critique of welfare programs as they relate to community disintegration, see John McKnight, "Do No Harm: Policy Options That Meet Human Needs," *Social Policy* 20 (Summer 1989).

42.   John Gardner, *Keynote Address* (Washington, D.C.: Independent Sector, 1978), p. 13.

43.   D. O'Neill, "Voucher Funding of Training Programs: Evidence from the GI Bill," *Journal of Human Resources* (Fall 1977).

44.   D. Rogers, R. Blendon, and T. Maloney, "Who Needs Medicaid?" *New England Journal of Medicine* (July 1, 1982).

45.   Committee on Ways and Means, U.S. House of Representatives, *Background Material and Data on Programs within the Jurisdiction of the Committee on Ways and Means, 1990 Edition* (Washington, D.C.: U.S. Government Printing Office, 1990), pp. 1154–61.

46.   David Linowes, *Privatization: Toward More Effective Government* (Washington, D.C.: U.S. Government Printing Office, 1988), p. 15.

47.   John Chubb and Terry Moe, "Choice *Is* a Panacea," *Brookings Review* (Summer 1990), pp. 4–12.

48.   Elaine Morley, "Patterns in the Use of Alternative Service Delivery Approaches," in *Municipal Year Book* (Washington, D.C.: International City Management Organization, 1989).

6

Options in Social Welfare Policy

Howard Jacob Karger
and David Stoesz

Securing a full-time job in the United States does not guarantee that a family will experience economic security. Thirty percent of jobs performed by Americans in 1990 were in-person service jobs (jobs that require little education and training and usually pay low wages and provide scanty benefits), and their numbers were growing rapidly. During the 1980s, well over 3 million *new* jobs were created in the United States in fast-food outlets, restaurants, and bars. This was more than the *total* number of existing jobs in the automobile, steelmaking, and textile industries combined.[1] As a consequence, more than half of the 32.5 million Americans whose incomes fell below the poverty line lived in households with at least one worker. Moreover, the number of impoverished working Americans rose by nearly 23 percent between 1978 and 1987. Among full-time, year-round workers that number climbed by 43 percent. Two-parent families with a full-time worker fell further below the poverty line than any other type of family, including single parents on welfare.[2]

Social policy toward families of the working poor has been haphazard at best—and at worst, punitive. Too often, social programs fail to reinforce the integrity of workers and their families. In many states, benefits are denied to workers simply because they persist in working, although their wages are so low that they are entitled to public assistance. Until recently, roughly half of state AFDC programs have contributed to family breakup, requiring one parent to leave home in order for children to be eligible for benefits. Under the Family Support Act of 1988, states not allowing grants for two-parent families will be required to do so, but could limit benefits to six months of a given year.[3] The idea that social policy could require an absent parent to move in and out of the home at six-month intervals so that children may receive necessary income and health

benefits does little to advance the notion that social policy is, in some
minimal sense, rational.

On the other hand, productivity, family, social cohesion, community,
and social choice are benchmarks around which future thinking about American
social welfare can be organized. Welfare policies must focus on these
principles in order to recast social welfare so that it is more congruent
with the American postindustrial experience. In tandem with these principles, then, we are proposing a "civic welfare state" composed of three
main programs: (1) the Family Conservation Program, (2) the Community
Revitalization Initiative, and (3) the National Service Program. These
three social programs illustrate how the principles of family, social cohesion, community responsibility, and social choice can be used to reconstruct the American welfare state.

THE FAMILY CONSERVATION PROGRAM

Any attempt to develop social policy initiatives that aim to preserve,
stabilize, and strengthen the American family must be composed of both
preventative and remediative components. The basic axiom for social
policy is the same as for physical medicine: it is far easier and less costly
to *prevent* diseases than to *treat* them. Thus, the preventative component
in any family preservation program must help to establish social conditions that encourage working families to conduct their lives with minimal
use of governmental income maintenance programs. The Family Conservation Program is divided into two parts: preventative programs, and
remediative programs. The preventative approach consists of eight core
programs designed to encourage family preservation: (1) the stabilization
of Unemployment Insurance; (2) the establishment of a minimum wage
that is annually adjusted to the regional average wage; (3) the creation of
a minimum benefits package; (4) the development of high quality and
affordable daycare; (5) the establishment of Individual Development Accounts;
(6) the creation of progressive Individual Retirement Accounts; (7) national health care; and (8) a universal Maternal and Child Health Program.
The remediative component of the Family Conservation Program consists
of the Stable Incomes Program (SIP), a comprehensive and nonredundant
income maintenance program designed to incorporate the principles of
reciprocity, productivity, and social choice into a viable and cost-effective income maintenance structure.

Preventative Approaches to Poverty: Firming-up
the Income Floor

Any preventative strategy to curb poverty must have as one of its primary goals the creation of a firm income floor for America's poor working

families—those who are poor, but not in immediate need of direct governmental welfare. Creating a firm income floor requires a three-pronged approach: stabilizing the unemployment insurance program, stabilizing family income by establishing a minimum wage that is keyed to the average wage, and establishing a national minimum benefits package. This minimum income/benefits security must then be complemented by an increased availability of viable daycare.

Stabilizing the Unemployment Insurance Program

Robert Reich argues that, because of the economic changes in the global economy, America is facing an increasingly stratified job market composed of routine production services (traditional production jobs), in-person services (person-to-person service jobs), and symbolic-analytic services (jobs characterized by problem-solving, problem-identifying, and strategic brokering activities). According to Reich, these first two job categories will experience more difficult economic times as high-paying manufacturing jobs become scarcer, and as in-person jobs are marked by greater competition and lower wage and benefit levels. On the other hand, workers in the third category should experience greater prosperity and higher standards of living. In effect, America will be marked by several economic boats, each one growing more economically independent from the other.[4] If Reich's theory is correct, it only reinforces the need to protect vulnerable economic groups from a capricious global marketplace in which they have little economic influence.

Workers facing job losses brought on by changes in the global economy turn first to the government's first line of defense: the Unemployment Insurance Program (UI). Initially designed to cushion the effects of employer layoffs for both individual workers and local economies, the UI program contracted sharply in the 1980s because of changes in federal and state laws. Unemployment insurance fell to record lows in the 1980s; and in 1990, only 37 percent of unemployed workers received benefits in an average month. This figure compares unfavorably to 1975, when more than 75 percent of unemployed workers received benefits. Even in the recession year of 1980, 50 percent of all unemployed workers received benefits.

Low levels of unemployment coverage contribute to high poverty rates, especially in a recession. Jobless workers without UI are more likely to descend into poverty—especially the long-term unemployed. Moreover, the protection offered by UI not only shields low-income workers, but also offers protection for the middle class. Byzantine eligibility guidelines promulgated by state and federal agencies either discourage many jobless workers from using the UI system, or deny them eligibility. In any case, the net result is the same: poor working-class families—already perched dangerously on a flimsy economic branch—are sent spiraling into poverty by the loss of just one or two paychecks. In order to inhibit this cycle, straightforward eligibility guidelines for UI should be promulgated on a national level. The UI system should also be administered by the federal government to ensure uniformity across all states. Moreover, UI benefits should be linked to regional differences in the cost of living. The compensation for lost income, especially for the working poor, is too important to be left to the caprice of individual state legislatures.

A Minimum Wage Program

In 1950 the minimum wage brought a worker to 56 percent of the average wage. Throughout the 1950s and 1960s (as can be seen from Table 6.1), the average minimum wage hovered between 44 and 56 percent (the mean being 50 percent) of the average wage. However, by 1980 the minimum wage had fallen to 46.5 percent of the average wage; and in 1988 it dropped even further, to 35.7 percent. Even with a minimum wage of $4.25 an hour in 1991, the minimum wage only equals about 41 percent of the average wage, bringing a family of three to about 85 percent of the poverty line. This figure is considerably below the 120 percent of the poverty level reached by the minimum wage in 1968.[5] For workers who were stuck with a minimum wage that was frozen from 1981 to 1989, the drop in earnings relative to the median income was significant, especially in light of the 40 percent rise in consumer prices during that period. Even with the current increase in the minimum wage to $4.25 an hour, it is $1.00 below its 1981 inflation-adjusted value. Furthermore, the $4.25 minimum wage is lower than it was in every year from 1956 to 1986, after adjusting for inflation.[6] The gulf between the minimum wage and the poverty line is illustrated by Table 6.1.

At the heart of the minimum wage debate is the argument that increasing the minimum wage would cause unacceptable effects on employment opportunities, particularly among teenagers and young adults. While liberals counter that job-loss arguments are predicated on outmoded and incorrectly interpreted data,[7] the reality is that many young and old Americans are working for wages that place them at $2,200 below the poverty line for a family of three. Some 18 million Americans—including 8 million children—live in a household with a working family member, but with an income that remains below the poverty line.[8]

In order to stabilize the income floor for working families, a minimum wage must be calibrated based on a fixed percentage of the average wage. If the minimum wage were seen as a parity issue—similar to farm parity— a benchmark year could be chosen by which to calibrate future minimum

Table 6.1 Value of the Minimum Wage, Selected Years

Year	Percent of Poverty Line for a Family of Three	Percent of Average Wage
1950	81.3%	56.0%
1955	73.1	43.9
1960	88.2	47.8
1965	103.4	50.8
1968	120.0	56.1
1970	107.4	49.5
1975	101.7	46.4
1980	98.2	46.5
1985	81.3	39.1
1988	73.6	35.7

Source: Adapted from Isaac Shapiro, *The Minimum Wage and Job Loss* (Washington, D.C.: Center on Budget and Policy Priorities, 1988), p. 3.

wage increases. Throughout the 1950s and 1960s, the minimum wage hovered between 44 and 56 percent of the average wage. We are proposing that the minimum wage be based on 50 percent of the average wage, adjusted yearly. Moreover, since the average wage differs regionally (supposedly reflecting differences in regional costs of living), the minimum wage should be calibrated to the regional average wage and be adjusted annually.

This formula would have several benefits. For one, an income floor would be established, assuring all working-class American families a minimum wage that would not fall below a certain percentage of the average wage of their fellow citizens. For another, this formula would help stem the growing economic disparity between the income brackets. By having a stable income floor adjusted in terms of the average wage, working Americans—if they did not do better economically—would at least not be doing worse in relative terms. Establishing a stable income floor would also ensure that decreasing wages as a percentage of the average wage would not provide a disincentive for labor market participation. Lastly, by creating an automatically adjusted minimum wage, the shrill political battles that mark minimum wage legislation would be less problematic, at least after the initial fray.

A Minimum Benefits Package

A major component of any attempt to fashion more equitable minimum wage legislation must include a minimum benefits package. Currently, many of the poor work in part-time or seasonal jobs, which are without benefits. Many sectors of the service industry—convenience stores and fast-food franchises, for instance—actually capitalize on avoiding paying benefits to employees by limiting the hours they work. Through a minimum benefits package, employees working 20 hours a week or more would be assured of health-care benefits (see the subsequent discussion of national health care), child daycare, and leave through portable benefits accounts that would follow them from one job to another.

Revenues for the minimum benefits package would be derived from several sources. Current appropriations for workfare under the Family Support Act—$3.5 billion over a five-year period—would establish a fund for the minimum benefits plan, which would be maintained by nominal mandatory contributions from employers and employees. In order to dissuade employers from further reducing an employee's hours in order to dodge participation in the program, a penalty—a "McTax"—would be levied against employers who hire workers for less than 20 hours per week. In order to keep employee and employer payroll tax levels low (so as to avoid interfering with job creation), the minimum benefits fund would be supplemented by earmarking a special tax expenditure: eliminating the deduction allowed business for meal and entertainment expenses. For 1991, the Congressional Budget Office calculated that $4 billion in revenues would be lost because of deductions for two-martini lunches, greens fees, and Las Vegas junkets.[9]

Daycare

In the early 1970s, President Richard Nixon vetoed a bill that would have provided a range of services for children, including daycare. Nixon's justification for the veto was that it would have "commit[ted] the vast moral authority of the federal government on the side of communal approaches to child-rearing as against the family-centered approach."[10]

Despite America's emphasis on a "family-centered" approach to child-rearing, the proportion of women who have children younger than 18 and are in the labor force rose from 40 to 65 percent between 1970 and 1988. Between 1976 and 1987, the labor force participation rates of mothers of infants (age one or younger) rose from 31 to 51 percent. In 1988, 10.2 million children under age six and 16.1 million children between the ages of six and thirteen had mothers who participated in the labor force. Some researchers estimate that, by 1995, two-thirds—14.6 million—of all preschool children will have mothers in the workforce.[11]

Most mothers work because of financial need, and about 25 percent are the primary wage earners for their children. Many two-parent families also require dual incomes to meet the basic necessities. Between 1973 and 1989 the median wages of hourly workers fell by 29 percent for men under 25 and by 19 percent for men 25 and older, after adjusting for inflation. In 1987 half of all families headed by a parent younger than 30 had yearly incomes below $18,500.[12]

In 1987 almost 50 percent of all children under age five with mothers in the workforce were cared for either in family daycare homes or in organized child-care facilities. Despite this large number, the federal government has not been actively involved in setting daycare standards, instead leaving that responsibility to the individual states. Even with state regulations (often spotty at best), about 43 percent of all children spend their days in out-of-home child-care facilities that are exempt from minimal health and safety standards.[13]

For most poor working-class families, quality private daycare services are virtually unaffordable. Moreover, nonpublic institutional child care is almost unaffordable for much of the middle class. For example, a survey conducted in 1990 found that the average annual cost for an infant in licensed child care ranged from almost $4,000 a year in Dallas to almost $11,000 a year in Boston. Even in Dallas, a single mother working at the minimum wage would have to spend half of her salary on daycare alone. Although child care costs differ by cities (as Table 6.2 shows), in all cases the costs are high enough to discourage workforce participation by at least one parent.

The three primary issues in child care are quality, cost, and accessibility. If the United States is to marshal its productive capacity more effectively, it must ensure that high-quality, affordable, and accessible daycare is available for all families requiring it. Moreover, if family preservation is a major national goal, then it is critical to ensure that poor working-class families are provided with opportunities to participate fully in the labor force. A minimum wage program and a minimum benefits package must be complemented by universal daycare services. Much of the physical and human infrastructure needed to establish a comprehensive daycare system can be accomplished as part of the Community Revitalization Program, a social policy initiative that is discussed more fully in a subsequent section of this chapter.

Preventative Approaches to Poverty: Building Economic Security

In order to develop a viable policy for family preservation, policymakers must take into account the relationship between strong families and eco-

Table 6.2 Child Care Costs Using Average Fees Charged in Licensed Child Care Centers, by Age Group, in Selected Cities, 1990

	Oakland CA	Boulder CO	Dallas TX	Orlando FL
Average annual cost of child care for a one-year-old child	$5,772	$6,604	$3,900	$4,212
Percentage of income low-income parents paid for average child care for their one-year-old child if they were:				
Single parent working full-time at the minimum wage	67.9%	77.7%	45.9%	49.6%
Two parents working full-time at the minimum wage	34.4%	38.8%	22.9%	24.8%
Average annual cost of child care for a four-year-old child	$4,836	$4,472	$3,380	$3,120
Percentage of income low-income parents paid for average child care for their four-year-old child if they were:				
Single parent working full-time at the minimum wage	56.9%	52.6%	39.8%	36.7%
Two parents working full-time at the minimum wage	28.4%	26.3%	19.9%	18.4%

Source: Children's Defense Fund, *The State of America's Children, 1991* (Washington, D.C.: Children's Defense Fund, 1991), p. 43.

nomic security. Economically unstable families are at a greater risk for dysfunctional behavior as well as for using governmental welfare programs. In American society, assets are in part the basis for much of the political, social, and economic power enjoyed by the middle class. To ensure that poor working-class Americans enter the economic mainstream, it is also necessary to ensure that they possess assets.

Individual Development Accounts

Recently, the concept of "stakeholding"—the substitution of assets for income transfers through social policy—has entered the social policy debate. Pioneered by Michael Sherraden of Washington University's George Warren Brown School of Social Work, stakeholding is advocated in response to the realization that the distribution of assets is even more skewed than income, and that the poor can gain directly from benefits that encourage "savings, investment, and asset accumulation rather than income, spending, and income." Accordingly, Sherraden has proposed the creation of Individual Development Accounts (IDAs) to bolster assets for the working poor. IDAs would be designated for specific purposes: housing, postsecondary education, self-employment, and retirement. The federal government would simply match IDA deposits made by people in qualifying low-income families. The amount of the federal supplement would vary with the importance of the activity—say, $5 in federal match to $1 saved for housing, or $2 in federal match to $1 saved for retirement.[14] Through IDAs the federal government could reinforce directly—and strongly—activities that strengthen families. One such strategy—the Human Investment Policy for Oregon—is now in a planning phase, having been approved by that state's legislature and governor.[15] Since the IDA focuses on the essentials of family life for the lowest wage workers, the fairest way to fund it is to levy a national sales tax on *nonessential* goods purchased by the more affluent. A 5-percent national sales tax (which would exempt food, housing, and medical care), for example, could net more than $52 billion in 1992.[16]

Progressive Individual Retirement Accounts

The IDA concept could advance retirement security for older Americans, as well. Despite the extensive coverage of Social Security, millions of the nation's elders remain in poverty. In order to encourage workers to plan ahead for their retirement, younger employees should be given clear incentives to supplement their contributions to Social Security. A feasible way to do this is by calibrating Individual Retirement Accounts (IRAs) so that tax deferments granted to poorer workers are greater than those given to the well-off. In 1985, when IRAs were available to all taxpayers according to a regressive formula, more than 15 percent of tax returns of those individuals who earned less than a $30,000 yearly adjusted gross income contributed to IRAs, their total IRA contributions exceeding $10 billion.[17]

The working poor underutilized IRAs for several reasons. First, the effective income tax on their income was relatively low, thereby providing little incentive to use the tax-saving feature of IRAs. Second, many believed that Social Security would take care of them when they retire. Third, the working poor had little disposable income and had pressing needs for immediate cash. If progressive IRAs are to have an effect, they will be required to provide bigger incentives for the working poor to invest. Moreover, information must be convincingly presented in illustration of the fact that Social Security alone is not sufficient to provide for a secure life-style after retirement. Then, given an aggressive education campaign directed at low-wage workers and a more favorable contribution formula, the working poor can be expected to do much more toward planning for their retirement income needs.

The current Social Security program can be enhanced by other, relatively modest changes. While an expansion of income security is desirable and should be shared equitably among workers, contributions should be assessed by a more progressive method than is currently used. The easiest method for increasing revenues for Social Security would be to remove the present cap on taxable earned income ($51,300 in 1990) so that the wealthy would be contributing their fair share. If the ceiling were lifted so that all income were taxed, approximately $18.5 billion would be added to income security coffers.[18] On the other hand, increases in the payroll tax as authorized by the 1983 amendments to the Social Security Act cannot be increased further without risking a decline in economic growth, or even intergenerational reprisal. Virtually ignored has been the possibility of increasing the supply of workers who contribute to Social Security. This is particularly significant since the ratio of workers to beneficiaries is plummeting—from 5.1 to 1 in 1960 to 2.0 to 1 in 2040.[19] Unless the supply of workers is increased dramatically, major adjustments will have to be made to maintain current benefit levels—adjustments such as doubling the payroll tax.

A straightforward solution to the need for more workers is to integrate immigration policy with income security policy. Approximately 7 million undocumented workers are in the United States, and every year hundreds of thousands enter the country illegally in search of employment.[20] The most recent initiative to address the influx of undocumented workers—the Immigration Reform and Control Act of 1986—offered a one-year window during which persons who had been in the United States since January 1, 1982, could apply for "amnesty." Since only 2 million people took advantage of this provision, the great majority of undocumented workers continue to work illegally without basic wage and workplace protections. Unfortunately, tens of thousands of these workers are contributing to a Social Security program from which they will never collect benefits.[21] Instead of a one-year period during which established workers could apply for legal residency status, immigration policy should incorporate a rolling amnesty date; workers and their families who have been in the United States for five years, say, could apply for legal residency status. Moreover, education, health, and social service benefits should be available to qualifying workers to encourage their participation in the labor force. A more humane amnesty provision for undocumented workers would go a long way toward assuring the baby-boomers that they will be supported in the manner to which they have become accustomed; and it would also ensure that undocumented workers are not exploited for their contributions to the nation.[22]

Preventative Approaches to Poverty: Health Care

Any meaningful proposal for preserving the American family must include the critical component of national health. Despite massive and uncontrollable infusions of funds, the United States fails to assure even minimal health care to 37 million citizens. Our deregulated and disorganized method of health-care provision is unnecessarily costly, particularly when compared to other industrial nations. The United States allocates 10.8 percent of gross domestic product (GDP) on health care, while its competitors spend much less: Germany, 8.2 percent; Japan, 6.7 percent.[23] The influence of high health-care costs on competitiveness was noted by Lee Iacocca, who observed that health-care costs added $700 to the price of a Chrysler car built in the United States, but only $223 if the same car were built in Canada.[24] Per-capita health-care expenditures in Canada were $1,370 in the mid-1980s, significantly lower than the United States' $1,926.[25] While U.S. government-sponsored health care for the poor is being rationed because of government funding rescissions,[26] American health care has come under increasing commercial pressure from large corporate health-care providers and insurance companies that continue to profit from skyrocketing health-care costs.[27]

National Health Care

Three options have been suggested for restructuring American health care: (1) a national health insurance modeled after Canada; (2) a national health service such as that of the United Kingdom; and (3) a mandatory-contribution plan through which employers would insure workers not covered under other plans.[28] The best candidate for a U.S. national health program is the first option, drawn from the Canadian national health program.[29] A national health service, such as the Veterans Administration operated by the federal government, is unlikely to respond adequately to market influences and consumer choices, while a mandatory-contribution scheme funded by employers simply adds one more piece to an already chaotic and unnecessarily costly *non*system of health care.

An optimal health program for the United States has been outlined by Harvard's David Himmelstein and Steffie Woolhandler. Under their "national health program," commercial health care would be gradually phased out in favor of a public insurance system that would cover all health costs for all citizens. Enrollees would be free to choose their provider, yet hospitals and physicians would be limited in the fees they could charge either by a binding fee schedule, a global budget allocated to institutions from which all costs would be paid, or a capitation arrangement. Costs would be negotiated annually between providers and government, which would be the sole source of payments.[30] The fiscal core of a National Health Insurance Program would be derived from current appropriations for the major governmental health-care programs—Medicare, Medicaid, and those of the Veterans Administration.

Much of the costs for extending health-care coverage to those now uninsured or subinsured would be derived from increased program-management efficiencies. For example, a National Health Insurance program would have saved $29.2 billion in 1983 had it been in place.[31] Supplemental revenues could be derived by simply making the payroll tax allocated for Medicare hospital insurance more progressive. By removing the cap on taxable income, an additional $3.5 billion would have been added to Medicare for 1991.[32] And one financing method that would broaden revenue sources would be to tax commercial health providers in order to create a pool from which care for the publicly insured would be paid. A modest 5-percent tax on occupied rooms in for-profit hospitals, similar to the hotel tax, could defray some of the costs of health care for the poor. When health care becomes a commercial activity, it should be taxed as such. Thus, much of the costs for a national health program would be met by simply constructing a system out of the present fragmentation that characterizes health care in the United States. Under a National Health Insurance plan, private providers would be honored, yet all Americans would be entitled to their choice of providers.

A Universal Maternal and Child Health Program

If family preservation is a primary focus of social policy, a commitment must be made to assure that all infants receive the best nutritional and health care possible. The absence of a universal Maternal and Child Health Program is a national embarrassment, and the consequences of this omission are predictable. The Women, Infants, and Children Supplemental Food Program (WIC) provides health and nutrition benefits to poor women, but only 40 percent of those who are eligible participate.[33] The social and psychological costs of fetal alcohol syndrome have been brought to public attention by Michael Dorris's award-winning book *The Broken Cord*.[34] Increasingly, delivery room personnel are presented with infants who were exposed to illegal drugs in utero. The Department of Health and Human Services predicts that 4 million infants and children who have been exposed to cocaine will require billions of dollars of care during the next ten years.[35] In California, some 72,000 infants are born each year with prenatal exposure to alcohol and illegal drugs.[36] It follows that a universal Maternal and Child Health Program is not only justifiable out of concern for the life opportunities of at-risk infants, but also because the nation cannot afford the costs of care for long-term disabilities. An American Maternal and Child Health Program could be created by consolidating the present Maternal and Child Health-care Block Grant, the WIC program, and relevant components of the Medicaid program. Funding to make the program universal, so that all mothers and children can participate, could be derived from increased excise taxes on cigarettes and alcohol. The indexing of modest increases in taxes on cigarettes and alcohol would have generated $10.1 billion in 1991,[37] which could have been earmarked as a special supplement to National Health Insurance for a universal Maternal and Child Health Program.

Taken together, these preventative programs can buffer America's most vulnerable workers from those events most likely to make them poor. Ensuring America's working-class families a stable income floor, the prospects for economic mobility, and optimal health means that the need for governmental income-maintenance programs will be reduced. Moreover, such investments in human capital will contribute to a more highly productive labor force that is better able to compete in a volatile international economy. By improving the productivity of American workers, social welfare programs thus improve the overall economic well-being of American society. Furthermore, greater social equality has the potential to translate into greater social stability. In the absence of such preventative programs, it is only a matter of time before the violence currently erupting in America's poorest communities will spill over, with a fierceness, into the more affluent communities. If, as Robert Reich suggests, we are not all in the same economic boat, we certainly all inhabit the same sea.

Combating Poverty: The Stable Incomes Program

Because of the profound economic changes under way, many Americans will require remedial economic help, even those who participate in the workforce full-time. The following proposal for a Stable Incomes Program (SIP) is intended as a starting point for examining alternatives to the present income-maintenance programs.

When most people try to understand the American welfare state, they are struck by the redundancy of welfare programs, the lack of a series of consistent and integrated social programs, the gaps in coverage, and the often arcane criteria for eligibility. On closer examination, one finds many welfare departments staffed by untrained workers who labor under nearly impossible conditions of low pay, poor supervision, and immense client caseloads, often numbering in the hundreds. State and federal manuals outlining baffling eligibility criteria and complex procedures can take up a full shelf of office space. It is not surprising, then, that clients often receive different assessments of their eligibility based on which welfare worker they happen to speak to on a given day. This situation is further complicated by the lack of follow-up and client tracking. At best, most welfare departments have become financial dispensaries, rather than purveyors of *social* services. Indeed, the public welfare department has disintegrated to the point that Alvin Schorr, a longtime supporter of public welfare initiatives, has admitted that "many human service departments cannot manage to answer the telephone, let alone conduct a civilized interview."[38]

The present welfare state represents a system out of control. With multiple, overlapping programs replete with complex eligibility criteria, few people—including many welfare administrators—fully understand the web of welfare services. This web is understood least of all by befuddled clients trying to make their way through a virtually incomprehensible maze of programs. Apart from its complexity, each welfare program represents an administrative structure that can consume upward of 10 or more percent of the potential benefits earmarked for clients. Thus, the complexity of welfare programs represents in itself a costly component of the welfare state.

Despite this confusion, many social activists continue to believe that the American welfare state represents a rational approach to rectifying the financial and social distresses of clients. On some level, welfare professionals want to believe that the present welfare structure represents a logical, systematic form of organization. However, instead of reflecting a well-thought-out and integrated series of social programs, the American welfare state is in fact a patchwork quilt cobbled together by last-minute negotiations, adroit political maneuvering, and key political concessions. Although when viewed separately most welfare programs embody good intentions and may be reasonably well thought out, taken as a whole the welfare state reflects a jumbled mix of redundant social programs. In that sense, the sum of the parts is less than the whole. It is to this redundancy that we will now turn.

The income maintenance component of the American welfare state is composed of three *major* income support programs:[39] AFDC (Aid to Families with Dependent Children), SSI (Supplemental Security Income), and the EITC (Earned Income Tax Credit) program. In addition, income supports are folded into other programs such as Food Stamps, the Low-Income Home Energy Assistance Program (LIHEAP), Section 8 housing, and the Women, Infants, and Children Program (WIC), to name a few. For example, a four-person family living in New Jersey in 1988 who had no income but who fully capitalized on their potential benefits could have received the following yearly grant: $8,346 in combined AFDC and Food Stamps, $388 in LIHEAP benefits, a minimum of $336 per year in WIC benefits, and a Section 8 subsidy that could total $3,000. This poverty family could have accrued through various sources a yearly income of $12,070, excluding the valuable Medicaid perk for which they would be automatically eligible.[40] That same family with two minimum-wage earners would have earned a yearly income of $12,864 plus the maximum EITC benefit of $658, thereby "earning" $13,522.[41] The difference of $1,452 between the working and welfare family would have been made up by the need to secure health-care insurance and daycare—costs that would result in far less net income for the working family than for the recipient family.[42] In effect, welfare state programs can provide a built-in incentive to choose welfare over work.

The redundancy of welfare programs also fosters an inequality among welfare recipients themselves. Recipients who are skilled at the manipulation of public assistance programs will do better than welfare novices who assume a passive stance in searching for benefits. The working poor—who qualify for some benefits, including Food Stamps—may be out of the welfare loop and thus may not be aware of the possibilities for welfare receipt. This may partly explain why more than 40 percent of eligible families did not receive Food Stamps in an average month in 1985.[43] Paradoxically, the very complexity of the welfare system sets up a Darwinian scramble for resources that rewards the most enterprising recipients at the cost of those less able to compete.

Separating out the EITC program (which is geared to the working poor) from AFDC and SSI leaves two programs that are similar in many respects. For example, both programs mainly serve people who do not fully participate in the labor force. Both programs also benefit the poor: AFDC is targeted for poor families with children; SSI is for the aged, blind, and disabled who are also poor. Likewise, both of these income-maintenance programs require no past history of labor force participation—no prior contribution—and pay low benefits that may in some instances be complemented by Food Stamps, housing, and utility assistance.

AFDC and SSI suffer from important structural problems. SSI is a national program that in 1990 served more than 4.6 million people at a cost of $12.5 billion. The federal benefits under SSI ($386 per month for a single person and $579 per month for a couple, in 1990) are so low that 16 states have opted to supplement it. While SSI benefits are standardized nationally and adjusted for inflation, they fail to respect regional economic differences. In many ways, the AFDC program is even more problematic than SSI. With 50 separate state-run programs, AFDC has only limited standardization in terms of service provision and benefits. Because benefits are not standardized, AFDC payments fluctuate widely from state to state, going from a low of $118 per month for a family of three in Alabama to a high of $846 per month for the same family in Alaska.

The EITC program is equally problematic. Enacted in 1975 as a means of targeting tax relief to working low-income taxpayers with children, of providing relief from Social Security payroll taxes, and in general of improving the incentive to work, the original EITC rebate equaled 10 percent of the first $4,000 of earned income (i.e., a maximum credit of $400). Under the Tax Reform Act of 1986, the maximum tax credit was increased to $800 (14 percent of the first $5,714 of earned income). The EITC is available to married individuals with a child, unmarried heads of households who maintain a household for a child, and certain other dependents. While economists Saul Hoffman and Lawrence Seidman agree with the basic principles of the EITC program, they also recognize its inherent problems. According to Hoffman and Seidman, the EITC program "provides benefits to one-third of all poor families and one-quarter of all black families. The EIC [sic] population is, however, predominantly white and non-poor. The typical EIC family has a low-to-moderate income that places it above the poverty line. . . . Finally, the average credits were quite low, so the contributions of the EIC program to the economic well-being of low- and moderate income families is certainly quite modest."[44] Indeed, with an average family credit of $595 in 1989, one is hard pressed to imagine that the EITC program makes a significant difference in the economic lives of the working poor. Lastly, the EITC program is plagued with the problem of nonfilers. In 1990 a family of four with income less than $13,650 would not owe any tax and would thus not be required to file an income tax return. If that family did not file a tax return, they would not receive the EITC credit for which they were entitled.[45]

Given the similarities and problems with AFDC, SSI, and the EITC program, it becomes increasingly difficult to justify the overlapping and expensive duplication of program administration and personnel. Fragmented welfare programs lead to a fragmented welfare state. To rectify the problems of program duplication and inequitable welfare benefits, redundant welfare programs should be integrated into one administrative unit, and geographically sensitive welfare benefits should be developed.

In effect, there is a pressing need to restructure the income maintenance programs of the American welfare state.

In order to restructure social welfare programs more rationally, AFDC, SSI, and EITC should be collapsed into one income-maintenance program—the Stable Incomes Program (SIP)—which would be under one administrative unit. In addition, all social programs within the American welfare state—including among others Food Stamps, WIC, LIHEAP, and Section 8[46]—should be scoured for their income support features, which would then be incorporated within the SIP structure. In effect, we are calling for a single income-maintenance program to replace the tangled web of social programs that currently provide income to the poor.

Restructuring social programs would also require restructuring the delivery of social services. Instead of receiving benefits piecemeal from the coffers of AFDC, SSI, EITC, Food Stamps, and so on, each client would receive a single income/benefits package developed with the assistance of a case manager. This income/benefits package would combine marketplace wages with a supplemental cash grant that would elevate the working and nonworking poor to a poverty threshold based on the median family income in a target region. This cash grant would be transferred to the welfare department from the IRS in the form of a per-capita payment for each recipient, and would be distributed directly to clients or to case managers in a quasi-public multiservice (MSA) agency. Case managers in the MSAs would determine whether SIP benefits should be awarded through a yearly grant or in monthly installments. The specific details of the SIP program are discussed more fully in the following sections.

Redefining Poverty

By allocating benefits according to the median family income in a target region, the SIP program would eliminate the current poverty classification. Formally adopted by the Social Security Administration (SSA) in 1969, the official poverty line provides a set of income cutoffs adjusted for the size of the household, the number of minor children (those under age 18), and the age of the household head. In order to ensure the same purchasing power each year, the SSA adjusts the poverty threshold by using the consumer price index (CPI). Through use of the CPI, the SSA estimates the yearly cash income required for individuals and families to satisfy their basic survival (food, clothing, medical, and shelter) needs. This absolute figure is calculated by making an estimate of the food costs for a household—based on the "Thrifty Food Plan" designed by the Department of Agriculture—and multiplying that number by three. (It is assumed that one-third of an average household budget is, or should be,

spent on food.) In 1989 the federal poverty index for a family of four was
set at $12,675 per year.[47] Looking at the poverty line in five-year incre-
ments (for a family of four), in 1970 the index was set at $3,968; in 1975
it rose to $5,500; and in 1980 it rose again, this time to $8,414.[48] For the
most part, these increases do not represent a liberalization of the poverty
index, but instead are due solely to the effects of inflation. Moreover,
poverty is assumed to be eliminated when the income of a family exceeds
this federal poverty line, regardless of any regional changes occurring in
the average household income.

Alleged to be objective, the poverty index is plagued with structural
problems. First, for example, while the poverty line is calculated by multiplying
the Thrifty Food Plan by three, and although food has jumped in price, it
has not escalated as sharply as rent, home heating fuel, and medical care.
Consequently, these necessities now comprise a larger share of the family
budget than they did 20 years ago when the USDA devised the poverty
index. Thus, while food costs may still constitute one-third of the family
budget, other costs consume a greater share of the remainder. Second, the
Thrifty Food Plan is based on an emergency diet and assumes the existence of an educated consumer able to discern nutritious and inexpensive
foods. Obviously, not every consumer is exemplary. Third, regional differences
are overlooked. One is hard pressed to imagine that the costs of food and
especially housing are similar in New York City and Houma, Louisiana.

The current poverty line is almost meaningless in terms of understanding poverty. For example, a single female who earned the minimum wage
and headed a four-person family in 1986 would have brought home $6,432
a year, thus bringing her to 57 percent of the poverty line. (To reach the
poverty line she would have had to earn about $5.00 an hour.) Her total
family income of $6,432 would have equaled only 19 percent of the median
family income ($34,716) for the United States in 1986. Even if she were
in a two-wage-earner family with both workers receiving the minimum
wage, their combined incomes would have equaled only 38 percent of the
median family income. Moreover, even if she reached the poverty line
for a family of four ($11,203), her income would have brought her to only
32 percent of the median family income.

This problem is exacerbated because, while the minimum wage is national,
median family income differs on a state-by-state basis, having gone from
a high in 1986 of $44,591 in New Jersey to a low of $26,763 in Mississippi. Thus, if our single mother in a four-person family earned the minimum
wage in New Jersey, she would have earned only 14 percent of the median
family wage of that state. Had she lived in Mississippi, she would have
earned 24 percent of the median family income—almost double that of
New Jersey. AFDC benefits are equally out of line with the current poverty

threshold. In 1990, combined AFDC and Food Stamp benefits for a family of three went from a low of $4,536 a year in Alabama to a high of $12,792 a year in Alaska. The median state had a combined AFDC and Food Stamp benefit of $7,212 a year, equaling 73 percent of the poverty line. On the other hand, the $7,212 a year in combined AFDC and Food Stamp benefits would have equaled only 23 percent of the average family income in 1988. In short, the difference between the minimum wage or combined AFDC and Food Stamp benefits and the median family income is sharp in all states, as Table 6.3 illustrates.

A more accurate and fair measure of poverty—one that is regionally sensitive—would be calculated based on a percentage of the median family income (which is influenced by differences in regional price levels) in specific areas. In other words, the country would be divided into target areas based on existing metropolitan statistical areas and rural economic sectors. Within each target area, the poverty line would be based on a percentage of the median family income for that region. Specifically, benefits would be set nationwide to equal 40 percent of the median family income in a regional area. This benefit level would correspond to 1.5 times the minimum wage; or put in another way, it would equal the wages of 1.5 full-time minimum wage earners. Because we are proposing a variable minimum wage that is regionally adjusted, the SIP benefits for eligible families would fluctuate nationally since they would be keyed to regional rather than national median family incomes.[49]

Moreover, because the SIP program would include a mandatory work requirement for *all* recipients who are judged capable of labor force participation, no incentive would exist to choose welfare over work, thus ending the inherent competition between minimum wage employment and welfare receipt. Looking at benefits on a national level, the welfare family that now claims all its benefits and receives about $12,000 per year would accrue about the same amount ($12,240) under this formula. However, the single female householder with a four-person family who earns a minimum wage of $4.25 an hour (a yearly salary of $8,160) would now also "earn" $12,240 under this formula. Because median family income does not vary widely with the size of the family (most American families have slightly over two children), there will also be no incentive to increase family size to gain greater benefits. Lastly, eligibility for the SIP program would be capped at 40 percent of the regional median family income. Redefining the poverty threshold in this manner would eliminate the yearly need to readjust the poverty line for inflation and would ensure a fairer and geographically more sensitive measure of poverty. In addition, a work requirement would positively influence the labor supply, thereby increasing the pool of Social Security contributors.

Table 6.3   Comparison of Median Family Income of a Four-person Family in Individual States with Combined AFDC and Food Stamp Benefits, and the Minimum Wage, 1986

State	Median Family Income	Combined AFDC and Food Stamp Benefits (Yearly Maximum)	AFDC and Food Stamps as Percent of Median Family Income	Minimum Wage as Percent of Family Income for a Single-wage Household
U.S.	$34,716	$8,904	26%	19%
Alabama	29,799	5,328	18	21
Alaska	41,292	13,392	32	16
Arizona	33,477	7,512	22	19
Arkansas	27,157	6,192	22	23
California	37,655	12,192	32	17
Colorado	36,026	9,492	26	18
Connecticut	44,330	10,692	24	14
Delaware	35,766	7,812	22	18
D. of Col.	35,424	8,760	25	18
Florida	33,368	7,140	21	19
Georgia	34,602	7,104	21	19
Hawaii	36,618	9,564	26	18
Idaho	27,075	7,320	27	23
Illinois	36,163	7,512	21	18
Indiana	32,026	7,368	23	20
Iowa	30,556	8,796	29	21
Kansas	32,512	8,424	26	20
Kentucky	28,464	6,646	23	23
Louisiana	29,614	6,156	21	22
Maine	31,297	11,832	38	21
Maryland	42,250	8,496	20	15
Mass.	42,295	10,692	25	15
Michigan	36,088	10,044	28	18
Minnesota	36,746	10,836	29	18
Mississippi	26,763	8,730	33	24
Missouri	33,149	7,368	22	19
Montana	29,130	8,604	30	22

Nebraska	31,484	8,544	27	20
Nevada	33,604	7,572	23	19
New Hamp.	39,503	8,982	23	16
New Jersey	44,591	9,084	20	14
New Mexico	27,474	7,080	26	23
New York	36,796	10,026	27	17
N. Carolina	31,787	6,816	21	20
N. Dakota	29,424	8,844	30	21
Ohio	34,038	8,022	24	19
Oklahoma	29,071	7,002	24	22
Oregon	31,392	9,252	29	20
Penn.	32,700	8,874	27	20
R. Island	35,837	10,080	28	18
S. Carolina	31,025	9,016	29	21
S. Dakota	27,008	8,190	30	24
Tennessee	29,568	7,236	24	22
Texas	32,442	6,126	19	20
Utah	30,635	8,748	29	21
Vermont	32,490	10,812	33	20
Virginia	37,885	7,670	20	17
Washington	35,071	10,332	29	18
W. Virginia	27,094	7,092	26	24
Wisconsin	33,739	11,202	33	19
Wyoming	28,742	8,136	28	22

Source: Adapted from U.S. Government, *1987 AFDC Recipient Characteristics, Annual Study, 1989* (Washington, D.C.: U.S. Government Printing Office, 1989); and U.S. Bureau of the Census, *Statistical Abstract of the United States, 1989* (Washington, D.C.: U.S. Government Printing Office, 1989).

Operationalizing SIP

The organizational auspices for the SIP program would be a community-based multiservice agency (MSA). This administrative unit would be a quasi-governmental entity—either a nonprofit agency under the aegis of a board of directors or a privately held human service collective. Individualized services would be provided by case managers who would be human service professionals specially trained in personal finance and domestic problems. Social workers would be logical candidates to provide case management services, since the SIP program would customize benefits to the social economy of eligible individuals. Eligibility for SIP would require that a client's income fall below 40 percent of the regional median family income, with assets limited to $30,000.

Case managers would classify SIP beneficiaries into four employability categories: (1) clients who cannot realistically be expected to participate in the labor force (e.g., the totally disabled); (2) clients who can participate in the labor force within a protected environment (e.g., handicapped or mentally ill clients requiring sheltered workshops); (3) clients who can participate in the labor force on a part-time basis (e.g., mothers with infants); and (4) clients for whom labor force participation on a full-time basis is possible. Clients who cannot participate in the labor force on any level will be required to substantiate their disability by undergoing thorough medical examinations and periodic case reviews. Firm criteria would be established to rate handicaps in terms of percentage of disability. In addition, through their intensive case reviews, state welfare departments would monitor clients judged unemployable by the local MSAs. Any MSA found to be consistently classifying employable clients as totally disabled would risk losing its accreditation.

All clients in the SIP program would work with their case managers to develop an individualized plan designed to maximize their welfare benefits, increase their human capital (i.e., further education, job training, etc.), and optimize their personal assets. Clients falling within each of the four above employability categories would be provided with a plan to maximize their life opportunities, particularly with reference to Individual Development Accounts (IDAs) as discussed earlier in the chapter. Totally and partially disabled clients would receive a plan that best helps them to use welfare and support service benefits. Because employment (either in the private labor market or in a community development agency) is mandatory for all able-bodied recipients, no incentive would exist to peg benefits lower for those who cannot possibly participate in the labor force. In effect, they would receive the same minimum benefit levels as people employed in the labor force. Those for whom limited or full labor-force participation is possible will have SIP plans that reflect job training and educational opportunities. Workers who are presently in the labor force full-time but who earn a wage that puts them below the eligibility threshold will be provided with a package that combines their labor market income with supplemental welfare funds, thus allowing them to be at 40 percent of the regional median income. Moreover, those in the workforce will be provided with plans containing incentives that encourage a greater share of their income to be derived from labor market sources. This may include job retraining opportunities, career counseling, or further education. Lastly, clients who fully meet the objectives of their plan yet still earn less than 40 percent of the regional median family income will receive a small supplemental benefit. (A mainstay of SIP must be to reward rather than punish initiative.)

Apart from formulating economic plans, case managers would also be responsible for helping clients budget their money. In the instance that a client is judged as incapable of managing their resources, the case manager would function as a broker, dispensing income on a monthly basis. The case manager would also be a constant point of contact for clients during their participation in the SIP program. Social service referrals and client tracking would be a major responsibility of the case manager. Apart from determining eligibility, case managers would also function as client advocates, ensuring that clients received the full benefits to which they are entitled. In effect, the case manager would be responsible for the client from the point of entry into the SIP program until his or her termination. Part of the mechanics of the SIP program is illustrated in Figure 6.1.

Social Service Vouchers

If independent providers are to supply the bulk of human services in postindustrial America, it is essential to devise a mechanism whereby social objectives are achieved while allowing professionals autonomy and clients freedom to choose the person or agency they deem best suited to help with their problem. The dispensing of social service vouchers is one method of providing a wide range of services to the poor in a manner that is both responsive and cost effective. Under the SIP program, clients eligible for financial management services could choose the MSA from which to seek services. For those seeking social services, vouchers would be provided allowing them to choose from a range of service providers who would be reimbursed by government through the MSA. Service providers from the private sector would be required to meet standards established by government for reimbursement purposes. Many of the existing private nonprofit agencies would participate; but a voucher system would also open up participation to the approximately 20,000 social workers in private practice since they could affiliate themselves with MSAs.[50]

Each MSA would be responsible for maintaining a client information center, which would update a roster of eligible service providers as well as their performance as evaluated by former clients. Jurisdictions would provide those services now assured through Title XX: home-based care, daycare for children, protective and emergency services for adults and children, as well as employment, education, and training services. Because the kind of service needed by the poor varies widely, an inclusive "service provision inventory" would be developed, similar to those already used in the provision of psychiatric and health care.[51] Reimbursement would be related to the type of care provided, and rates would be negotiated annually between providers and the state.

Since the implementation of social service vouchers would make the public welfare department a regulatory agency, a substantial reduction in personnel would occur. Direct service employees of the welfare department would be encouraged to affiliate with MSAs. The most desirable outcome would be the formation of MSAs that are privately held, community-based social service collectives.[52] The funding for social service vouchers would be derived from the $2.7 billion appropriated for Title XX, although states and localities would be free to supplement this for special needs. In applying market principles to the delivery of social services, the use of vouchers can be expected not only to replicate successes in other areas of service delivery, but also to provide low-income beneficiaries the same measure of choice accorded their more affluent compatriots.

Released from their prime responsibility of providing services, welfare departments would function as financial and administrative conduits, regulators, and evaluators. Specifically, welfare departments would certify individual MSAs as well as their professional affiliates. The welfare department would then be responsible for regulating, monitoring, and investigating the services provided. This would occur in the same way that state agencies are responsible for monitoring the services provided by group homes for the mentally ill or mentally retarded. For example, welfare departments could make unannounced visits in order to evaluate the progress of individual client plans and the quality of services provided. Released from the conflicting role of being the funder, provider, and monitor of its own social services, welfare departments would be free to concentrate on ensuring that clients receive competent and effective income maintenance and social services. Moreover, instead of being accused of encouraging client dependency, welfare departments could help to ensure that recipients move in a direction of greater economic independence and mobility.

Funding SIP

The initial funding for SIP would come from the reallocation of funds from AFDC, SSI, EITC, Food Stamps, WIC, and the income support allocations contained within other social programs. These funds would then be transferred to a specially modified coffer in the Internal Revenue Service. Through SIP, these funds would supplement the wages of those in the labor force as well as provide benefits for those outside of the labor force.

Thus, funding for the SIP program would come from reallocating the $6 billion refunded by EITC, the $18 billion spent on AFDC, the $15 billion spent on SSI, and the $13 billion spent on Food Stamps—a total of $52 billion. The SIP program would also receive additional funds from absorbing the income-maintenance features of other social programs, including the WIC program ($2 billion), LIHEAP ($2.3 billion), Section 8 housing,

Figure 6.1

The Proposed Stable
Incomes Program (SIP)

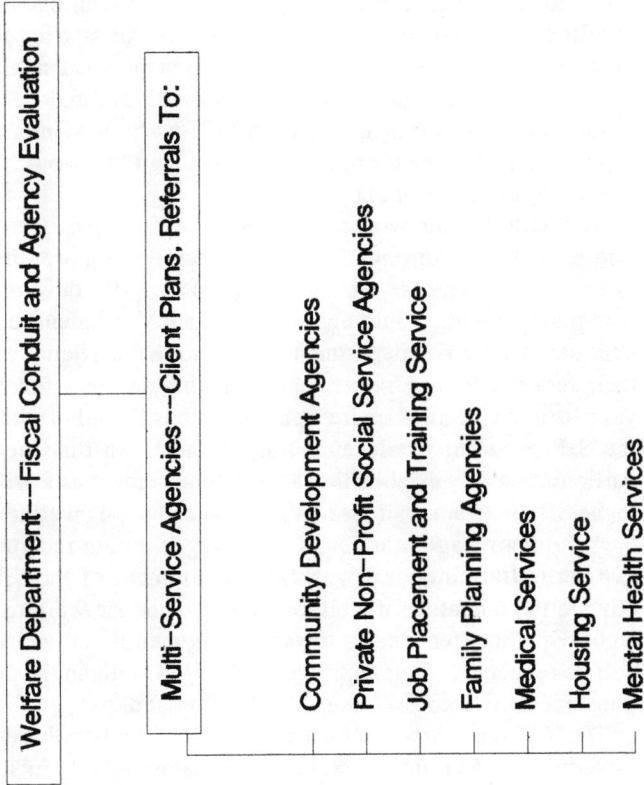

Welfare Department—Fiscal Conduit and Agency Evaluation

Multi-Service Agencies—Client Plans, Referrals To:

- Community Development Agencies
- Private Non-Profit Social Service Agencies
- Job Placement and Training Service
- Family Planning Agencies
- Medical Services
- Housing Service
- Mental Health Services

and so forth.[53] Collateral funding for MSAs and case managers would come from reallocating the sizable administrative costs associated with AFDC, SSI, and Food Stamps. For example, administrative costs in 1990 for each AFDC family totaled $776 (a total of $3 billion); for SSI it was $465 (a total of $1 billion); and for Food Stamps, more than $600 per family (a total of $2.5 billion). Taken together, the administrative savings from collapsing these programs would amount to $6.5 billion[54]—an amount sufficient to fund MSAs.

Under the SIP program, the MSAs would be reimbursed on a capitation basis; in other words, they would be given a specific sum for each client enrolled in a particular MSA. Seed money for starting and maintaining the administration of MSAs would come from the substantial savings realized by collapsing the administrations of SSI, AFDC, and Food Stamps. Part of this money could then be lent to MSAs as a low-interest loan for purposes of establishing the organization—a loan that would be repaid as part of the capitation formula.

The SIP program would offer several advantages over traditional welfare programs. For one, SIP would target help more directly on clients through intensive case-management services. By developing individualized plans, clients would avoid being made dependent (as presently happens at most welfare departments) and thus have a better chance of getting their real needs met, rather than receiving services for which they may have little use. Furthermore, because help is linked to work requirements, the SIP program would encourage rather than discourage labor force participation. By establishing a work requirement as a primary ingredient in the SIP program, there is no longer a need to peg welfare benefits below the minimum wage in order to discourage welfare receipt over work. In that sense, the universal workfare requirement of the SIP program will obviate the incentive of welfare clients to choose welfare over work. As a consequence, tendencies toward intergenerational welfare dependency will be reduced as recipients accumulate job skills in the public sector and translate them into private-sector employment.

The SIP program would also address the administrative confusion caused by redundant welfare structures. A streamlined administrative structure with minimal overlap would result in more money available for client programs, more cost-effective social programs, and more effective client programming. The SIP program would also decentralize welfare services and thus offer clients freer social choice in choosing their service providers. A standardized welfare program coupled with a geographically sensitive poverty threshold could also result in less client migration to states with higher welfare benefits.

Perhaps the most important advantage of the SIP program is that it reestablishes the idea of an interdependent society. By building a more solid income floor under poverty, the poor will have less distance to climb back to reach the median wage. As the economic distance between the poor and the middle class is shortened, those in poverty may experience more hope (and thus more motivation) to raise themselves to middle-class levels of economic security based on their own personal assets.

THE COMMUNITY REVITALIZATION INITIATIVE

Any serious welfare reform proposal must address the social deterioration of American communities. During the past two decades there has been a marked slowdown in public investment in infrastructure, including schools, public buildings, highways, bridges, airports, and public utilities. According to Robert Kuttner, nonmilitary public capital grew at an average annual rate of 4.1 percent from 1948 to 1969 (greater than the rate of economic growth). However, from 1969 to 1987, those same expenditures grew at only 1.6 percent; and during the Reagan years of the 1980s, they plummeted to 0.9 percent per year, or less than half the rate of overall growth.[55] This cut in public spending had a differential effect on communities. While the affluent communities of the 1980s saw the building of new schools, roads, and public utilities, the poor inner-city neighborhoods became more desolate as their infrastructures (both physical and human) rotted from a lack of attention. As such, the quality of life in many American communities dropped precipitously during the 1980s. When Claude Brown returned to Harlem 20 years after the publication of his *Manchild in the Promised Land*, he was shocked by the casual viciousness of gang members toward their victims.[56] "In many if not most of our major cities, we are facing something very like social regression," wrote Daniel Patrick Moynihan. "It is defined by extraordinary levels of self-destructive behavior, interpersonal violence, and social class separation intensive in some groups, extensive in others."[57] The social pathology attributed to economic dislocation was exacerbated by policies of the Reagan, then Bush, administrations. Failing to institute a coherent community development policy, these administrations have had to rely on economic growth as a vehicle for benefiting lower-income workers; but the trickle-down has been mere seepage. As a consequence, an oxymoron entered the nation's vernacular: for the first time there was frequent reference to an American "underclass" (see the discussion in Chapter 4).

Community Enterprise Zones

To strengthen poor communities a Community Enterprise Zone (CEZ) program should be created that would provide technical assistance and time-limited grants for the purpose of generating basic commodities, such as jobs and housing. The geographic basis of a CEZ would be an economic catchment area with a population of from 4,000 to 50,000, to accommodate rural and urban environments. Eligibility for community development grants would depend on the social and economic conditions of the catchment area as determined by specific socioeconomic indicators: incidence of poverty, unemployment, and business closings. Catchment areas in which the rates for two of these three indicators exceeded one standard deviation above the national average would be eligible for benefits.

Two types of aid would be provided. For those in which the infrastructure had deteriorated substantially, CEZ benefits would consist of technical assistance and development grants. Rather than provide assistance directly, government would contract services from existing organizations that have established a successful track record in economic development, such as the Enterprise Foundation or the Local Initiatives Support Corporation. For communities experiencing acute dislocation, a system of incentives—including tax credits—would be instituted to retain and promote entrepreneurial activity.

Funding for the CEZ program would be derived from a Community Enterprise Zone Fund created by combining Community Development Block Grants ($3.1 billion for 1991) and Economic Development Administration appropriations ($210 million for 1991), supplemented by nominal limits on mortgage interest deductions and a tax on capital gains from home sales in excess of $125,000 (a figure that totaled $900 million in 1991).[58] The resulting $4.21 billion could be doubled by imposing a modest 1-percent tax on new construction in the United States,[59] yielding a total fund of more than $8 billion. In addition, much of the $1.75 billion allocated in 1990 to the Job Training Partnership Act could be transferred to the CEZ program. In effect, CEZ funding would insure communities against economic dislocation by providing a safety net for all communities in economic distress.

The Community Revitalization Program

In the past, welfare advocates have justified taxing the haves in order to provide assistance to the have-nots on the basis that a particular status entitled someone to welfare benefits. When resources are scarce, however, unconditional welfare is perceived by the public as wasteful. Worse, unconditional welfare is popularly viewed as eroding the individual initiative necessary for self-support. Programs that provide unconditional payments—especially the means-tested programs such as AFDC—have taken a drubbing largely because they have been associated with welfare dependency.[60] Despite evidence that only a small minority of welfare beneficiaries is made up of generational recipients,[61] the fact that some *are* is unacceptable in an era of fiscal belt-tightening. Further, increases in unwed parenthood, particularly among African American teenagers, raises a fundamental question about the relationship between welfare grants and family stability.[62] Whatever the causes for the rise in adolescent parenthood, the consequences are clear: a lower probability that parents will be able to support themselves through work, and a higher probability that mother and child will have to rely on public assistance for support. Welfare advocates have been implicated in this social tragedy because they have not included reciprocity—that a standard of conduct be a condition of eligibility for benefits—in social welfare policies.[63]

During the past decade, a series of community work experience programs administered by the Manpower Demonstration Research Corporation (MDRC) showed that workfare could prove an effective strategy for reducing welfare costs, depending on the presence of supports for job training and employment, as well as the availability of nearby jobs. While initial assessments of the workfare demonstrations were cautious,[64] later studies revealed an unexpected finding: since the most-dependent of AFDC recipients consumed the most program resources, they also represented the greatest program savings once they were participating in workfare.[65] Studies such as these provided the justification for incorporating workfare in the Family Support Act of 1988.

Unfortunately, a serious deficiency of the Family Support Act workfare component remains: namely, aside from engaging in job-seeking activity, no expectation is manifested in the legislation as to *which* employment is considered ultimately desirable. "In structuring jobs programs, policymakers have paid insufficient attention to the types of service performed," argued Charles Moskos. "Only when training programs involve young adults in the delivery of vital services to the community can they hope to inculcate the values that make for good citizenship."[66]

Incorporating civic content into workfare could be accomplished by tying the SIP program in with a Community Revitalization Program through which public assistance beneficiaries would contribute to the neighborhoods in which they live. Under a Community Revitalization Program, public assistance beneficiaries who were deemed employable but who were not working or in education/training activities would be referred by their case manager to a community development agency to which their benefits would be assigned. In order to collect benefits, those on welfare would have to engage in joblike tasks identified by the community development agency. Community development entities would be nonprofit organizations meeting standards of the state department of social services relating to personnel and benefit management, but would otherwise be free to define community development projects and assign beneficiaries to them.

In contrast to the dependency associated with public welfare, beneficiaries would be treated like employees of the community development agency. Although still receiving public assistance, beneficiaries could develop a track record that would be of use in the private labor market. Thus, the benefit assignment strategy addresses a major flaw in the AFDC program. "You cannot get good at welfare," William Raspberry shrewdly observed. "It does no good for a welfare mother to impress her caseworker with her quick grasp of her sense of responsibility or her willingness to take on an extra task. There is no way for a welfare client to distinguish himself, in any economically useful way, from any other welfare client. There are no promotions on welfare."[67]

In order to encourage the responsiveness of community development agencies toward beneficiaries, welfare recipients would have a choice among community development agencies in which to enroll. Once enrolled, beneficiaries could transfer to another community development agency— or to other employment—much like employees change jobs in the labor market. Such an arrangement would assure a measure of social responsibility on the part of welfare beneficiaries in a way that directly benefits the communities in which they live. Moreover, such an arrangement would allow the reciprocity goals of the SIP program to be realized, even for the difficult to employ. In effect, those judged employable (but not in other job-related programs) by their case manager would be referred to a community development agency where they would be required to contribute their labor in exchange for social welfare benefits.

Apart from helping clients to develop positive work attitudes and job skills, community development agencies could also help to rebuild the decaying physical and social infrastructure of poor communities. As such, work teams under the auspices of community agencies could be used to demolish or renovate abandoned buildings (places that are often used as ad-hoc crack houses and gang headquarters) and to rebuild roads, bridges, schools, and other public buildings. In addition, work projects developed by community agencies could be used to build new community institutions, including daycare centers, parks, schools, shopping areas, and industrial parks.

Rebuilding a poor community's physical infrastructure must be accompanied by rebuilding its *social* infrastructure. As part of a renewed commitment to community revitalization, low-cost daycare centers must be developed that allow poor families the opportunity to participate fully in the labor force. In addition, effective preschool and child health and immunization programs must also be developed. Lastly, community development agencies can provide the economic and social leadership to help communities effectively compete in a complex economy. This could be done by helping to establish building-trade cooperatives, personnel agencies, and the like, and by creating economic incentives that would encourage small and medium-size industries to relocate in inner-city communities. As part of these economic incentives, the community must be able to ensure both its inhabitants and the potential industries of their security from bodily and property crimes. This goal could be accomplished by creating local security teams that work in conjunction with police departments to patrol neighborhoods and, where appropriate, to make arrests.

A revitalized community infrastructure can accomplish several goals. For one, it can lead to a renewed sense of local self-initiative. This goal is particularly important since a fiscally paralyzed and politically fractured federal government cannot be expected to develop the innovative programs necessary to restore economic and social vibrancy to poor neighborhoods. Also, a revitalized infrastructure may succeed in attracting back a portion of the black middle class that fled inner-city areas during the past three decades, thus restoring some of the social and economic leadership that has been lost.[68] Lastly, vital communities can better capture and exploit the human capital that is wasted by abject poverty, poor education, drug and alcohol abuse, and criminal activities. Recapturing human capital will help not only the poor communities, but also the larger society that must effectively marshal its human capital to compete successfully in a new economic theater.

Social Intervention Teams

Public confidence in social programs has diminished as policies failed to deal effectively with people identified as being harmful to themselves or capable of doing harm to others. While the individual consequences of self-destructive behavior are often recognized—and, as a result, subject to legal sanction—the aggregate consequences are not. When the number of individuals who are harmful to themselves and others proliferates and is concentrated in one community, the result is not simply an arithmetic increase in the number of destructive persons; it destroys, also, the very competence of the community. The community is no longer able to maintain its essential functions, one of which is to assure the safety of its residents.

Unavoidably, human service professionals are held responsible by the public when people known to public officials engage in life-threatening behavior. Two current problems illustrate this: homelessness and child abuse. As a result of deinstitutionalization, thousands of psychiatric patients were discharged from state hospitals to often nonexistent community programs during the 1970s. Unable to maintain themselves independently, ex-patients have become a prominent part of the urban landscape as homeless street people. Because many of the homeless have severe emotional disorders that make personal management difficult, New York City has instituted Project Help, a program through which mobile teams of psychiatric professionals interview and involuntarily hospitalize seriously disordered street-people.[69]

The social control issue also contributes to what has become a crisis in the various existing child protective services (CPS). Douglas Besharov, a social worker and fellow of the American Enterprise Institute, noted that "of the 1,000 children who die under circumstances suggestive of parental maltreatment, between 35 and 50 percent were previously reported to child protective agencies."[70] And New York City acknowledged that half of its deaths due to child abuse and neglect "occurred in families already reported to the public child welfare agency."[71] Larry Brown, author of the American Humane Association's standards for CPS, has observed that "the biggest indictment of [CPS] today is that there are plenty of children in the system whose victimization is not treated appropriately."[72] By 1988, the CPS situation had degenerated to the point that the Supreme Court agreed to determine if governments were liable for the failure of CPS workers to discharge their duties properly.[73]

A more realistic approach to both of these social control difficulties is simply to consider life-threatening behavior a public safety problem, rather than a human service problem. Accordingly, child and adult protective service workers should be reassigned to the local police departments, where they would work with police officers in Social Intervention Teams.[74] Social service studies and field experiments with police street patrols suggest that police-social work teams can be established, and that they can effectively manage a wide range of problems that social service departments are not prepared to manage alone.[75] Police and social work personnel have quite different orientations to human problems, of course. In order to bridge this difference, special training programs would be established as part of a national Police Corps—an undergraduate student aid program that would supply public safety departments with officers trained to help communities manage social control problems.[76] Funding for college grants would be derived from targeting Pell grants and consolidating portions of the existing training programs in mental health and social services. Much of the funding for maintaining Social Intervention Teams would come from combining the existing appropriations for police and protective service personnel.

THE NATIONAL SERVICE PROGRAM

Social policy is beset by several paradoxes. For one, postindustrial America has witnessed the unparalleled success of some citizens while many more have experienced a serious deterioration in their standard of living. What's more, many of those who have benefited from the expansion of the service sector have been those very professionals who, despite their pledge to promote the common welfare, have failed to provide services to their disadvantaged compatriots. In a development that would have been implausible a generation ago, the corporate sector has exploited what have been rapidly emerging markets in human services such as hospital management, health maintenance, nursing care, and even corrections—in many instances, extracting a profit from human misfortune. These developments speak to the commercialization of compassion, a subjugation of goodwill to market forces (the very dynamics that too often generated the need for services in the first place). To the extent that commercialization has denigrated the nation's voluntary spirit, it is necessary to bolster America's service ethic. This is not a matter to be left to vacuous rhetoric (e.g., a defunded "thousand points of light" foundation); instead, it must be an urgent priority for social policy.

The National Service Corps

In 1960, John F. Kennedy sparked the idealism of young Americans by giving them the opportunity to help others through a short-term commitment to live and work in disadvantaged communities. The Peace Corps, and later VISTA, provided many poor communities abroad and in the United States with technical assistance they could not otherwise afford, and it provided young people with an exposure to other peoples they would never have encountered. Recently, six states have followed up on this idea by creating conservation services, the most well-known being the California Conservation Corps.[77] The popular support these programs enjoy indicates that a range of income groups would participate in a national service program.

A National Service Corps, according to a proposal fielded by Charles Moskos, would allow volunteers to elect one-year stints in a nationwide program for which they would be paid $100 per week plus benefits and would, upon completion of service, be eligible for "generous postservice educational and job training benefits." Enrolling approximately 600,000 youth (excluding those enlisting in the military), a National Service Corps would make a substantial contribution toward reconstructing distressed communities. Volunteers would engage in such activities as establishing tutorial programs for schoolchildren, helping residents in slums rehabilitate housing, assisting the frail elderly who need assistance to stay out of nursing homes, and organizing child care services, among others. Approximately half of the budget for the Moskos proposal of $7 billion could be derived from consolidating current jobs and training programs,[78] the remainder coming from CEZ appropriations (see the discussion earlier in this chapter). A promising start for a National Service Corps was enacted with the National and Community Service Act of 1990, which set aside $56 million in 1991 for demonstration projects in five states.[79]

A National Service Corps is appealing for several reasons. For one, it would make available to hard-pressed communities personnel that they would not otherwise attract. Significantly, national service would expose affluent volunteers to the circumstances of their less well-off compatriots, and it would demonstrate to less advantaged Americans that others are not indifferent to their plight. Perhaps most significantly, a National Service Corps would perform an essential democratizing function in this political economy that constantly pushes the social classes apart, by "increasing the variety of class mixing situations."[80] A national service also complements the need to reinvigorate the voluntary sector. "With our tradition of voluntary organizations," noted Moskos, "coupled with comprehensive national service, we could set our country on an entirely new course of effective yet affordable delivery of human services."[81]

Volunteer Tax Credit

The institutional origins of social welfare in the United States are reflected in the myriad nonprofit agencies of the voluntary sector. Organizations such as the Red Cross, Boys' and Girls' Clubs, Boy Scouts and Girl Scouts, the Ys, and various sectarian agencies have contributed incalculable benefits to American communities. More recent innovations have addressed a variety of new problems besetting the United States: the first sale of a federally subsidized housing project in Washington, D.C., to its tenants, engineered by Kimi Gray; the construction of a model facility for the homeless in San Diego by Father Joe Carroll; the establishment of a school for inner-city African American children in Chicago by Marva Collins; the development of a youth development program for delinquency-prone minority adolescents in Philadelphia by Sister Falakah Fattah; and the organization of an international home ownership program for low-income families—Habitat for Humanity—by Millard Fuller. Nonprofit social agencies offer virtues that strike a chord with most Americans: local control, neighborliness, and community well-being.

Yet, these organizations are besieged by increased demand for service while government support has ebbed. Between 1977 and 1984, government funding of nonprofit social service agencies dropped from 53.5 to 43.9 percent of their revenues.[82] For each of the years from 1982 to 1984, federal aid to nonprofits that provided nonhealth-related services dropped *$26 billion*. But increased efforts at fund raising the following year recouped only one-eighth of that amount.[83] Traditionally, the voluntary sector

has relied on individual and corporate contributions to balance governmental aid; but neither promise to offset the loss of governmental revenues. Individual contributions are unlikely to increase substantially, since
half of all charitable giving to nonprofits comes from families making less
than $25,000 per year[84]—families whose income has stagnated since the
mid-1970s. Corporate contributions flagged with the October 1987 stock
market crash.[85] Facing a probable recession after so many years of economic expansion, few corporate directors are willing to risk capital reserves to bail out the nonprofit sector.

To revitalize the voluntary sector, people should be given incentives to
contribute to local nonprofit social service agencies. The most immediate
way to do this is to restore the deduction allowed for charitable contributions by nonitemizing taxpayers, which was withdrawn by the Tax Reform
Act of 1986. If voluntary agencies are to fill the void left by government
cuts in social expenditures, however, it will be necessary to raise more
revenues than deducted contributions would produce; thus, the individual
deductions should be changed to a partial tax credit. Moreover, the relationship between altruistic citizens and nonprofit social service agencies
could be strengthened by rewarding those who commit substantial time as
volunteers. For all practical purposes, these volunteers become quasi-
employees, often assuming a function that cannot be provided by a sala-
ried employee because of inadequate agency funding. Therefore, persons
committing more than 30 hours per month to a tax-exempt social service
agency should be able to establish Volunteer Tax Credits that would allow
them to deduct a portion of the economic equivalent of their volunteering
against their tax liability. The amount that this tax expenditure would
represent as a loss to the U.S. Treasury would be negligible compared to
the value of investment it would encourage in community institutions. In
all likelihood, it would exceed the paltry $5 million earmarked (then withdrawn
by President Bush's 1992 proposed budget) for voluntary agencies in 1991
through the Points of Light Foundation, as part of the National and Community Service Act of 1990.[86]

Nondiscrimination in Service Provision

To the extent that the private sector continues to provide a major portion of human services, it is essential to assure that people have the right
of access to services. For-profit health and human service firms have
discriminated against people with complex problems who are dependent
on government insurance. Instances of preferential selection (when providers skim more treatable, less costly clients for care) and dumping (when
indigent clients are capriciously transferred to public facilities without
provision of necessary care) have been documented.[87] Even voluntary-

sector agencies have been criticized for avoiding multiproblem clients.[88] Hence, welfare departments will carefully monitor individual MSAs to make certain that they do not cream off the higher functioning families and individuals, while rejecting the multiproblem families.

Severe penalties should be levied against *all* private-sector service providers who discriminate against clients with public sponsorship. This is a fair price to pay on the part of proprietary firms that are profiting from human misfortune. Parenthetically, modest regulation would correct market incentives that now tend to disadvantage a provider willing to serve a disproportionate number of high-cost clients, by spreading the obligation among all providers. And a nondiscriminatory requirement would be incontrovertible for voluntary-sector agencies who profess primary concern for community welfare in order to become tax exempt. Nonprofits that demonstrate a pattern of discrimination would lose their tax-exempt status, and MSAs their governmental certification.

As a related measure, a nondiscriminatory clause should be included in professional licensing standards. Professions are granted the exclusive right to use particular skills by the state—thereby establishing the professional monopoly—in exchange for the assurance that service to the community will be a priority in the application of their skills. For some time, the community's welfare has suffered as some professionals have used the freedom to practice as license for personal aggrandizement. Flagrant disregard of the interests of the broader community are no less than a violation of the social contract between a profession and the state. When human service professions cease to function in the interest of society, the state reserves the authority to oblige them to do so as a condition of the exclusive right to practice. Accordingly, if a state licensing authority determines that a human service professional or an MSA shows a pattern of discriminatory practice against certain people seeking and eligible for care, then the provider's license or the agency's mandate to practice should be revoked. Penalties already exist that punish discrimination restricting access to education, housing, and employment; human services should also be included. The costs to the public of assuring access to services through regulation of human service professionals should be borne by providers through increases in licensing fees.

THE FUTURE OF AMERICAN SOCIAL WELFARE

The social policy initiatives described above—stable incomes, community revitalization, and national service—can serve as the basis for reorganizing welfare programs in a manner that is more consistent with the American experience. These strategies recognize the influence of capitalism on the labor force as well as the human service professions. They enhance the altruistic capacity of a voluntary sector that has always played a prominent role in American culture. These proposals acknowledge the deterioration of families and institutions, particularly in poor communities. However, instead of relying on the federal government for redress, local communities are encouraged to seek solutions to their own problems. Whenever possible, the revenues for these policy initiatives are derived from the restructuring of existing programs and from reasonable, modest taxes on activities related to or earmarked for particular objectives. In some instances, social objectives can be achieved without increased revenues, by simply clarifying the social contract among involved parties. The result is an arrangement that is peculiarly American.

Oddly enough, this arrangement for social welfare policy may also serve as a prototype for social policy in the more established welfare states of Europe. In a provocative analysis, Scott Lash and John Urry have proposed that postmodern "disorganized" capitalism such as that evident in the postindustrial era requires a different form of social policy than that characteristic of the fully articulated welfare states of Northern Europe. The nature of future social welfare will be "less bureaucratized, more decentralized and in cases more privatized . . . as the welfare state of organized capitalism makes way for a much more varied and less centrally organized form of welfare provision in disorganized capitalism."[89] If that is the case, the underdeveloped American welfare state may not be the institutional laggard it is often portrayed as, but instead a model for future social welfare policy among the industrial nations.[90]

Because the model of social welfare proposed here is indigenous to the American experience, the likelihood of its adoption rests with contemporary political forces, the nature of which we shall now examine.

NOTES

1. Robert Reich, *The Work of Nations* (New York: Alfred A. Knopf, 1991), p. 177.

2. David Ellwood, *Poor Support: Poverty in the American Family* (New York: Basic Books, 1988), p. 99

3. Committee on Ways and Means, U.S. House of Representatives, *Overview of Entitlement Programs* (Washington, D.C.: U.S. Government Printing Office, 1990), p. 546.

4. Reich, *Work of Nations*.

5. Isaac Shapiro, *The Minimum Wage and Job Loss* (Washington, D.C.: Center on Budget and Policy Priorities, 1988).

6. Center on Budget and Policy Priorities, "The Bush Administration's Minimum Wage Proposal," Washington, D.C., March 31, 1989.

7. Ibid.

8. Center on Budget and Policy Priorities, "Many Black and Hispanic Workers Harmed by Minimum Wage Bill Veto, Analysis Finds," Washington, D.C., June 15, 1989.

9. Congressional Budget Office, *Reducing the Deficit: Spending and Revenue Options* (Washington, D.C: U.S. Government Printing Office, 1990), p. 410.

10. Jansson, *The Reluctant Welfare State* (Belmont, Calif.: Wadsworth, 1984), p. 337.

11. Children's Defense Fund, *The State of America's Children, 1991* (Washington, D.C.: Children's Defense Fund, 1991), p. 38.

12. Ibid.

13. Ibid.

14. See Michael Sherraden, *Stakeholding: A New Direction in Social Policy* (Washington, D.C.: Progressive Policy Institute, 1990); and Michael Sherraden, *Assets and the Poor* (Armonk, N.Y.: M. E. Sharpe, 1991).

15. Oregon House of Representatives, "Oregonians Investing in Oregonians," Salem, 1991.

16. Congressional Budget Office, *Reducing the Deficit*, p. 417.

17. Committee on Ways and Means, House, *Overview of Entitlement Programs*, p. 821.

18. Figures were used from Congressional Budget Office, *Reducing the Deficit*.

19. Committee on Ways and Means, U.S. House of Representatives, *Background Material and Data on Programs within the Jurisdiction of the Committee on Ways and Means, 1985 Edition* (Washington, D.C.: U.S. Government Printing Office, 1985), p. 261.

20. Sam Fulwood III, "Uncountable Problem at the Border," *Los Angeles Times* (May 17, 1990).

21. Ted Conover, *Coyotes* (New York: Vintage, 1987), p. 207.

22. The need to revise immigration policy so as to account more adequately for undocumented workers is underlined by two developments: the proliferation of *maquiladora* plants along the U.S.-Mexico border; and the recent interest in a North American trade alliance, consisting of the United States, Canada, and Mexico, in response to consolidation of the European Economic Community in 1992.

23. Howard J. Karger and David Stoesz, *American Social Welfare Policy* (White Plains, N.Y.: Longman, 1990), p. 207.

24. Lee Iacocca, "The Competitive Pull to National Health Care," *Los Angeles Times* (April 16, 1989), p. V-5.

25. Michael Specter, "Searching for the Best Medical Care Money Can't Buy," *Washington Post Weekly* (December 25-31, 1989), p. 3.

26. See Melinda Beck, "Not Enough for All," *Newsweek* (May 14, 1990); and Victor Cohn, "Rationing Our Medical Care," *Washington Post Weekly* (August 13-19, 1990).

27. David Stoesz, "Corporate Health Care and Social Welfare," *Health and Social Work* (Summer 1986); Eli Ginzberg, "For-profit Medicine," *New England Journal of Medicine* 319, 12 (September 22, 1988).

28. Alain Enthoven and Richard Kronick, "A Consumer-choice Health Plan for the 1990s," *New England Journal of Medicine* 320, 1 (January 5, 1989).

29. Theodore Marmor and Jerry Mashaw, "Canada's Health Insurance and Ours: The Real Lessons, the Big Choices," *American Prospect* 3 (1990), pp. 18-29.

30. David Himmelstein and Steffie Woolhandler, "A National Health Program for the United States," *New England Journal of Medicine* 320, 2 (January 12,1989).

31. David Himmelstein and Steffie Woolhandler, "Cost without Benefit: Administrative Waste in U.S. Healthcare," *New England Journal of Medicine* 314, 7 (February 13, 1986), p. 442.

32. Congressional Budget Office, *Reducing the Deficit*, p. 399.

33. Dana Hughes, et al., *The Health of America's Children* (Washington, D.C.: Children's Defense Fund, 1987), p. 84.

34. Michael Dorris, *The Broken Cord* (New York: Harper and Row, 1989).

35. Denise Hamilton, "Crack's Children Grow Up," *Los Angeles Times* (August 24, 1990).

36. "Drug-exposed Births Exceed 72,000 a Year," *San Diego Union* (July 14, 1990).

37. Congressional Budget Office, *Reducing the Deficit*, p. 429.

38. Quoted in Howard Jacob Karger and David Stoesz, "Welfare Reform: Maximum Feasible Exaggeration?" *Tikkun* 4 (March/April 1989), p. 121.

39. We have segregated the Social Security Program from the means tested public welfare programs for several reasons. First, unlike means-tested public assistance programs, Social Security benefits correspond to individual contributions made to the system. Second, Social Security is a nonstigmatized program. On the other hand, SSI and AFDC are highly stigmatized income-maintenance programs that require no contribution or past labor force participation. While the EITC program requires present labor force participation, its benefits are not based on actual contributions to the system. In that sense, it is not a social insurance program. Third and lastly, despite some theoretical proximity, Social Security is viewed by the public as being as removed from AFDC and SSI as are apples from oranges.

40. This scenario assumes that welfare beneficiaries actually are enrolled in all of the programs for which they qualify. However, in 1988 residents of New Jersey had less than a 40-percent chance of receiving subsidized housing, and almost half of WIC eligible women and children were not on the program. See Karger and Stoesz, *American Social Welfare Policy*, p. 252; and Committee on Ways and Means, House, *Overview of Entitlement Programs*, p. 1318.

41. Calculations were based on statistics found in the Committee on Ways and Means, House, *Overview of Entitlement Programs*, and in Karger and Stoesz, *American Welfare Policy*.

42. While the bulk of income-maintenance benefits are concentrated in the three main programs, the supports found in the smaller programs make it difficult to calculate actual welfare benefits.

43. Karger and Stoesz, *American Social Welfare Policy*, p. 264.

44. Saul D. Hoffman and Lawrence S. Seidman, *The Earned Income Tax Credit* (Kalamazoo, Mich.: W. E. Upjohn Institute for Employment Research, 1990), p. 34.

45. Ibid., p. 82.

46. Although the Food Stamp Program is generally not considered to be an income-maintenance program, it does, nevertheless, provide income support for working and nonworking poor families. With more than 18 million participants, Food Stamps cost the federal government over $14 billion in 1988. Despite these expenditures, a USDA study found that most families whose food expenditure equaled the maximum Food Stamp benefit level lacked adequate diets, and only one-tenth of those families received adequate nutrition. Moreover, one-third of those eligible for Food Stamps receive no assistance. These problems are complicated by the brisk black market for Food Stamps found in most poor communities—a submarket where poor families often sell their Food Stamps at a fraction of their face value. In short, the idea that the provision of Food Stamps ensures that poor families will use them solely for food is basically conjecture. What is not conjecture, however, is that the Food Stamp Program is a stigmatized form of assistance—which discourages many poor working-class families from obtaining them. While Section 8 housing, LIHEAP, and WIC are also not generally considered income maintenance programs, they too function as income supports.

47. *Federal Register* 53, 46 (Washington, D.C.: U.S. Government Printing Office, Friday, March 20, 1987), p. 9518.

48. U.S. Bureau of the Census, *Statistical Abstract of the United States, 1984* (Washington, D.C.: U.S. Government Printing Office, 1984), p. 447.

49. While it would be possible to ascertain accurate median incomes in most regions of the United States, we recognize that certain geographical areas will have skewed incomes that will require specific adjustments to be made in the benefit formula.

50. Telephone interview with Donna DeAngeles, National Association of Social Workers, September 27, 1990.

51. The *Diagnostic and Statistical Manual III* (DSM III) used by mental health professionals and the Diagnosis Related Group system developed by Medicare are prototypes.

52. Privately held, community-based collectives have demonstrated their superiority to governmental and corporate forms of service provision. See David Stoesz, "The Family Life Center," *Social Work* 26 (September 1981); Jonathan Rowe, "Up from the Bedside," *American Prospect* (Summer 1990).

53. These figures were compiled from the Committee on Ways and Means, House, *Overview of Entitlement Programs*, 1990.

54. Ibid.

55. Robert Kuttner, *The End of Laissez-faire* (New York: Alfred A. Knopf, 1991), p. 275.

56. Claude Brown, *Manchild in the Promised Land* (New York: Macmillan, 1965); Claude Brown, "Manchild in Harlem," *New York Times* (September 16, 1984).

57. Daniel Patrick Moynihan, *Came the Revolution* (San Diego: Harcourt Brace Jovanovich, 1988), p. 291.

58. Congressional Budget Office, *Reducing the Deficit*, pp. 279-81.

59. Computations based on the U.S. Bureau of the Census, *Statistical Abstract of the United States, 1990* (Washington, D.C.: U.S. Government Printing Office, 1990), p. 711.

60. See Martin Anderson, "Welfare Reform," in P. Duignan and A. Rabushka (eds.), *The United States in the 1980s* (Stanford, Calif.: Hoover Institution, 1980); and Charles Murray, *Losing Ground* (New York: Basic Books, 1984).

61. Committee on Ways and Means, U.S. House of Representatives, *Children in Poverty* (Washington, D.C.: U.S. Government Printing Office, 1985), pp. 43-47.

62. In 1982, 80 percent of births to black teenagers were to unwed mothers, compared to 37 percent of births to white teenagers. The out-of-wedlock rate for black teenagers aged 15-19 doubled from 1940 to 1972; by 1977 it was more than six times the rate for white teenagers. See Ruth Sidel, *Women and Children Last* (New York: Penguin Books, 1986).

63. See Lawrence Mead, *Beyond Entitlement* (New York: Free Press, 1986); and Stuart Butler, "A Conservative Vision of Welfare," *Policy Review* (Spring 1987).

64. Judith Gueron, "Work for People on Welfare," *Public Welfare* (Winter 1986), pp. 30-41.

65. D. Friedlander, *Subgroup Impacts and Performance Indicators for Selected Welfare Employment Programs* (New York: Manpower Demonstration and Research Corporation, 1988).

66. Charles Moskos, *A Call to Civic Service* (New York: Free Press, 1988), p. 90.

67. William Raspberry, "Welfare's Limits," *Washington Post* (April 11, 1988), p. A-15.

68. For a discussion of black flight from inner cities, see William Julius Wilson, *The Truly Disadvantaged* (Chicago: University of Chicago Press, 1987).

69. John Goldman, "Vans Still Pluck Mental Patients from N.Y. Streets," *Los Angeles Times* (July 11, 1990).

70. Douglas Besharov, "Contending with Overblown Expectations," *Public Welfare* (Winter 1987), p. 7.

71. Leroy Pelton, "Resolving the Crisis in Child Welfare," *Public Welfare* (Spring 1988), p. 20.

72. Larry Brown, "Questions and Answers," *Public Welfare* (Winter 1987), p. 21.

73. National Association of Social Workers, "High Court Review Urged on Foster Care Liability," *NASW News* (July 1988).

74. Pelton, "Resolving the Crisis," makes this recommendation with regard to child protective services.

75. H. Treger, *The Police-Social Work Team* (Chicago: Jane Addams School of Social Work, 1975).

76. Progressive Policy Institute, *The Police Corps and Community Policing* (Washington, D.C.: Progressive Policy Institute, 1990).

77. Moskos, *Call to Civic Service.*

78. Ibid., pp. 155-60.

79. U.S. House of Representatives, "National and Community Service Act of 1990," Report 101-893, December 31, 1990.

80. Timothy Noah, "We Need You: National Service, An Idea Whose Time Has Come," *Washington Monthly* (November 1986), p. 38.

81. Moskos, *Call to Civic Service*, p. 154.

82. V.A. Hodgkinson and M. S. Weitzman, *Dimensions of the Independent Sector* (Washington, D.C.: Independent Sector, 1986), pp. 119-20.

83. Ibid., p. 2.

84. Brian O'Connell, *Origins, Dimensions, and Impact of America's Voluntary Spirit* (Washington, D.C.: Independent Sector, 1984), p. 2.

85. C. Skrzycki, "Pace of Giving by U.S. Firms Slowed in 1987," *Washington Post* (January 2, 1988).

86. House,"National and Community Service Act of 1990."

87. Stoesz, "Corporate Health Care and Social Welfare."

88. Richard Cloward and Irwin Epstein, "Private Social Welfare's Disengagement from the Poor," in M. Zald (ed.), *Social Welfare Institutions* (New York: Wiley, 1965).

89. Scott Lash and John Urry, *The End of Organized Capitalism* (Oxford, England: Basil Blackwell, 1987), p. 231.

90. Christopher Pierson, "The 'Exceptional' United States: First New Nation or Last Welfare State?" *Social Policy and Administration* (November 1990).

7

The Civic Welfare State

David Stoesz

Events of the past quarter-century have conspired to force a reappraisal of liberal orthodoxy regarding the American welfare state. The question that has emerged is whether liberals should adhere to the format that has guided the elaboration of social programs since the New Deal—in other words, *preserve* the welfare state—or, in the face of a conservative tide that continues to run high, strike out for new ideological ground and *reconstruct* the welfare state. While many progressives still defend the American welfare state, cracks in the foundation of welfare state liberalism have been recognized by at least some liberal welfare philosophers. Some of these philosophers alerted the public about the new "pluralism" in welfare,[1] that the American welfare state was "adrift,"[2] and that "rethinking social welfare" was in order.[3] These were contemporaneous with the attempt by the right to contract the welfare state by formulating a conservative "new paradigm" for domestic policy.[4]

The decline of the American welfare state has split social advocates into three camps: (1) those who strive to erase, abruptly or through attrition, the liberal imprimatur on social policy and institutions; (2) those who want to preserve the ideological orientation toward social welfare much as it has been articulated since the New Deal; (3) and those who want to reconstruct social programs around a postindustrial ideological orientation.

REWRITING THE SOCIAL CONTRACT: THE DEVOLUTION OF WELFARE

Recent efforts to reverse the momentum of the welfare state can be traced to conservative antipathy toward governmental social programs. Traditionally, conservative objections toward welfare were relatively simple:

social programs eroded the work ethic, were financed by revenues that could otherwise have been used for capitalization of the business sector, and subverted the altruism evident in indigenous community activities. The most cynical of critics identified social programs as payoffs to constituencies of liberal Democrats—chiefly women who sought economic independence, minorities who demanded equality of opportunity, and a well-educated class of civil servants who designed, administered, and evaluated the programs. The beneficiaries of social programs had become the political constituents of liberal Democratic party politics, and welfare program benefits in exchange for votes was the dynamic that provided momentum to the expansion of the American welfare state. No minor irritant to conservatives was their observation that the bureaucracy growing up around social programs was staffed by civil servants who, despite their status as public officials, invariably identified with liberal notions of public policy. How, conservatives came to wonder, was it possible to make public policy more consistent with public sentiment when the political, economic, and administrative features of social programs guaranteed not only their persistence, but their expansion?

This interpretation—that social programs were part of a self-sustaining system outside of the realm of public politics—framed conservative tactics toward social policy during the 1980s. As noted in earlier chapters, conservatives invoked multiple strategies to reshape social policy, from creating a conservative public philosophy to condemning the negative outcomes of social programs. Intermixed in these strategies were two distinctly different orientations toward the conservative mission in social policy. On one side stood the New Right—those who wished to roll back social programs to a pre-welfare state period. Religious fundamentalists, traditionalist romantics, and laissez-faire marketeers found that their interests converged with the political objectives of Ronald Reagan. The Reaganauts found in the presidency the ultimate podium from which to make a range of pronouncements on social affairs. The Institute for Cultural Conservatism inveighed against the underclass and against welfare programs that condoned, in effect, "crime, drugs, and casual sex."[5] Think tanks of the New Right lent the intellectual capital necessary to close the deal. The Heritage Foundation led the assault on liberal social programs, offering private sector surrogates for Social Security, Medicare, and urban development. "The crisis of the modern welfare state is not just a crisis of government," averred Marvin Olasky, the Bradley scholar at Heritage. "The more effective provision of social services will ultimately depend on their return to private and especially to religious institutions." Putting the issue in historical perspective, Olasky concluded that "most of our 20th-century schemes have failed. It's time to learn from the warm hearts and hard heads of the 19th."[6]

Facing the Reaganauts were conservative incrementalists who were willing to recognize the legitimacy of the institutional basis for the American welfare state, but who had qualms about what they perceived to be the massive—and conceivably infinite—revenue commitment to welfare that liberal social programs seemed to require. Ironically, the ranks of the incrementalists were populated with academically well credentialed former liberals who had misgivings about liberal public policy. Accordingly, these neoconservatives provided much of the intelligence behind what was to become the conservative assault on the welfare state. Policies that expanded the Earned Income Tax Credit while trimming poverty programs, that shifted program responsibility from the federal government to the states, that contained the growth of social entitlements, and that used deficit-control legislation to limit welfare expenditures can be traced to these conservative intellectuals who were willing to concede an American welfare state but insisted on paring it back. That incrementalist neoconservatives were not anti-welfare per se, but worked under the ideological umbrella of the arch-anti-welfare Reaganauts, explains how the programmatic structure of the American welfare state remained intact despite the vehemence directed at it by the New Right. During the first Reagan term, the New Right established a highly charged political climate in which the American welfare state was blasted time and time again by the Reagan radicals; yet, by the time the final regulations were posted in the *Federal Register*, the incrementalists had won the day. Most of the damage to social programs consisted of budget rescissions and program consolidation, not the wholesale destruction that right-wing rhetoric had demanded.

The preconditions for retrenchment of the American welfare state were well in place by the time George Bush assumed the presidency. While many liberals anticipated further raids on social programs, these were hardly necessary. Expenditure limits imposed because of an enormous deficit precluded new social programs unless savings from other programs or additional revenues were identified. Under these constraints, liberals found the doors to the federal treasury locked until at least the mid-1990s. In response to the worsening of several social problems, the Bush administration had little choice but to design "new" initiatives that were little more than facades. In the proposed budget for 1992, existing programs were cannibalized in order to create the illusion of a federal response to a host of deteriorating circumstances. White House Chief of Staff John Sununu was more explicit, maintaining that an absence of domestic initiatives was a positive posture for the Bush presidency. Do-nothing domestic policy, after all, had several advantages: its direct costs were negligible; policy initiatives would be left for Democrats to sort out, primarily at the state and local levels; and Republicans would not face the prospect of being hoisted by the petard of program evaluators—the fate of post-War on Poverty liberal Democrats—if they did nothing. Herbert Hoover would have applauded.

The problem for conservatives who were intent on retracting the welfare state was their inability to assemble an alternate vision. In *Out of the Poverty Trap*, Stuart Butler and Anna Kondratas of Heritage present such a vision; but by the time of the book's publication in the late 1980s, the conservative momentum in social policy had expired. Sensing an opportunity that has slipped from grasp, Butler and Kondratas admit candidly that "conservative scholars generally have presented no picture [of welfare] that the American people can judge in its entirety."[7] Naively, conservatives believed that economic growth was a sufficient answer to the problems related to social welfare. "The conservative prescription for trimming the modern welfare system [was] based on the belief that social problems [would] be more adequately addressed through economic growth rather than redistributive policies and the conviction that no alternative could obviate the need to choose between these two approaches."[8] Nevertheless, while parroting the benefits of economic growth for the poor, conservatives could hardly resist the temptation to retrench social programs. Even when it became clear that the poor were not benefiting from the economic expansion of the 1980s, conservatives shamelessly continued their crusade to exorcise the evils of dependency, sloth, and waste from poverty programs. If the conservatives can be *faulted* for decimating government social programs, they should be *indicted* for their failure to optimize on the political and economic forces that they unleashed during the 1980s and that could have been used to put in place measures to ameliorate poverty and related problems.

The outline for such an initiative is not hard to imagine. In the late 1970s, Peter Berger and Richard Neuhaus had published *To Empower People: The Role of Mediating Structures in Public Policy*,[9] a not so thinly disguised brief against welfare state liberalism. It would have required little imagination to translate Berger and Neuhaus's empowerment thesis into a conservative initiative in domestic policy: enterprise zones to foster jobs in poor communities; incentives for voluntary-sector agencies to assume more of the welfare burden; transfers of revenue to states and cities to defray increased program costs; inducements for disadvantaged children to do well in school and thus participate maximally in the labor force. Yet, a coherent package failed to emerge from conservatism during the 1980s.

Instead, the New Right expended its influence on a "social" agenda consisting of diatribes about abortion, school prayer, and homosexuality. Apparently content to leave the lightning to the Reagan radicals, the incrementalist neoconservatives opportunistically pared social programs to the bone. The result was a decade of unnecessary misery for millions of Americans. What could have been a series of visionary experiments on a scale reminiscent of the New Deal or the War on Poverty—yet under Republican leadership—might well have evolved early in the Reagan presidency, had conservatives put themselves to the task. The 1980s were, after all, a conservative decade—a period when the right put its considerable intellectual, social, and political capital on the line for major policy initiatives: investments in high-tech weapons systems, an overhaul of federal tax laws, and the deregulation of entire industries. But when it came to questions of poverty and welfare policy, bold initiatives were framed in rhetoric only. In retrospect, it may simply have been easier to hatchet programs for the poor than to conceive of solutions to their deteriorating circumstances. Nonetheless, for all the social injustice that this omission generated, it represented a measure of poetic justice. Indeed, while Republicans rejoiced as the remnants of state socialism crumbled in Eastern Europe, at home they had created a social group that Marx himself would have predicted: an American underclass.

Although the Reagan administration failed to launch a policy initiative that clearly reflected the empowerment premise, the idea did not remain dormant indefinitely. Early in the Bush administration, White House aide James Pinkerton and HUD Secretary Jack Kemp stirred conservative complacency about domestic policy by suggesting that a "new paradigm" be the basis for domestic policy. And despite the ridicule of Budget Director Richard Darman, features of the new paradigm surfaced in Bush's 1991 State of the Union Address. By the time the Bush administration's proposed 1992 budget appeared, however, the program and budget commitments to either empowerment or a new paradigm had, for all practical purposes, vanished.

REFORM THROUGH INCREMENTALISM:
THE PRESERVATIONISTS

Preservationists draw their influence from the legacy of federal social programs that define the American welfare state. A precept of American liberalism has long been that, through gradual accretion, economically marginal and politically disenfranchised populations could be folded into the protections assured by the governmental welfare state established in

1935. Until the 1980s, this seemed a reasonable expectation. After all, the American welfare state seemed to fluctuate between bursts of innovation under Democratic presidents (Roosevelt and Johnson) interrupted by consolidation and expansion when Republicans (such as Richard Nixon) held the White House. Both political parties invested heavily in social programs during the first half of the century.

By the late 1970s, however, social and political developments began to strain a faultline within welfare state liberalism. The American welfare state had been constructed around two basic types of programs: social insurance for those who worked, and poverty programs for those who did not. During periods of prosperity this distinction was blurred; but when income for middle-class families contracted during the late 1970s, support for poverty programs plunged. In short order, conservatives exploited the opportunity primarily by splitting the relatively well funded and defended social insurance programs such as Social Security and Medicare from the more vulnerable poverty programs such as Aid to Families with Dependent Children (AFDC) and Medicaid. While welfare state expenditures continued to creep higher despite the Reagan administration's reductions, most of this occurred in the popular social insurance programs rather than the poverty programs, which at best stagnated. While total federal social welfare expenditures *did* increase between 1975 and 1987, as a percentage of GNP they had stalled. During the decade beginning in 1978, expenditures for means-tested poverty programs also increased, but as a percent of GNP they actually declined.[10] In fact, much of the erosion of poverty programs could be attributed to inflation—a problem avoided by the social insurance programs, which tended to be protected by Cost of Living Allowances. The House Ways and Means Committee, for example, noted that between 1970 and 1990 the true value of AFDC benefits *declined* 39 percent due to inflation.[11] By the end of the 1980s, conservatives had effectively halted expansion of the American welfare state.

In response to conservative assaults on social programs, many liberals defended the welfare state, insisting that the integrity of existing programs be respected. For social activists schooled in the New Deal, the state offered the best protection against the vicissitudes of nature and capitalism. While preservationists might concede that governmental social programs of the United States were less adequate than those of most industrial nations, they held fast to the notion that citizens have a right to basic protections assured by the state. If there were problems in the American welfare state, they were in execution, not in formulation. For welfare state preservationists, more work needed to be done toward realizing the vision of replicating the European model of the welfare state in the United States.

The ideology of welfare state preservation is firmly lodged in the liberal policy institutes such as the Brookings Institution and the Urban Institute. When neoconservative influences drove social policy to the right, some liberals organized new institutes to promote governmental social programs, including Marian Wright Edelman of the Children's Defense Fund and Robert Greenstein of the Center on Budget and Policy Priorities. Toward the end of the 1980s, three widely read liberal intellectuals—Paul Starr, Robert Kuttner, and Robert Reich—founded *The American Prospect* journal to invigorate liberal thought in the United States. In 1990 a point-by-point defense of welfare state liberalism was presented: "we do not argue that America has in place *all* the social welfare programs that would be compatible with the nation's constant commitments," argued Theodore Marmor, Jerry Mashaw, and Philip Harvey, "only that the major features of our most substantial programs are *compatible* with our relatively stable post-New Deal political ideology."[12]

If preservationists were besieged by Reaganites from the far right, they also encountered opposition from the Democratic center. Neoliberal Democrats (to be considered below) distanced themselves from traditional Democratic commitments to welfare. As the momentum of Democratic party politics swung toward the center, traditional liberal Democrats sought to revive ebbing loyalty to the New Deal. Early in the 1990s, resurgent Democratic liberalism was institutionalized as the Coalition for Democratic Values (CDV), under the chairmanship of Senator Howard Metzenbaum. The CDV placed its platform squarely in opposition to centrists of the rival Democratic Leadership Council (DLC).[13] With pointed reference to the DLC Tories, the CDV executive—Heather Booth—quipped condescendingly, "We do not need *two* Republican parties."[14]

The strongest case for preservation of the American welfare state is found in the social insurance programs: Social Security, Disability Insurance, and Unemployment Compensation established in 1935, and Medicare in 1965. The problem for preservationists is that the only social insurance to be established subsequently—Catastrophic Health Insurance—was repealed. Worse, the budget deficit and increasing conservatism of the political climate greatly diminish the possibility of launching a new social insurance program. And if recent history has been at all informative, it has indicated the unwillingness of the public to tolerate higher taxes for means-tested welfare programs. Thus, without increased support for poverty programs, welfare advocates face a conundrum. The popular social insurances of Social Security and Medicare hold their own, while programming for the poor diminishes. The contradictions in this situation are lost on an unsympathetic American middle class that has seen its economic prospects stagnate. As the experience with government health care has shown, few Americans look kindly upon a welfare state that requires them to become poor in order to receive Medicaid, yet provides Medicare to anyone over 65.

These circumstances place preservationists in an untenable position. Their strongest case for the American welfare state is built on social insurance programs that have prospered, while they are vulnerable on the question of desperately needed poverty programs. As social conditions for the poor have worsened and public support has not been forthcoming, pressure has been building to convince the public that it should abandon its commitment to social insurance. If programs for the poor are badly needed, the question goes, why continue less needed social insurance benefits for the nonpoor? From this question, it is but a short distance to the idea of converting the social insurance programs to poverty programs that are targeted at the poor through a means test. The traditional liberal solution to this problem would be to institute new social insurances, but the public seems unwilling to finance such initiatives. This inconvenience notwithstanding, preservation of the American welfare state remains contingent on the implementation of new social insurance programs.

THE RECONSTRUCTIONISTS

Reconstructionists have their intellectual origins in the civic republican critique of unchecked individualism that is evident in both contemporary liberalism and conservatism. Moreover, they argue that ideologues from both the left and the right err by focusing excessively on the individual— liberals, through welfare benefits; conservatives, through corporate salaries. Both of these demands are made at the expense of community and national solidarity. According to William Sullivan, "the notion of *citizen* is unintelligible apart from that of *commonwealth*, and both terms derive their sense from the idea that we are by nature political beings. . . . [S]elf-fulfillment and even the working out of personal identity and a sense of orientation in the world depend upon a communal enterprise."[15] Sullivan's sentiments reverberated with community organizers of the left such as Harry Boyte, who popularized civic philosophy in *CommonWealth*.[16]

Reconstructionism soon found a niche among younger Democrats. Smarting from losses of liberal presidential candidates and in search of a public philosophy to replace liberalism, Democrats were drawn to civic philosophy. In 1989, the Progressive Policy Institute (PPI) was spun off from the Democratic Leadership Council (DLC), and soon was organizing its domestic policy proposals within a "Center for Civic Enterprise." PPI fellow

David Osborne charted PPI's ideological vector. According to Osborne, "the traditional liberal and conservative ideologies that competed with the New Deal paradigm did not fail; they simply outlived their usefulness. . . . They evolved in response to the realities of the industrial age, and that era is over."[17] To date, PPI's policy suggestions have included an expansion of the EITC to bring poor workers out of poverty; the creation of individual development accounts so low- and middle-income workers can buy homes, establish pensions, attend college, and start businesses; and a police corps to make communities more secure. While some PPI initiatives may resemble New Deal-style programs, the intent is to fashion a new ideological base for domestic policy.

The tangent taken by the DLC stretched liberal precepts within the party and caused a split within Democratic ranks. At a 1991 meeting in Cleveland—a meeting preempted by a CDV preservationists meeting in Des Moines the week before—the DLC presented its "New American Choice" resolution. "Choice" meant that the DLC was "genuinely committed to the idea of using government to meet legitimate social needs," but not at the expense of economic growth and individual liberties.[18] Precisely what that meant for New Deal social programs was left unclear. Neoliberals who had initially suggested such radical departures from mainstream liberalism as means-testing Social Security were more modest as the conservative juggernaut moved through the 1980s. Yet, what was to distinguish the civic orientation to social policy from liberalism remained problematic.

While reconstructionists enjoy a certain advantage by virtue of the originality of their ideas, significant problems loom ahead. Without a coherent and plausible ideological base, reconstructionism can either disintegrate into an opportunistic pragmatism or be interpreted as an appendage—however awkward—to welfare state liberalism. If short on ideology, reconstructionists are long on credibility. Their emphasis on solidarity and community resonates with many who despair about the disintegration of social institutions. Their vision of welfare and the wealthy is decidedly unromantic: the former are expected to work for benefits, the latter to pay their way through higher taxes *and* community service. The strong point for reconstructionists is that they expect unqualified and positive outcomes from social policy. Their weakness is how to finance programs. Reconstructionism promises political payoffs for investments in the working-class and middle-income families—a powerful idea until it founders on the shoals of the budget deficit. Until its adherents can solve the fiscal riddle, reconstructionism will remain a promising but implausible idea, much like the industrial policy of the 1980s.

THE CHALLENGE OF AMERICAN SOCIAL WELFARE

Given these countervailing forces, what are the prospects for the American welfare state? As noted above, those who would contract, preserve, or reconstruct the infrastructure of the social programs of the American welfare state have decidedly different answers. Yet, even after those formulations are dissected, a larger question emerges for the public: Is the welfare state worth pursuing as an objective of public policy? This is a compelling question if we are sincere in believing that *social* policy should be *public* policy.

As in most matters of social policy, the answer is multifaceted. To fashion a response is to enter the yet to be explored regions of a labyrinth constructed of polity, economy, and society. For direction, we have little more to depend on than the ideological tools of the past. Unfortunately, these guides—liberalism and conservatism—have proved less and less useful to the task; this reality is yet to be realized by many academics, but is not lost on the public. The result is a doldrums spell in social welfare policy, a rudderless American welfare state about to founder in rising seas.

While as a nation we may be less sure of where to go with social welfare policy, the consequences of following our current course are becoming more and more evident. Homelessness, the spread of AIDS, overcrowded prisons, illiteracy, and poverty have become intransigent features of our social landscape. At this point, we are unable to mount adequately even those programs about which we have had a great deal of confidence— programs such as Head Start and childhood vaccinations against communicable disease. Among our worst calculations was the expectation that the destitute, if driven to the abyss, would object and demand more benefits. Instead, the poorest Americans have turned inward—defeated by insuperable forces—to become an underclass. One of the more perverse lessons to come from the 1980s is that we have underestimated the capacity of those most deprived to self-destruct. "In the great cities of America, class division is rapidly moving toward class war," observed Richard Goodwin, a Democratic liberal, "not so much the very poor against the more affluent, but the hopeless against the hopeless."[19] Benign neglect has given way to malignant neglect, with the attendant escalation of cost.

It is difficult to be sanguine about conventional responses to this set of worsening domestic ills. Burdened by debt, the federal government has left it to the states to fashion solutions; but even the once prosperous states, such as Michigan and California, are cutting deeply into social welfare expenditures.[20] Except for hollow presidential appeals to altruism via "a thousand points of light," there has been no significant initiative toward bolstering the capacity of the nonprofit sector to absorb more of the responsibility for social welfare. Concurrently, the human service professions have demonstrated a glaring disregard for their obligation to advance the common good, intent as they are instead on self-aggrandizement.

The result of this is an exhausted public sector. As the market extends globally, governments—both state and federal—are less able to tax highly mobile corporate entities in order to restore depleted revenues. While the corporate sector has deftly dodged its tax obligations, it has nevertheless assured its employees a range of health and welfare benefits. Perversely, some corporations have exploited human service markets and are profiting from a whole list of human needs, many of which are compensated through government social programs. Approaching the end of the twentieth century, social welfare in the United States is rapidly evolving toward a "corporate welfare state." Those having the wages and perks attendant with the commercial sector have prospered, often at the expense of those dependent on governmental programs and nonprofit social service agencies.

A necessary complement to a corporate postindustrial economy is the crafting of civic culture through social policy. A civic orientation to social welfare would strengthen social relations among the diverse groups comprising American society, reinforce the productivity of American workers, and restore the vitality of essential institutions in American communities. By and large, these concerns have been at the margin of conventional liberal and conservative prescriptions for social welfare. In the absence of diligent attention to these features of American life, the culture begins to fragment. In this respect the ostentation of Wall Street parvenus (condemned by liberals) is but the other side of the coin of welfare dependency (condemned by conservatives). Unbridled individualism has reached beyond the analyses of social scientists to become popularized in the media. The bourgeois narcissism portrayed in Tom Wolfe's novel *Bonfire of the Vanities* is matched by the underclass hedonism of Dennis Hopper's movie *Colors*. In both instances, there is little that connects individuals to a larger constructive purpose.

The implications for public policy are substantial. There is little "social" about social policies that promote individualism at the expense of social unity. Paradoxically, the American welfare state has become less of a *social* welfare state as it reinforces the social atomism so conducive to the machinations of corporate and governmental bureaucracies. By focusing on relational dynamics, a "civic welfare state" presents a clearer purpose for *social* policy than that endorsed by liberals through the current "governmental welfare state." Moreover, assiduous attention to the cultivation of social and economic relations ameliorates the divisive tendencies of a "corporate welfare state" favored by conservatives, the damage of which is already apparent.

Consistent with the notion of commonwealth, the purpose of a social policy that would be consonant with a civic welfare state is to bind the wounds an untended society inflicts on so many citizens: poverty for those who do not produce, alienation for those who do not belong, apathy for those who have given up, and overindulgence for those who have lost their sense of purpose. In this respect, a civic welfare state would address many of the deficiencies evident from policies that are generated by liberals and conservatives. Harry Boyte, a senior fellow at the Humphrey Institute of Public Affairs at the University of Minnesota, noted that "the commonwealth tradition forms an alternative to the politics of modern capitalism and socialism alike . . . one that has a renewed relevance for the years ahead."[21]

What is the feasibility of evolving a new paradigm for social policy? Public opinion research suggests that the prospects of reconstructing social welfare are actually quite good. Most Americans—perhaps 70 percent—support social programs that help the disadvantaged, although they balk at subsidizing a governmental bureaucracy that is associated with expensive and wasteful welfare programs.[22] The implications of this are ominous for welfare statists who insist that government is the sine qua non of social welfare. In order to capitalize on such public sentiment, liberals must get beyond the knee-jerk response of defending programs grounded in the New Deal, and begin to reconstruct social welfare so that it reflects the social, political, and economic imperatives of contemporary American culture. This, to be sure, will require the perseverance of imaginative and committed people. But it need not be a pedantic exercise. American progressives have often seen the pathos and the humor in "the good fight"— a quality they will surely need for the next decade. Jim Hightower, a progressive who lost his position as commissioner of the Texas Department of Agriculture when agribusiness objected to his strident populism, is a lesson in point. "The water won't ever clear up," he said alluding to the conservative 1980s, "'til you get the hogs out of the creek."[23] The future of American social welfare rests with those who profess to help the disadvantaged, and with their capacity to conceive of new—indeed, "popular"—ways to serve the public interest.

Historically, American social activists *have* responded to adversity, and the result has been the expansion of social provision. It is worth noting, however, that this response has varied: progressives focused on state government and philanthropy; New Dealers focused on the federal government. Although contemporary circumstances are daunting, they are probably no more so than those faced by Jane Addams, a progressive and pioneer of the settlement movement; by Harry Hopkins, a liberal who conceived many of the programs of the New Deal; or by Wilbur Cohen, a welfare professional and architect of the Great Society. The past decade indicates that a commensurate degree of creativity will be necessary to meet America's social needs during the 1990s.

NOTES

1. Sheila Kamerman, "The New Mixed Economy of Welfare," *Social Work* 28 (January/February 1983); Michael Walzer, "Toward a Theory of Social Assignments," in W. Knowlton and R. Zeckhauser (eds.), *American Society: Public and Private Responses* (Cambridge, Mass.: Ballinger, 1986); Norman Johnson, *The Welfare State in Transition* (Amherst: University of Massachusetts Press, 1987); David Stoesz, "A Theory of Social Welfare," *Social Work* 34 (January/February 1989).

2. Neil Gilbert, "The Welfare State Adrift," *Social Work* 31 (July/August 1986).

3. Robert Morris, *Rethinking Social Welfare* (White Plains, N.Y.: Longman, 1986).

4. Stuart Butler, "A Conservative Vision of Welfare," *Policy Review* (Spring 1987); Stuart Butler and Anna Kondratas, *Out of the Poverty Trap: A Conservative Strategy for Welfare Reform* (New York: Free Press, 1987); J. Risen, "White House Split on How to Beef Up Domestic Policy," *Los Angeles Times* (December 9, 1990); J. DeParle and P. Applebome, "Ideas to Aid Poor Abound, But Consensus Is Wanting," *New York Times* (January 29, 1991).

5. Institute for Cultural Conservatism, *Cultural Conservatism: Toward a New National Agenda* (Washington, D.C.: Institute for Cultural Conservatism, 1987), pp. 80-89.

6. Marvin Olasky, "Beyond the Stingy Welfare State," *Policy Review* (Fall 1990), p. 14.

7. Butler and Kondratas, *Out of the Poverty Trap*, p. 7.

8. Sar Levitan and Clifford Johnson, *Beyond the Safety Net* (Cambridge, Mass.: Ballinger, 1987), pp. 9-10

9. Peter Berger and Richard Neuhaus, *To Empower People: The Role of Mediating Structures in Public Policy* (Washington, D.C.: American Enterprise Institute, 1977).

10. Theodore Marmor, Jerry Mashaw, and Philip Harvey, *America's Misunderstood Welfare State* (New York: Basic Books, 1990), pp. 84, 94.

11. Committee on Ways and Means, U.S. House of Representatives, *Overview of Entitlement Programs* (Washington, D.C.: U.S. Government Printing Office, 1990), p. 560.

12. Marmor, Mashaw, and Harvey, *America's Misunderstood Welfare State*, p. 20; original emphasis.

13. Robert Shogan, "Rival Factions Vie to Mold Democratic Agenda," *Los Angeles Times* (May 5, 1991).

14. Jacob Weisberg, "Family Feud," *New Republic* (May 20, 1991), p. 22.

15. William Sullivan, *Reconstructing Public Philosophy* (Berkeley: University of California Press, 1986), pp. 157-58.

16. Harry Boyte, *CommonWealth: A Return to Citizen Politics* (New York: Free Press, 1989).

17. David Osborne, *Laboratories of Democracy* (Boston: Harvard Business School Press, 1988), p. 321.

18. Robert Shogan, "Centrists Seek to Alter Democrats' Course," *Los Angeles Times* (May 7, 1991), p. A-24.

19. Richard Goodwin, "The People Can Do Better than Two Parties in a Pod," *Los Angeles Times* (May 16, 1991), p. A-1.

20. Jason DeParle, "As Funds for Welfare Shrink, Ideas Flourish," *New York Times* (May 12, 1991).

21. Boyte, *CommonWealth*, p. 13.

22. "The Public's Agenda," *Time* (March 30, 1987).

23. Jim Hightower, "What Is to Be Done?" *New Republic* (May 20, 1991), p. 29.

Selected Bibliography

Aaron, Henry. *Politics and the Professors.* Washington, D.C.: Brookings Institution, 1978.

Abramovitz, Mimi. "Why Welfare Reform Is a Sham." *Nation* (September 26, 1988), p. 239.

Abramson, Alan and Lester Salamon. *The Nonprofit Sector and the New Federal Budget.* Washington, D.C.: Urban Institute, 1986.

Adams, J. R. *The Big Fix: Inside the S&L Scandal.* New York: Wiley, 1990.

Alperovitz, Gar and Jeff Faux. *Rebuilding America.* New York: Pantheon, 1984.

Amidei, Nancy. "How to End Poverty: Next Steps." *Food Monitor* (Winter 1988), p. 52.

Anderson, Martin. "Welfare Reform." In Peter Duignan and Alvin Rabushka (Eds.), *The United States in the 1980s.* Stanford, Calif.: Hoover Institution, 1980, pp. 145–64.

Aronowitz, Stanley. *False Promises.* New York: McGraw-Hill, 1973.

Atherton, Charles. "The Welfare State: Still on Solid Ground." *Social Service Review* 63 (Fall 1989), p. 167–79.

AuClaire, Philip. "Public Attitudes toward Social Welfare Expenditures." *Social Work* 29 (March/April 1984), pp. 141–50.

Auletta, Ken. *The Underclass.* New York: Random House, 1982.

Bachrach, Peter and Morton S. Baratz. *Power and Poverty.* New York: Oxford University Press, 1979.

Balzano, Michael. *Federalizing Meals on Wheels.* Washington, D.C.: American Enterprise Institute, 1979.

Bell, Winifred. *Contemporary Social Welfare.* New York: Macmillan, 1983.

Berger, Brigitte and Peter Berger. *The War over the Family.* New York: Anchor, 1983.

Berger, Peter and Richard Neuhaus. *Empower People: The Role of Mediating Structures in Public Policy.* Washington, D.C.: American Enterprise Institute, 1977.

Berkowitz, Edward and Kim McQuaid. *Creating the Welfare State.* New York: Praeger, 1980.

Bernstein, Blanche. "Welfare Dependency." In Lee D. Bawden (Ed.), *The Social Contract Revisited.* Washington, D.C.: Urban Institute Press, 1984.

Besharov, Douglas. "Contending with Overblown Expectations." *Public Welfare* (Winter 1987), pp. 6–12.

Blau, Joel. "Theories of the Welfare State." *Social Service Review* 63 (March 1989), pp. 226–37.

Block, Fred, Richard Cloward, Barbara Ehrenreich, and Frances Fox Piven (Eds.). *The Mean Season: The Attack on the Welfare State.* New York: Pantheon, 1987.

Bluestone, Barry and Bennett Harrison. *The Deindustrialization of America.* New York: Basic Books, 1982.

Blumenthal, Sidney. "Chapped Lips." *New Republic* (July 30 and August 6, 1990), pp. 20–25.

Blumenthal, Sidney and Thomas Edsall (Eds.). *The Reagan Legacy.* New York: Pantheon, 1988.

Boskin, Michael. "Social Security and the Economy." In Peter Duignan and Alvin Rabushka (Eds.), *The United States in the 1980s.* Stanford, Calif.: Hoover Institution, 1980.

Bowles, Samuel, David M. Gordon, and Thomas E. Weisskopf. *Beyond the Wasteland.* Garden City, N.Y.: Anchor Press, 1983.

Boyte, Harry. *CommonWealth: A Return to Citizen Politics.* New York: Free Press, 1989.

Bradbury, Kathleen. "The Shrinking Middle Class." *New England Economic Review* 16 (September/October 1986), pp. 41–55.

Brenner, Harvey M. *Estimating the Effects of Economic Change on National Health and Social Well-being.* Washington, D.C.: U.S. Government Printing Office, 1984.

Brown, Claude. *Manchild in the Promised Land.* New York: Macmillan, 1965.

Brown, Larry. "Questions and Answers." *Public Welfare* (Winter 1987), p. 21.

Buchanan, James and R. Tollison (Eds.). *Theory of Public Choice.* Ann Arbor: University of Michigan Press, 1972.

Buchanan, James and R. Wagner (Eds.). *Democracy in Deficit.* New York: Academic Press, 1977.

Burtless, Gary. "Public Spending for the Poor." In Sheldon Danziger and Daniel Weinberg (Eds.), *Fighting Poverty.* Cambridge, Mass.: Harvard University Press, 1986.

Butler, Stuart. "A Conservative Vision of Welfare." *Policy Review* (Spring 1987).

Butler, Stuart and Anna Kondratas. *Out of the Poverty Trap: A Conservative Strategy for Welfare Reform.* New York: Free Press, 1987.

Cassidy, Harry. *Social Security and Reconstruction in Canada.* Boston: Bruce Humphries, 1943.

Center on Budget and Policy Priorities. *Smaller Pieces of the Pie.* Washington, D.C.: Center on Budget and Policy Priorities, 1985.

———. *Analysis of Poverty in 1987.* Washington, D.C.: Center on Budget and Policy Priorities, 1987.

Children's Defense Fund. *The State of America's Children, 1991.* Washington, D.C: Children's Defense Fund, 1991.

Chubb, John and Terry Moe. "Choice *Is* a Panacea." *Brookings Review* (Summer 1990), pp. 4–12.

Cloward, Richard and Irwin Epstein. "Private Social Welfare's Disengagement from the Poor." In M. Zald (Ed.), *Social Welfare Institutions.* New York: Wiley, 1965.

Committee on Ways and Means, U.S. House of Representatives. *Background Material and Data on Programs within the Jurisdiction of the Committee on Ways and Means, 1989 Edition.* Washington, D.C.: U.S. Government Printing Office, 1989.

———. *Overview of Entitlement Programs.* Washington, D.C.: U.S. Government Printing Office, 1990.

Congressional Budget Office. *Current Housing Problems and Possible Federal Responses.* Washington, D.C.: U.S. Government Printing Office, 1988.

———. *Reducing the Deficit: Spending and Revenue Options.* Washington, D.C.: U.S. Government Printing Office, 1990.

Conover, Ted. *Coyotes.* Vintage: New York, 1987.

Corrigan, Paul and Peter Leonard. *Social Work Practice under Capitalism.* London: Macmillan, 1978.

Danziger, Sheldon and David Feaster. "Income Transfers and Poverty in the 1980s." In J. Quigley and D. Rubinfeld (Eds.), *Agenda for Metropolitan America*. Berkeley: University of California Press, 1985.

Danziger, Sheldon and Daniel Weinberg. *Fighting Poverty*. Cambridge, Mass.: Harvard University Press, 1986.

Dasgupta, Sugata. "Towards A No-Poverty Society." *Social Development Issues* 12 (Winter 1983).

Davis, Kenneth. *FDR: The New Deal Years 1933–1937*. New York: Random House, 1986.

Day, Phyllis. "The New Poor in America: Isolationism in an International Political Economy." *Social Work* 35 (1989), pp. 227–33.

Dearborn, Philip. "Fiscal Conditions in Large American Cities, 1971–1984." In McGeary and L. Lynn (Eds.), *Urban Change and Poverty*. Washington, D.C.: National Academy Press, 1988.

Diamond, Sara. *Spiritual Warfare: The Politics of the Christian Right*. Boston: South End Press, 1989.

DiNitto, Diane M. and Thomas R. Dye. *Social Welfare: Politics and Public Policy*. Englewood Cliffs, N.J.: Prentice-Hall, 1987.

Doble, John and Keith Melville. "The Public's Social Welfare Mandate." *Public Opinion* 11 (January/February 1989), pp. 59–67.

Doeringer, Peter B. and Michael Piore. *Internal Labor Markets and Manpower Analysis*. Armonk, N.Y.: M. E. Sharpe, 1985.

Domestic Policy Council. *Up from Dependency*. Washington, D.C.: White House Domestic Policy Council, December 1986.

Dorris, Michael. *The Broken Cord*. New York: Harper and Row, 1989.

Duncan, Greg, Richard D. Coe, et al. *Years of Poverty, Years of Plenty*. Ann Arbor, Mich.: Institute for Social Research, 1984.

Easterbrook, Gregg. "Ideas Move Nations." *Atlantic Monthly* (January 1986), pp. 190–97.

Economic Policy Institute. *Family Incomes in Trouble*. Washington, D.C.: Economic Policy Institute, 1986.

Elias, Robert. *The Politics of Victimization*. New York: Oxford University Press, 1986.

Ellwood, David. *Poor Support: Poverty in the American Family*. New York: Basic Books, 1988.

Enthoven, Alain and Richard Kronick. "A Consumer-choice Health Plan for the 1990s." *New England Journal of Medicine* 320, 1 (January 5, 1989).

Esping-Andersen, Gosta. "After the Welfare State." *Public Welfare* 44 (Winter 1983).

Estes, Richard. *The Social Progress of Nations.* New York: Praeger, 1984.

———. *Trends in World Social Development: The Social Development of Nations, 1970–1987.* New York: Praeger, 1988.

Etzioni, Amitai. "The Fast-food Factories: McJobs Are Bad for Kids." *Washington Post* (August 24, 1986).

Feather, N. T. and P. R. Davenport. "Unemployment and Depressive Affect: A Motivational and Attributional Analysis." *Journal of Personality and Social Psychology* 6, 41 (1981), pp. 422–36.

Ferrara, Peter. *Social Security Reform.* Washington, D.C.: Heritage Foundation, 1982.

———. *Rebuilding Social Security.* Washington, D.C.: Heritage Foundation, 1984.

Filer, John. "Editorial Notes: Commission on Private Philanthropy and Public Needs." *Social Casework* (May 1976), p. 342.

Finnegan, Daniel. "Federal Categorical Grants and Social Policies." *Social Service Review* 63 (December 1988), pp. 625–29.

Fisher, Jacob. *The Response of Social Work to the Depression.* New York: Schenkman Books, 1980.

Fisk, D., H. Kiesling, and T. Muller. *Private Provision of Public Service.* Washington, D.C.: Urban Institute, 1978.

Ford Foundation Project on Social Welfare and the American Future. *The Common Good: Social Welfare and the American Future.* New York: Ford Foundation, 1989.

Friedlander, D. *Subgroup Impacts and Performance Indicators for Selected Welfare Employment Programs.* New York: Manpower Demonstration and Research Corporation, 1988.

Friedman, Milton and Rose Friedman. "The Tide in the Affairs of Men." In Annelise Anderson and Dennis Bark (Eds.), *Thinking about America: The United States in the 1990s.* Stanford, Calif.: Hoover Institution, 1988.

Furniss, Norman and Timothy Tilton. *The Case for the Welfare State.* Bloomington: Indiana University Press, 1977.

Galper, Jeffry. *The Politics of Social Services.* Englewood Cliffs, N.J.: Prentice-Hall, 1975.

———. *Social Work Practice: A Radical Perspective.* Englewood Cliffs, N.J.: Prentice-Hall, 1980.

Gans, Herbert. "The Uses of Poverty: The Poor Pay All." *Social Policy* 2, 2 (July/ August 1971), pp. 20–24.

———. *Middle American Individualism*. New York: Free Press, 1988.

George, Vic and Paul Wilding. *Ideology and Social Welfare*. London: Routledge and Kegan Paul, 1976.

Gil, David. *Unraveling Social Policy*. Boston: Schenkman, 1981.

Gilbert, Neil. *Capitalism and the Welfare State*. New Haven, Conn.: Yale University Press, 1983.

———. "The Welfare State Adrift." *Social Work* 31 (July/August 1986), pp. 251–56.

Gilder, George. *Wealth and Poverty*. New York: Basic Books, 1981.

Ginzberg, Eli. "For-profit Medicine." *New England Journal of Medicine* 319, 12 (September 22, 1988).

Glasgow, Douglas. *The Black Underclass*. New York: Vintage, 1981.

Glazer, Nathan. "The Social Policy of the Reagan Administration." *Public Interest* (Spring 1984), pp. 97–102.

Glazer, Nathan and Daniel Patrick Moynihan. *Beyond the Melting Pot*. Cambridge, Mass.: MIT Press, 1970.

Gordon, David, Richard Edwards, and Michael Reich. *Segmented Work, Divided Workers*. New York: Cambridge University Press, 1982.

Gough, Ian. *The Political Economy of the Welfare State*. London: Macmillan, 1979.

Greenberg, Stanley. "Reconstructing the Democratic Vision." *American Prospect* (Spring 1990), p. 83.

Greenstein, Robert. "Losing Faith in 'Losing Ground.' " *New Republic* (March 25, 1985).

Greenstein, Robert and Scott Barancik. *Drifting Apart*. Washington, D.C.: Center on Budget and Policy Priorities, 1990.

Gueron, Judith. "Work for People on Welfare." *Public Welfare* 44, 1 (Winter 1986), pp. 7–12.

———. *Reforming Welfare with Work*. New York: Ford Foundation, 1987.

Guttman, Herbert. *Work, Culture, and Society*. New York: Vintage Books, 1977.

Habenstreit, Barbara. *The Making of America*. New York: Julian Messner, 1971.

Habermas, Jurgen. *Legitimation Crisis*. Boston: Schenkman, 1975.

Harrington, Michael. *The New American Poverty*. New York: Pantheon, 1984.

Harrison, Bennett and Barry Bluestone. *The Great U-Turn*. New York: Basic Books, 1988.

Haveman, Robert. *Starting Even*. New York: Simon and Schuster, 1988.

Himmelstein, David and Steffie Woolhandler. "Cost without Benefit: Administrative Waste in U.S. Healthcare." *New England Journal of Medicine* 314, 7 (February 13, 1986), p. 442.

————. "A National Health Program for the United States." *New England Journal of Medicine* 320, 2 (January 12, 1989).

Hirschman, Albert O. *Shifting Involvements: Private Interest and Public Action*. Princeton, N.J.: Princeton University Press, 1982.

Hodgkinson, Virginia and Murray Weitzman. *Dimensions of the Independent Sector*. Washington, D.C.: Independent Sector, 1986.

Hoffman, Saul and Lawrence Seidman. *The Earned Income Tax Credit*. Kalamazoo, Mich.: W. E. Upjohn Institute for Employment Research, 1990.

Horowitz, Irving. *C. Wright Mills: An American Utopian*. New York: Free Press, 1983.

Howe, Irving. *Beyond the Welfare State*. New York: Schocken Books, 1982.

Hughes, Dana. *The Health of America's Children*. Washington, D.C.: Children's Defense Fund, 1987.

International Monetary Fund. *Directory of Trade Statistics Yearbook: 1989*. Washington, D.C.: International Monetary Fund, 1989.

Jacoby, Russell. *The Last Intellectuals*. New York: Basic Books, 1987.

Jansson, Bruce. *The Reluctant Welfare State: A History of American Social Welfare Policies*. Belmont, Calif.: Wadsworth, 1988.

Jencks, Christopher. "Deadly Neighborhoods." *New Republic* (June 13, 1988).

Jencks, Christopher and Kathryn Edin. "The Real Welfare Problem." *American Prospect* 1 (Spring 1990), p. 49.

Johnson, Norman. *The Welfare State in Transition*. Amherst: University of Massachusetts Press, 1987.

Johnston, William, Arnold Packer, et al. *Workforce 2000*. Washington, D.C.: U.S. Department of Labor, 1987.

Judis, John. "Conservatism and the Price of Success." In Sidney Blumenthal and Thomas Edsall (Eds.), *The Reagan Legacy*. New York: Pantheon, 1988, pp. 135–71.

Kamerman, Sheila. "The New Mixed Economy of Welfare." *Social Work* 28 (January/February 1983).

Kanter, R. *The Changemasters*. New York: Simon and Schuster, 1983.

Karger, Howard J. *Social Workers and Labor Unions.* New York: Greenwood Press, 1988.

Karger, Howard J. and David Stoesz, "When Welfare Reform Fails." *Tikkun* 4 (March/April 1989).

———. *American Social Welfare Policy: A Structural Approach.* White Plains, N.Y.: Longman, 1990.

Kasarda, John. "Jobs, Migration, and Emerging Urban Mismatches." In M. McGeary and L. Lynn (Eds.), *Urban Change and Poverty.* Washington, D.C.: National Academy Press, 1988.

Katz, Michael. *In the Shadow of the Poorhouse: A Social History of Welfare in America.* New York: Basic Books, 1986.

Kaus, Mickey. "The Work-Ethic State." *New Republic* (July 7, 1986).

Kirlin, John and Dale Marshall. "The New Politics of Entrepreneurship." In Lawrence Lynn, Jr. (Chair), *Urban Change and Poverty.* Washington, D.C.: National Academy Press, 1988.

Kornblum, William. "Lumping the Poor." *Dissent* (Summer 1984), p. 296.

Kuttner, Robert. *The Economic Illusion.* Boston: Houghton Mifflin, 1984.

———. "The Poverty of Economics." *Atlantic Monthly* (February 1985), p. 74.

———. *The Life of the Party.* New York: Viking, 1987.

———. "The Welfare Strait." *New Republic* (July 6, 1987), p. 20.

———. *The End of Laissez-faire.* New York: Alfred A. Knopf, 1991.

Lake, Celinda and Stanley Greenbert, "What's Left of Liberalism?" *Public Opinion* 11 (March/April 1989).

Lane, Chuck. "The Manhattan Project." *New Republic* (March 25, 1985).

Lash, Scott and John Urry. *The End of Organized Capitalism.* Oxford, England: Basil Blackwell, 1987.

Lee, Bradford. "The Welfare State Reconsidered." *Wilson Quarterly* 6 (Spring 1982), pp. 69–70.

LeGrand, Julian and Ray Robinson. *Privatization and the Welfare State.* London: George Allen and Unwin, 1984.

Lemann, Nicholas. "The Origins of the Underclass." *Atlantic Monthly* (June/July 1986), pp. 15–25.

Lind, William and William Marshner. *Cultural Conservatism: Toward a New National Agenda.* Washington, D.C.: Free Congress Research and Education Foundation, 1987.

Lindblom, Charles and David Braybrooke. *Strategy of Decision.* New York: Free Press, 1970.

Linowes, David. *Privatization: Toward More Effective Government.* Washington, D.C.: U.S. Government Printing Office, 1988.

Lipsky, Michael. "Bureaucratic Disentitlement in Social Welfare Programs." *Social Service Review* 33, 4 (March 1984), pp. 81–88.

Longman, Phillip. "Catastrophic Follies." *New Republic* (August 21, 1989).

Lubove, Roy. *The Professional Altruist.* New York: Atheneum, 1969.

Macarov, David. *The Design of Social Welfare.* New York: Holt, Rinehart, and Winston, 1978.

McIntyre, Robert. "The Populist Tax Act of 1986." *Nation* 246, 13 (April 2, 1988), p. 445.

McIntyre, Robert and Robert Folen. *Corporate Income Taxes in the Reagan Years.* Washington, D.C.: Citizens for Tax Justice, 1984.

McKnight, John. "Do No Harm: Policy Options That Meet Human Needs." *Social Policy* 20 (Summer 1989).

McLanahan, Sara, Irwin Garfinkel, and Dorothy Watson. "Family Structure, Poverty, and the Underclass." In M. McGeary and L. Lynn (Eds.), *Urban Change and Poverty.* Washington, D.C.: National Academy Press, 1988.

Magaziner, Charles and Robert B. Reich. *Minding America's Business.* New York: Harcourt Brace Jovanovich, 1982.

Marmor, Theodore and Jerry Mashaw. "Canada's Health Insurance and Ours: The Real Lessons, the Big Choices." *American Prospect* 3 (1990), pp. 18–29.

Mead, Lawrence. *Beyond Entitlement.* New York: Free Press, 1986.

———. "The New Welfare Debate." *Commentary* (March 1988), pp. 44–52.

Merton, C. and Joan Broadshaug Bernstein. *Social Security: The System That Works.* New York: Basic Books, 1987.

Meyer, J. (Ed.). *Meeting Human Needs.* Washington, D.C.: American Enterprise Institute, 1981.

Midgley, James. "The New Christian Right, Social Policy, and the Welfare State." *Journal of Sociology and Social Welfare* 17 (Winter 1990).

Miller, S. M. "Notes toward the Re-formulation of the Welfare State." In Helga Nowotny (Ed.), *Thought and Action in Social Policy: Social Concerns for the 1980s.* Vienna: European Centre for Social Welfare Training and Research, 1984, pp. 69–74.

Miringoff, Marc and Sandra Opdycke. *American Social Welfare: Reassessment and Reform.* Englewood Cliffs, N.J.: Prentice-Hall, 1986.

Mishra, Ramesh. *The Welfare State in Crisis.* New York: St. Martin's Press and Sussex, England: Wheatsheaf, 1984.

———. "Riding the New Wave: Social Work and the Neo-conservative Challenge." *International Social Work* 32 (1989), pp. 171–82.

Moffitt, Robert and Douglas Wold. "The Effect of the 1981 Omnibus Budget Reconciliation Act on Welfare Recipients and Work Incentives." *Social Service Review* 61 (June 1987), pp. 248–52.

Morley, Elaine. "Patterns in the Use of Alternative Service Delivery Approaches." In *Municipal Year Book.* Washington, D.C.: International City Management Organization, 1989.

Morris, Robert. *Rethinking Social Welfare.* White Plains, N.Y.: Longman, 1986.

———. *Testing the Limits of Social Welfare.* Hanover, N.H.: University of New England Press, 1988.

Moskos, Charles. *A Call to National Service.* New York: Free Press, 1988.

Moynihan, Daniel Patrick. *Maximum Feasible Misunderstanding.* New York: Free Press, 1969.

———. *Came the Revolution.* San Diego: Harcourt Brace Jovanovich, 1988.

———. "Toward a Post-industrial Social Policy." *Public Interest* 96 (Summer 1989).

Muller, Thomas, et al., *The Fourth Wave.* Washington, D.C.: Urban Institute, 1985.

Murray, Charles. *Losing Ground.* New York: Basic Books, 1984.

———. "The British Underclass." *Public Interest* 99 (Spring 1990).

Nadelmann, Ethan. "The Case for Legalization." *Public Interest* (Summer 1988), p. 14.

Newland, Kathleen. *Infant Mortality and the Health of Societies.* Washington, D.C.: Worldwatch Institute, 1981.

Nielson, Waldemar. *The Third Sector: Keystone of a Caring Society.* Washington, D.C.: Independent Sector, 1980.

Noah, Timothy. "We Need You: National Service, An Idea Whose Time Has Come." *Washington Monthly* (November 1986).

Noble, K. "Are Program Cuts Linked to Increased Infant Death?" *New York Times* (February 13, 1983).

Novak, Michael. *Toward a Theology of the Corporation.* Washington, D.C.: American Enterprise Institute, 1981.

————. (Ed.). *The New Consensus on Family and Welfare.* Washington, D.C.: American Enterprise Institute, 1987.

O'Connell, Brian. *Origins, Dimensions, and Impact of America's Voluntary Spirit.* Washington, D.C.: Independent Sector, 1984.

————. *Philanthropy in Action.* Washington, D.C.: Foundation Center, 1987.

O'Connor, James. *The Fiscal Crisis of the State.* New York: St. Martin's Press and London: St. James Press, 1973.

Odendahl, Theresa. *Charity Begins at Home.* New York: Basic Books, 1990.

Offe, Claus. *Contradictions of the Welfare State.* Cambridge, Mass: MIT Press, 1984.

O'Neill, D. "Voucher Funding of Training Programs: Evidence from the GI Bill." *Journal of Human Resources* (Fall 1977).

Osborne, David. *Laboratories of Democracy.* Boston: Harvard Business School Press, 1988.

Ozawa, Martha. "The 1983 Amendments to the Social Security Act." *Social Work* 29 (March/April 1984).

Painton, F. "Reassessing the Welfare State." *Time* (April 15, 1981), p. 32.

Palmer, John L. and Isabel Sawhill (Eds.). *The Reagan Record.* Cambridge, Mass: Ballinger, 1984.

Pelton, Leroy. "Resolving the Crisis in Child Welfare." *Public Welfare* (Spring 1988), pp. 20–31.

Peters, Charles. *How Washington Really Works, Revised Edition.* Reading, Mass.: Addison-Wesley, 1983.

————. "A Neoliberal's Manifesto." *Washington Monthly* 9 (May 1983), pp. 32–43.

————. "A New Politics." *Public Welfare* 18 (1983), p. 34.

Phillips, Kevin. *Staying on Top: The Business Case for a National Industrial Policy.* New York: Random House, 1984.

————. *The Politics of Rich and Poor.* New York: Random House, 1990.

Pierson, Christopher. "The 'Exceptional' United States: First New Nation or Last Welfare State?" *Social Policy and Administration* (November 1990), pp. 15-21.

Piliavin, Irving. "Restructuring the Provision of Social Services." *Social Work* 13 (1968), pp. 34–41.

Pines, Burton. *Back to Basics.* New York: William Morrow, 1982.

Piore, Michael. "The Dual Labor Market." In D. Gordon (Ed.), *Problems in Political Economy.* Lexington, Mass.: D.C. Heath, 1977, pp. 23–35.

Piven, Frances Fox and Richard A. Cloward. *Regulating the Poor: The Functions of Public Welfare*. New York: Vintage Books, 1971.

————. *Poor People's Movements*. New York: Pantheon, 1977

————. *The New Class War*. New York: Pantheon, 1982.

Platt, S. "Unemployment and Suicidal Behavior: A Review of the Literature." *Social Science and Medicine* 9 (1984), pp. 93–115.

President's Commission on Privatization. *Privatization: Toward More Effective Government*. Washington, D.C.: U.S. Government Printing Office, 1988.

Progressive Policy Institute. *The Police Corps and Community Policing*. Washington, D.C.: Progressive Policy Institute, 1990.

Rabushka, Alvin. "Tax and Spending Limits." In P. Duignan and A. Rabushka (Eds.), *The United States in the 1980s*. Stanford, Calif.: Hoover Institution, 1980, pp. 100–26.

Reich, Robert. *The Next American Frontier*. New York: Times Books, 1983.

————. *Tales of a New America*. New York: Times Books, 1987.

————. *The Insurgent Liberal*. New York: Times Books, 1989.

————. "As the World Turns." *New Republic* 200 (1989), p. 23.

————. "Blackboard Jingle." *American Prospect* 3 (Fall 1990).

————. *The Work of Nations*. New York: Alfred A. Knopf, 1991.

Reischauer, Robert. "America's Underclass." *Public Welfare* 45, 4 (Fall 1987), pp. 28–36.

Rogers, D., R. Blendon, and T. Maloney. "Who Needs Medicaid?" *New England Journal of Medicine* (July 1, 1982).

Rothenberg, Randall. *The Neoliberals*. New York: Simon and Schuster, 1984.

Rowe, Jonathan. "Up from the Bedside." *American Prospect* (Summer 1990).

Sandel, Michael. "Democrats and Community." *New Republic* (February 22, 1988), p. 21.

Schlesinger, Arthur Jr. *The Cycles of American History*. Boston: Houghton Mifflin, 1986.

Schneider, W. "JFK's Children: The Class of '74." *Atlantic Monthly* 263 (1989), pp. 35–58.

Schorr, Lisbeth. *Within Our Reach*. New York: Anchor Press, 1988.

Schultze, Charles. *The Public Use of Private Interest*. Washington, D.C.: Brookings Institution, 1977.

Seaberg, James. "Family Policy Revisited." *Social Work* 35 (November 1990), pp. 550–55.

Shapiro, Robert. *An American Working Wage: Ending Poverty in Working Families*. Washington, D.C.: Progressive Policy Institute, 1990.

Sharkansky, Ira. *The United States: A Study of a Developing Country*. New York: Longman, 1975.

Sherraden, Michael. *Stakeholding: A New Direction in Social Policy*. Washington, D.C.: Progressive Policy Institute, 1990.

————. *Assets and the Poor*. Armonk, N.Y: M. E. Sharpe, 1991.

Steinfels, Peter. *The Neoconservatives*. New York: Simon and Schuster, 1979.

Stoesz, David. "The Family Life Center." *Social Work* 26 (September 1981).

————. "Corporate Welfare." *Social Work* 31 (July/August 1986), pp. 245–49.

————. "The Functional Conception of Social Welfare." *Social Work* 33 (March 1988), pp. 58–59.

————. "Human Service Corporations." *Administration in Social Work* 13, 3/4 (1989), pp. 190–92.

————. "A Theory of Social Welfare." *Social Work* 34 (January/February 1989), pp. 101–7.

Stoesz, David and Howard Karger. "Welfare Reform: From Illusion to Reality." *Social Work* 35 (March 1990), pp. 35–40.

Sullivan, William. *Reconstructing Public Philosophy*. Berkeley: University of California Press, 1986.

Thornberry, T. P. and R. L. Christenson. "Unemployment and Criminal Involvement." *American Sociological Review* 49 (1984), pp. 398–411.

Thurow, Lester C. *The Zero-sum Society*. New York: Basic Books, 1980.

————. *The Zero-sum Solution*. New York: Simon and Schuster, 1985.

————. "A Surge in Inequality." *Scientific American* 256 (May 1987).

Tilman, Rick. *C. Wright Mills: A Native Radical and His American Intellectual Roots*. University Park: Pennsylvania State University Press, 1984.

Titmuss, Richard. *Commitment to Welfare*. New York: Pantheon, 1968.

————. *Essays on the Welfare State*. Boston: Beacon Press, 1969.

————. *The Gift Relationship*. New York: Pantheon, 1971.

Trattner, William. *From Poor Law to Welfare State*. New York: Macmillan, 1974.

Treger, H. *The Police-Social Work Team.* Chicago: Jane Addams School of Social Work, 1975.

Walker, Alan. "The Strategy of Inequality: Poverty and Income Distribution in Britain 1979–89." In I. Taylor (Ed.), *The Social Effects of Free Market Policies.* Sussex, England: Harvester-Wheatsheaf, 1990.

Walzer, Michael. "Toward a Theory of Social Assignments." In W. Knowlton and R. Zeckhauser (Eds.), *American Society: Public and Private Responses.* Cambridge, Mass.: Ballinger, 1986.

Wilensky, Harold. *The Welfare State and Equality.* Berkeley: University of California Press, 1975.

Wilensky, Harold and Charles Lebeaux. *Industrial Society and Social Welfare.* New York: Free Press, 1965.

Wilson, William Julius. *The Truly Disadvantaged.* Chicago: University of Chicago Press, 1987.

————. "American Social Policy and the Ghetto Underclass." *Dissent* (Winter 1988), pp. 63–74.

Wodarski, John, T. M. Jim Parham, Elizabeth Linsey, and Barry W. Blackburn. "Reagan's AFDC Policy Changes: The Georgia Experience." *Social Work* 31 (July/August 1986), pp. 277–81.

Wolock, Isabel, et al. "Forced Exit from Welfare: The Impact of Federal Cutbacks on Public Assistance Families." *Journal of Social Service Research* (Winter 1985/Spring 1986), pp. 94–99.

Index

Aaron, Henry, 45

Abramovitz, Mimi, 60–61

Addams, Jane, 150, 172

adoption, 113

affirmative action, 87

Aid to Families with Dependent Children (AFDC), xxiv, 10, 11, 12, 29, 30, 36, 47, 51, 52, 59, 60, 61, 62, 63, 85, 95, 105, 106, 111–13, 119, 132–39, 142, 144, 146–48, 166; effect of 1981 budget cuts on, 30; effect on family breakup, 119; problems in, 134

AIDS, 115, 170

American Association of Retired Persons (AARP), 64, 65

American Enterprise Institute (AEI), 43–44, 47, 50, 93

American welfare state, xviii, xxiv-xxv, xxvi, xxix, 4, 5, 16; attitude of American public toward welfare, 27; challenge to, 25; civic, 17, 171; client critique of, 25, 26; conservative critique of, 26, 27, 161; containment of, 15; corporate, 16, 171; crisis of, 104;

development of, 109; devolution of, 23; expenditures, 166; future of, 172; governmental, 3; inadequacy of benefits, 25; new paradigm, 161, 165; reconstruction of, 17; reluctant welfare state, 16; *see also* welfare state

Anderson, Martin, 49, 80, 107, 147

Andrews Air Force Base, 65

Associated Charities of Denver, 8

Atherton, Charles, 13

Balanced Budget and Emergency Deficit Control Act, 55

Balzano, Michael, 41, 44

Baroody, William, 44, 55

Bendick, Marc, xxiv

Berger, Peter, 41, 112, 114, 164

Beveridge Report, xiv

Blau, Joel, 27, 107

Bluestone, Barry, 32, 34, 89

Block, Fred, 87, 94

Blumenthal, Michael, 28, 35

Blumenthal, Sidney, 86

Booth, Heather, 167

About the Authors

DAVID STOESZ is Associate Professor of Social Work at San Diego State University. He has worked as a community organizer, a public welfare caseworker and administrator, and a planner of mental health services. With Howard Jacob Karger he is the coauthor of *American Social Welfare Policy* (White Plains, N.Y.: Longman, 1990). He is currently working on *Human Services in Postmodern America*, a critical examination of social welfare in the United States.

HOWARD JACOB KARGER is Associate Professor of Social Work at Louisiana State University. He is the author of *The Sentinels of Order* (Lanham, Md.: University Press of America, 1987), *Social Workers and Labor Unions* (New York: Greenwood Press, 1988), and *American Social Welfare Policy* (with David Stoesz). He is currently editing a book titled *Controversial Issues in Social Policy* (New York: Allyn and Bacon, forthcoming).